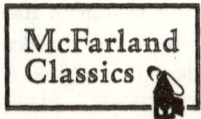

McFarland
Classics

1997–1998

Archer. *Willis O'Brien*

Cline. *In the Nick of Time*

Frasier. *Russ Meyer—The Life and Films*

Hayes. *3-D Movies*

Hayes. *Trick Cinematography*

Hogan. *Dark Romance*

Holland. *B Western Actors Encyclopedia*

Jarlett. *Robert Ryan*

McGee. *Roger Corman*

Okuda & Watz. *The Columbia Comedy Shorts*

Pitts. *Western Movies*

Selby. *Dark City*

Warren. *Keep Watching the Skies!*

West. *Television Westerns*

1999–2000

Benson. *Vintage Science Fiction Films, 1896–1949*

Cline. *Serials-ly Speaking*

Darby & Du Bois. *American Film Music*

Hayes. *The Republic Chapterplays*

Hill. *Raymond Burr*

Horner. *Bad at the Bijou*

Kinnard. *Horror in Silent Films*

McGhee. *John Wayne*

Nowlan. *Cinema Sequels and Remakes, 1903–1987*

Okuda. *The Monogram Checklist*

Parish. *Prison Pictures from Hollywood*

Sigoloff. *The Films of the Seventies*

Slide. *Nitrate Won't Wait*

Tropp. *Images of Fear*

Tuska. *The Vanishing Legion*

Watson. *Television Horror Movie Hosts*

Weaver. *Poverty Row HORRORS!*

Weaver. *Return of the B Science Fiction and Horror Heroes*

Also by Anthony Slide

Early American Cinema (1970; *revised* 1991)
The Griffith Actresses (1973)
The Idols of Silence (1976)
The Big V: A History of
the Vitagraph Company (1976; *revised* 1987)
Early Women Directors (1977; *revised* 1984)
Aspects of American Film History Prior to 1920 (1978)
Films on Film History (1979)
The Kindergarten of the Movies:
A History of the Fine Arts Company (1980)
The Vaudevillians (1981)
Great Radio Personalities in Historic Photographs (1982)
A Collector's Guide to Movie Memorabilia (1983)
Fifty Classic British Films: 1932–1982 (1985)
A Collector's Guide to TV Memorabilia (1985)
The American Film Industry: A Historical Dictionary (1986)
The Great Pretenders (1986)
Fifty Classic French Films: 1912–1982 (1987)
The Cinema and Ireland (1988)
Sourcebook for the Performing Arts
(*with* Patricia King Hanson *and* Stephen L. Hanson, 1988)
The International Film Industry: A Historical Dictionary (1989)
Silent Portraits (1990)
The Television Industry: A Historical Dictionary (1991)

With Edward Wagenknecht

The Films of D. W. Griffith (1975)
Fifty Great American Silent Films: 1912–1920 (1980)

Editor

Selected Film Criticism: 1896–1911 (1982)
Selected Film Criticism: 1912–1920 (1982)
Selected Film Criticism: 1921–1930 (1982)
Selected Film Criticism: 1931–1940 (1982)
Selected Film Criticism: 1941–1950 (1983)
Selected Film Criticism: Foreign Films 1930–1950 (1984)
Selected Film Criticism: 1951–1960 (1985)
International Film, Radio, and Television Journals (1985)
The Best of Rob Wagner's Script (1985)
Selected Theatre Criticism: 1900–1919 (1985)
Selected Theatre Criticism: 1920–1930 (1985)
Selected Theatre Criticism: 1931–1950 (1986)
Filmfront (1986)
Selected Radio and Television Criticism (1987)
Selected Vaudeville Criticism (1988)
The Picture Dancing on a Screen (1988)

NITRATE WON'T WAIT

A History of Film Preservation in the United States

by
Anthony Slide

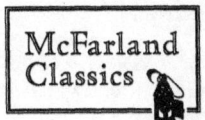

McFarland & Company, Inc., Publishers
Jefferson, North Carolina, and London

The present work is a reprint of the library bound edition of Nitrate Won't Wait: A History of Film Preservation in the United States, *first published in 1992. McFarland Classics is an imprint of McFarland & Company, Inc., Publishers, Jefferson, North Carolina, who also published the original edition.*

Library of Congress Cataloguing-in-Publication Data

Slide, Anthony.
    Nitrate won't wait : a history of film preservation in the United States / by Anthony Slide.
       p.   cm.
    Includes bibliographical references and index.
    ISBN 0-7864-0836-7 (softcover : 50# alkaline paper) ∞
    1. Motion picture film—Preservation and storage—United States—History. I. Title.
TR886.3.S55   2000   778.5'8—dc20   91-50948

British Library cataloguing data are available

Cover images © 2000 Digital Vision

Manufactured in the United States of America

McFarland & Company, Inc., Publishers
  Box 611, Jefferson, North Carolina 28640
    www.mcfarlandpub.com

For Robert Gitt
who preserves films

CONTENTS

Bibliographies:

ACKNOWLEDGMENTS

This is a factual account of the history of film preservation in the United States, but it is also a highly opinionated volume. The opinions are my own (although shared by quite a few others). For the facts I am grateful to many. I must thank the staffs of the Margaret Herrick Library of the Academy of Motion Picture Arts and Sciences, and of the Louis B. Mayer Library of the American Film Institute. The chapter on the American Film Institute could not have been written without the help of Lawrence F. Karr (who also read the manuscript), and I am also grateful to Richard Kahlenberg for his comments. At the international Museum of Photography at George Eastman House, Jan-Christopher Horak and Paolo Cherchi Usai were both helpful. The history of film preservation at the Library of Congress could not have been documented without the reminiscences of Howard Walls, and without the additional help of the Library's Assistant Public Affairs Officer, Jean E. Tucker. At the UCLA Film and Television Archive, I would like to thank William Ault, Blaine Bartell, Dan Einstein, Robert Gitt, and Jere Guldin. Other institutional staff who provided valuable information are William T. Murphy, chief of the Motion Picture, Sound and Video Branch of the National Archives; Stanley Yates, curator of the American Archives of the Factual Film; Wendy Shay, director of the Human Studies Film Archives; and G. William Jones of the Southwest Film/Video Archives. In Scandinavia, thanks to Rolf Lindfors and Gunner Almer at the Swedish Film Institute, Arne Pedersen of the Norwegian Film Institute, Ib Monty at the Danish Film Museum, and Timo Muitonen of the Finnish Film Archive.

I am also grateful to Eileen Bowser, Pete Comandini and Richard Dayton at YCM Laboratory, Bob Epstein, Michael Friend, Sam Gill, Lewis Jacobs, Edith Kramer at Pacific Film Archive, Sam Kula, Robert E. (Bob) Lee, Dick May of Turner Entertainment, George J. Mitchell, David Pierce, Mildred Simpson, and Lori Wagoner of Underground Vaults & Storage, Inc.

I would also like to acknowledge the many individuals who, upon hearing I was writing a book on the history of film preservation, offered suggestions as to what might be included. It was disturbing to me, and should be to archivists, that in general what I was asked to include were negative comments on the manner in which American archival institutions are managed.

Finally a comment on semantics. In that the legitimate archival community (which does not necessarily embrace film) uses the plural word "archives" as a singular noun, it is so used here. If any argument can be made for the insistence of the National Film Archive in London and the UCLA Film and Television Archive in Los Angeles to use the noun in its singular form, it is that there can be no such entity as a film archive or a film archives, and, therefore, the archival community can adopt any title it so desires.

The established definition of an archives is "the noncurrent records of an organization or institution preserved because of their continuing value." Quite obviously, film meets no such definition, unless one is willing to define the entire motion picture industry as a corporation or organization.

All the research materials gathered in the compilation of this book have been deposited with the Popular Culture Library of Bowling Green State University, Ohio.

"It was, I think, the advent of the talkies and—by that time—their prevalence which had slowly made us realize what we lacked or had lost. True enough, we had seen, heard, and rejoiced in *Public Enemy*, the first husky words of Garbo in *Anna Christie*. Yet something, not only of technique, seemed missing. Should we never again experience the same pleasure that *Intolerance*, *Moana*, or *Greed* had given with their combination of eloquent silence, visual excitement, and that hallucinatory 'real' music from 'real' orchestras in the movie theaters which buoyed them up and drifted us with them into bliss? No question but that had furnished an experience different in kind. But the silent films and the orchestras had vanished forever and when could one hope to see even the best of the early talkies again? How could movies be taken seriously if they were to remain so ephemeral, so lacking in pride of ancestry of of tradition?"

—Iris Barry "The Film Library and How It Grew," *Film Quarterly*, Summer 1969, page 20.

INTRODUCTION

"Nitrate Won't Wait!" has become the rallying cry for film archivists, in their efforts to raise funds as well as public consciousness of the need for such funds in the preservation of the world's film heritage. It is a phrase whose origins and history are as convoluted as the history of film preservation. It was originally coined in the late 1960s by Sam Kula, archivist at the American Film Institute from the summer of 1968 to the summer or 1973, in the form of "Nitrate Will Not Wait." He used it at a conference organized by the International Federation of Film Archives, which reformulated it as "Nitrate Can't Wait." Australian film archivists went one word better and adopted the term, "Nitrate Won't Wait." In 1973, a new American Film Institute archivist, Lawrence F. Karr, decided to adopt the Australian version of the phrase for the American film preservation movement.

To understand why nitrate won't wait and why film preservation is so important, it is necessary to understand the physical properties of film itself. Nitro-cellulose, commonly called nitrate film, was first utilized by the Eastman Kodak Company in 1899 as roll film for still photography. With the advent of moving pictures, it became obvious that nitro-cellulose film was the only suitable medium for film production, and remained so until 1949, when a satisfactory acetate-based, or safety film was introduced by Eastman Kodak for professional use. (For its efforts, the Eastman Kodak Company received a Special Academy Award, "for the development and introduction of an improved safety base motion picture film.") The transfer from nitrate to safety film took a number of years, and although most American films from 1950 onwards were shot on acetate stock, some foreign productions utilized nitrate film as late as 1955.

With its high silver content and its rich tones, there was, and for many still is, no better film for black-and-white photography than nitrate film. However, it had two major drawbacks (at least from today's viewpoint): it was highly flammable and it would eventually decompose. Nitrate film's chemical composition is very similar to that of guncotton, used in the manufacture of explosives, resulting in its burning 20 times as fast as wood, and containing sufficient oxygen to continue burning underwater. It can self-ignite at 300

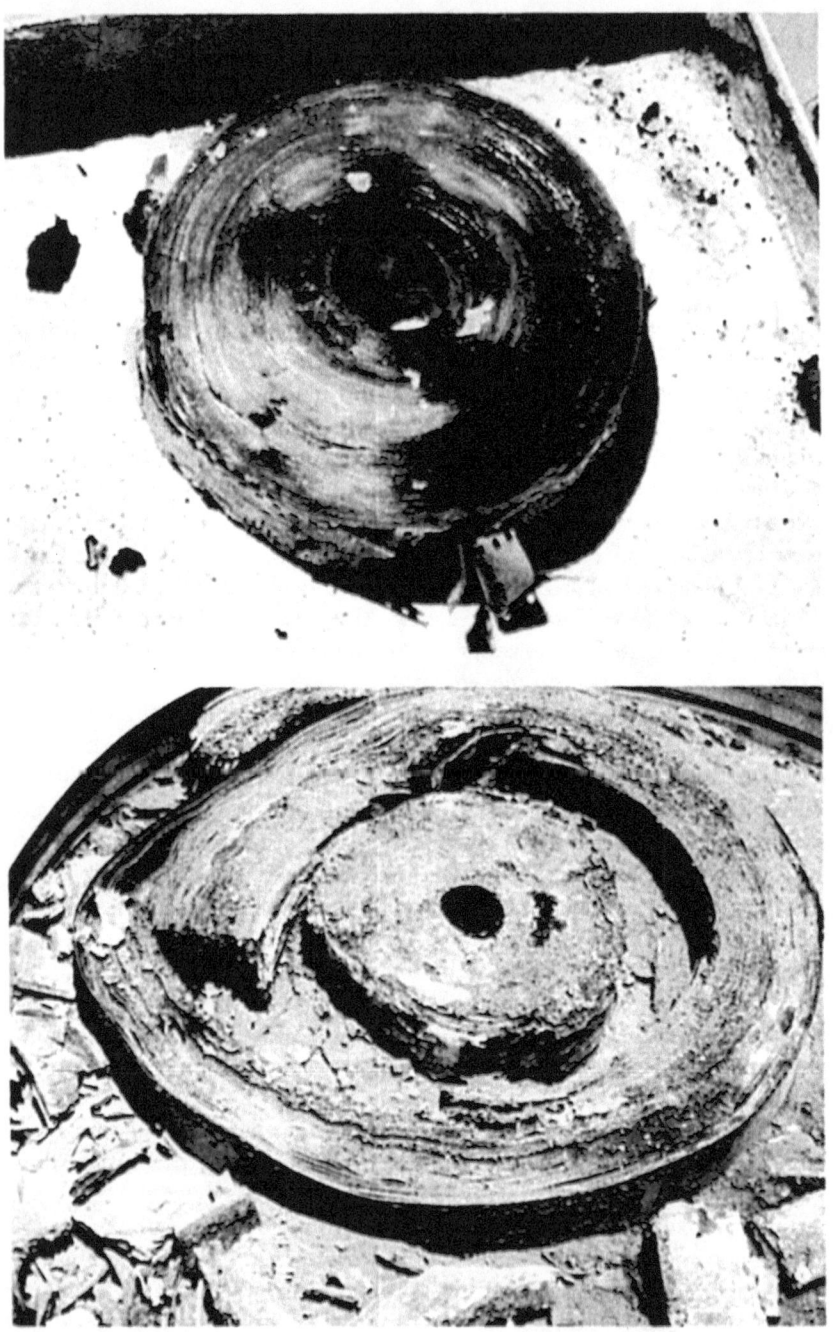

The decomposition of nitrate film (photographs by Blaine Bartell).

degrees or less, and the burning nitrate film gives off a gas which can form nitric acid in the lungs, possibly leading to death.

Because nitrate film is chemically unstable, it is in a perpetual state of decomposition. Such decomposition may take less than two decades or more than two generations. Nitrate film makes its own rules. If kept at a low temperature and humidity, it can be stored safely and indefinitely. Nitrate film from the 1890s can often be found in perfect condition, while film from the Second World War period, processed on inferior stock, has already decomposed.

Generally, under normal circumstances, nitrate film does not self-ignite. Eastman Kodak has found that a decomposing reel of nitrate film could be kept at 106 degrees for 17 days, tightly wrapped in a can, before it self-combusted. However, in the summer of 1949, a number of fires in New York City resulted from storage of decomposing nitrate film, and it was determined that self-ignition was taking place at a temperature of 106 degrees.

Nitrate decomposition starts with the discoloration of the picture image. Noxious fumes are given off by the film. Gooey bubbles appear and form a brown, frothy foam, and when the foam dries, all that is left is a fine powder.

Throughout its history, there have been stories of the dangers of nitrate film. In 1909, Earl C. Long wrote in the trade paper, *The Nickelodeon*:

> Throughout its commercial history, celluloid has suffered a disastrous reputation for Imflammability [sic]. Its supposedly mysterious properties, and the fact that it is made from guncotton, have afforded the newspapers unlimited opportunity for scare-head stories. In this they were supported by those interests who were affected by the possibility substitution of celluloid for horn, tortoise-shell, ivory, and other materials. Tales were told of ladies' hair burnt off by the ignition of celluloid combs; of yard-high flames shooting from some celluloid ornament brought near a flame; of explosion and spontaneous combustions. It was even reported that flaming celluloid was impossible to extinguish.

Concerning the impossibility of extinguishing a nitrate fire, Long continued,

> How absurd these statements are is well known to all who handle the material. Celluloid can ignite only when brought into direct contact with flame, or when heated to such a degree that it gives off inflammable vapors; and the so-called celluloid "explosions" are merely the igniting of quantities of the vapor which has been given off under such conditions. The substance itself ignites very little easier than does paper or muslin; and like them, its flames are easily extinguished.
>
> It is probably that the search for a non-flammable celluloid has been actuated as much by the unfortunate stigma upon the article as by any actual danger in its handling. But since the demand was created, the product was certain to follow.*

The Eastman Kodak Company first introduced safety-based film in 1909. In France, the Pathé Company had already begun the use of safety film in 28mm, for use in noncommercial situations, such as homes, churches and

---

*Long, Earl C., "The Story of Non-Inflammable Film," The Nickelodeon, August 1909, p. 51.

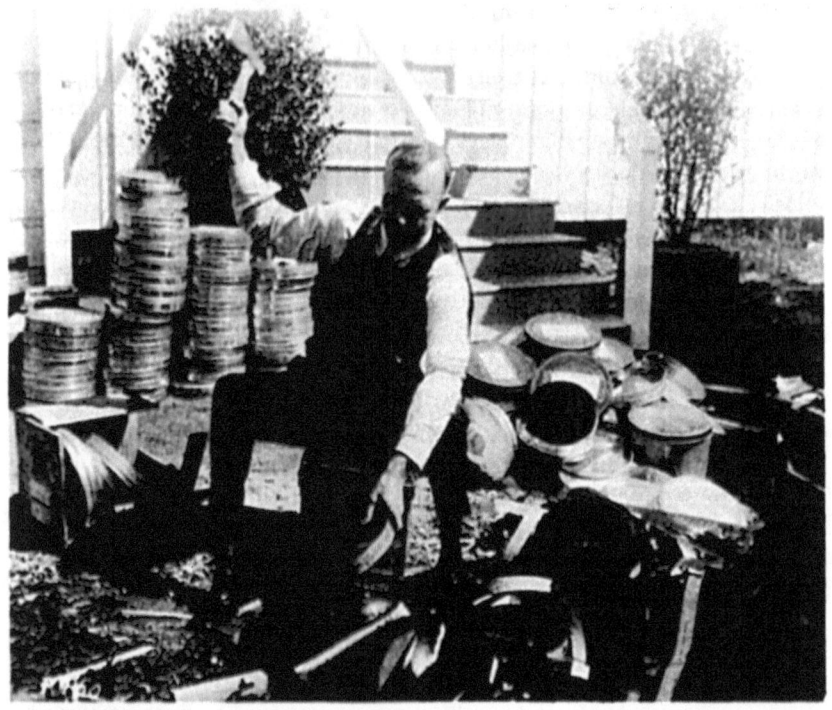

The destruction of unwanted reels of film during the silent era. The reels are physically axed into two to prevent possible piracy of the films.

schools—although it now seems certain that 28mm contains a small percentage of nitrate film. There was considerable interest in the industry in the new film—in December 1910, the Motion Picture Patents Company suggested that its members should use only nonflammable film—but the stock proved to be brittle and subject to shrinkage, and was generally unsuitable for day-to-day commercial use. Eastman Kodak continued to experiment with safety film, introducing it for 16mm use in 1923, and for 8mm in 1932.

Fire companies throughout the country lobbied for the use of safety film by the industry. However, the lobby was up against two insurmountable objections: the cost of safety film was greater than that of nitrate film, and its durability and effciency were not as high.* In the July 1936 issue of the *National Fire Protection Quarterly*, Harry Anderson explained:

> The motion picture industry uses nitrocellulose film because cellulose acetate film will not stand up under the severe conditions to which film is subjected. The average print now fulfills 40 playing dates, or about 200 showings. If cellulose

*Benedict, V. L., "Motion Picture Production Hazards," National Fire Protection Quarterly, vol. 15, no. 3, January 1922, p. 230.

acetate film were used, not more than 10 playing dates or 50 showings could be made, and it would therefore be necessary to make four times as many prints as are now being used on any given picture. Chemists of the film manufacturers have not yet found a way to stop cellulose acetate film from warping and buckling after being subjected to the high intensity arc lights which are generally used in theatres.*

One might ponder how many "lost" films might have survived had the safety lobby won its case. In reality, there might be no difference, for it seems very certain that the film industry would have continued to use nitrate film for its negatives, and only resorted to safety film for the making of release prints. Those release prints would have experienced a far shorter life than the nitrate prints and been quickly destroyed.

In recent years, archivists have discovered that safety film is not without its problems. Poor storage can cause shrinkage and resultant problems in copying. High heat and humidity, coupled with chemical contamination, can cause safety film base to decompose. Because safety film so decomposing gives off a vinegar odor, this form of safety decomposition has come to be known as "The Vinegar Syndrome." Color film fades in time, and creates its own specific preservation problem. The introduction of videotape in television has created further preservation problems.

The increased concern for film preservation has not resulted in an increase in the number of laboratories capable of handling the many problems relevant to the copying and restoration of nitrate films. Few, if any, major film laboratories, such as DeLuxe, or CFI, are capable of handling archival preservation needs. Only a handful of laboratories—YCM, Film Technology, Cinetech, and John E. Allen—exist to handle specialized preservation requirements.

No one really knows just how many films have survived and how much has been lost. It is often claimed that 75 percent of all American silent films are gone and 50 percent of all films made prior to 1950 are lost, but such figures, as archivists admit in private, were thought up on the spur of the moment, without statistical information to back them up.† Based on reports from other countries, it may well be that the percentage of films which have survived is a lot higher. For example, Britain's National Film Archive holds an amazing 73 percent of all British films produced between 1929 and 1975.

What is more to the point, there still remains more than 100 million feet of nitrate film of American origin awaiting preservation, in American and foreign archives, vaults of producers and distributors, and in the hands of private collectors. From the silent era, it is true that only a handful of original

---

*Anderson, Henry, "Fire Safety in the Motion Picture Industry," National Fire Protection Quarterly, vol. 30, no. 1, July 1936, pp. 26–27.

†In a letter to the author, March 3, 1991, Lawrence F. Karr points out, "True, these figures may well have been spur-of-the-moment, but I did check them at AFI using BIB [Broadcast Information Bureau] films available for TV book, actual counts from the BFI catalogs and FIAF and American archives lists, etc. The results basically confirmed these figures. Hence I continued to use them."

negatives remain, but a considerable number of original prints have survived and have been copied—several thousand American silent films are preserved at the Library of Congress alone. In terms of major "lost" films, the problem involves dozens rather than hundreds of titles, and the problem is often not that a film does not survive, but that it survives in an incomplete, cut version. Orson Welles' *The Magnificent Ambersons* (1942) is an obvious example.

The major problem facing film preservationists in the 1990s is one of selectivity. It is easy to garner public enthusiasm and funding for the preservation of familiar titles, but these are not the films in need of preservation. As film historian David Shepard commented, "There's so much material to be attended to. Archivists can become very competitive, and they'll choose to lavish their care on the films that'll garner the most attention and funding. They'll focus their energies on 'important' people."* For every "glamorous" restoration project, such as *A Star Is Born* or *Lawrence of Arabia*, there are literally hundreds of "little" films, forgotten "B" pictures, Westerns, and serials in desperate need of preservation.

"Glamorous" restorations projects have also glamorized film preservation, which is, in reality, a far from glamorous occupation. The "glitter factor" has resulted in the appearance of many dilettantes and "johnny-come-latelys" on the preservation scene; few have a working understanding of preservation techniques, but all are eager for public recognition of their supposed involvement in the field. The glamorization of film preservation is only one of many transitions which the film archives movement has undergone through the years.

At its beginning, film archives were dominated by personalities who loved film but who steadfastly protected their treasures from anyone unwilling to nourish their egos. These early archivists were cult figures, wallowing in the adulation of their young admirers. They loved film, but often the film decomposed or was destroyed in fires because they were unwilling even to share the labor of preservation with others. James Card in the United States and Henri Langlois in France were collectors institutionalized along with their collections.

Henry Langlois (1914–1977) of the Cinémathèque Française personified the independent-minded, highly autocratic film archivist, in love with films and the power which their ownership bestowed. Obese (he loved food as much as films) and charming, he manipulated the young breed of French filmmakers of the 1950s to such an extent that when the French minister of culture, André Malraux, tried to take the Cinémathèque away from him in 1968, there was no filmmaker in France—from François Truffaut to Jean-Luc Godard— unwilling to support Langlois. As a result, he was reinstated. Films at the Cinémathèque continued to decompose, while Langlois mischievously adopted

---

*Quoted in Deutsch, Joel, "Save Our Films!" DGA Newsletter, June/July 1990, p. 15.

adopted the attitude that the only legitimate way to save nitrate film was to transfer it to new nitrate film stock — no matter that such stock was no longer manufactured. Langlois loved mystery, to such an extent that he hid a considerable number of films in the Cinémathèque collection, and they remain "lost" to this day. *The New York Times* (December 4, 1977) reported that after Langlois' death as many as 25,000 titles were "missing."

Langlois was worshipped by filmmakers the world over. The writer recalls being present at a 1977 luncheon in Beverly Hills at which King Vidor offered a toast to Langlois for saving his and all the other films of his generation of American filmmakers. It was so pitifully untrue that it was laughable, and yet Vidor's fellow directors joined him in the benediction — it did not occur to one of them that their films might, in reality, have survived thanks to the efforts of American film archivists. Similarly, François Truffaut was an ardent Langlois supporter, but when he needed to view films for his book on Alfred Hitchcock, he went not to the Cinémathèque Française, but to Jacques Ledoux's Cinémathèque Royale in Brussels.

As the old guard slowly died off, or individuals were replaced as a result of official intervention, it was supplanted by a somewhat younger breed of film archivist, one with perhaps some slight training in the medium, but still with a genuine, if more restrained, love of film. Typical of this later breed is Eileen Bowser at the Museum of Modern Art, with her quiet, behind-the-scenes manner of getting the work done. At the American Film Institute, Lawrence F. Karr was accused of treating film as a commodity, which he notes is true, "since I was more dispassionate toward films and preferred analytical and statistical approaches to managing the preservation problem."*

In more recent years, a third generation of film archivists has arisen, a group which is in many ways representative of the Ronald Reagan "Me Generation," with no great interest in film except to the extent that its preservation would profit the individual curator or the individual institution. The new generation is bureaucratic in nature. But its members are not bureaucrats in the way that Ernest Lindgren, who founded Britain's National Film Archive in May 1935 (as the National Film Library), was a civil servant. Lindgren had many faults and many detractors, but still he was able to create one of the greatest film archives in the world. Today's most archival bureaucrats are not interested in film preservation, only in self-preservation.

Bureaucratic or not, all archives and archivists stand behind what is the only internationally recognized document on film preservation, "Recommendation for Safeguarding and Preservation of Moving Images," adopted by the General Assembly of UNESCO at its 21st session in Belgrade, Yugoslavia, on October 27, 1980.

Through it all, almost miraculously, film preservation has continued, not

In a letter to the author, March 3, 1991.

only survived but advanced in scope—archives which once could do nothing more than "safeguard" films by careful storing of them are now heavily involved in the physical preservation. Despite the politics which permeate the entire film archives movement in the 1980s and 1990s, both on the national and international levels, many dedicated preservationists are at work, assuring that a 20th century art form survives into the 21st century. This book is an attempt to document their work, and the historical background of film preservation and restoration in the United States.

1 EARLY YEARS AND THE MUSEUM OF MODERN ART

"When I used the word 'preservation,' the public didn't even know the word," commented Fay Kanin in reference to her 1979 appearance on the Academy Awards show.* "The past 15 years can be viewed as the birth of the preservation 'movement,'" wrote Frank Hodsoll, then chairman of the National Endowment for the Arts, in 1983. "A handful of separate institutions was doing excellent work before 1967, but national recognition and response to the problem is a relatively recent phenomenon."† In 1983, with great hoopla, the American Film Institute launched The Decade of Preservation. In 1990, the director of the National Center for Film and Video Preservation at the American Film Institute announced that "1990 is the year for dramatic action, growth and forward movement," concluding her message with the words, "So let the trip begin."§

In reading such comments, the casual observer might be led to believe that film preservation is a recent phenomenon, a product of the sixties and beyond. In reality, the concern for and interest in film preservation is almost as old as the film industry itself.

The first industry trade paper, *Views and Film Index* (later retitled *The Film Index*), began publication on April 25, 1906. In the first year of its life, on December 1, 1906, it published an editorial on the need for film preservation:

> We often wonder where all the films that are made and used a few times go to, and the questions come up in our minds, again and again: Are the manufacturers aware that they are making history? Do they realize that in fifty or one hundred years the films now being made will be curiosities? In looking through the maker's catalogues, we observe specially important subjects of great public interest, such as President Roosevelt at gatherings, Veterans processions, Scenes in busy streets, Political meetings, Prominent senators, and a host of other subjects

*Quoted in Variety, May 29, 1985, p. 2.
†"Our Heritage Must Be Saved," Variety, January 19, 1983, p. 132.
§"A Message from the Director," F/TAAC Newsletter, vol. 2, no. 3, Winter 1990, p. 2.

too numerous to mention, all of which are of value to the present generation; but
how much more so will they be to the men and women of the future?

We are making such rapid strides nowadays, the march of improvement is so
great that we hardly keep in touch with what a few short years ago we thought
wonderful. A large section of a city is torn down, another built in a few weeks'
time, and the former state forgotten except to the film or photograph. Perhaps
the day will come when motion pictures will be treasured by governments in their
museums as vital documents in their historical archives. Our great universities
should commence to gather in and save for future students films of national importance.*

Nine years later, another trade paper, *Motography*, also editorialized on
the need to preserve films as a record of historical events, and also raised,
perhaps for the first time, the problem of nitrate decomposition:

Now that the greatest event in world history is transpiring [World War I], so to
speak, before our cameras, the historians are offered their first extraordinary opportunity to establish archives of film records, to preserve into the indefinite future
the exact replicas of today's actions. It is reported that the German government
is doing just that; it is taking and filing away motion pictures of every important
action of the war. The British authorities, on the other hand, in spite of earnest
appeals by their own countrymen, have so far refused to consider the matter. This
course has been attributed, naturally, to the well-known Anglican conservatism.
The British Museum officials decline to store film because of its inflammable
nature and the consequent necessity for a special vault for its safekeeping.

One might suppose that even the conservative British mind would be sufficiently
impressed with the importance of the occasion to overcome the trifling obstacle
of proper storage space for such records. The cost of an adequate vault, and even
the labor (just now a more important factor) to build it, or adapt one already built,
is surely inconsiderable in view of the opportunity to imbue future sons of
England with a proper patriotism. Of course this argument has been presented
to the British authorities; and in rebuttal they bring against the films a charge
more serious, in the premises, than that of inflammability.

It is stated that for many years British scientists have been studying the problem
of whether the existing form of motion picture film will retain its properties after
years have aged it. And they claim to have made the discovery that after an unused
film has been placed in an airtight vault and left untouched for five years the
celluloid becomes covered with a fungus growth. They therefore dismiss at once
the possibility of preserving films for a hundred years or more.

There has always been some doubt as to the permanency of the emulsion whose
chemical changes make the photographic image causing the word permanency in
terms of centuries rather than years. But that the passive and inert vehicle which
carries that emulsion should be subject to disease is, we confess, a theory new to
us.

In this country there are doubtless many reels of film which have reposed idly
on vault shelves for more than five years. It will be noted that the British scientists
mention an airtight vault: whether that means a vault whose door is never opened
we do not know. We have no such storage spaces for films in this country, and
cannot see why the condition is necessary anywhere. If circulation of air will

*"*History and Motion Pictures,*" Views and Film Index, *vol. 1, no. 32, December 1, 1906, p. 1.*

remove the alleged curse, it surely could be provided for very readily. If mere darkness and time will grow fungus on celluloid some of our own scientists must have encountered it.

We would be glad to hear from any one familiar with the condition referred to, and to examine any specimens of celluloid film so afflicted.*

A few of the comments made by *Motography* with regard to the attitude of the British Government are unfair. Although Britain's National Film Archive (then titled the National Film Library) did not come into being until May 1935, the British government did establish the Imperial War Museum in 1917, and two years later it began the task of acquiring motion picture footage of the First World War. For its enlightened attitude towards film, the Imperial War Museum deserves credit as the oldest-surviving, noncommercial film archives in the world. The footage gathered by the Imperial War Museum was utilized for a series of postwar documentary features, compiled by director Walter Summers: *Ypres* (1925), *Mons* (1926) and *The Battles of the Coronel and Falkland Islands* (1927).

The United States government was also becoming aware, albeit slowly, of the dangers of nitrate film. In 1929, Dr. Charles E. Monroe, whose title was chief explosive chemist of the Bureau of Mines, warned that stored nitro-cellulose films presented a triple menace of fire, explosion and wholesale gas poisoning.†

The danger of a nitrate-related fire has, arguably, been understated through the years by the film industry. While it is true that nitrate film had been in use, with comparatively few problems, for more than 50 years, it has been the verified cause of several fires. The most tragic of nitrate-caused fires took place on May 4, 1897, at the Paris Charity Bazaar. Nitrate film caught fire while passing through a Lumière projector. One hundred-eighty people were killed, including prominent members of the French nobility and political life. The first major nitrate fire in the United States resulted in no loss of life, but it did cause two million dollars' worth of damage to the Thomas A. Edison plant in Orange, New Jersey, on December 9, 1914.

Six months later, on June 13, 1914, an explosion caused by spontaneous combustion of nitrate film destroyed the storage vault of the Lubin Film Manufacturing Company at Twentieth Street and Indiana Avenue in Philadelphia. According to *The Moving Picture World* (June 27, 1914),

> The explosion came about 10 o'clock in the morning without the slightest warning. No one was in the vault at the time and that it was tightly closed up is given as the reason for the force of the let-go which was sufficient to blow out an entire wall of brick and concrete eighteen inches thick.
>
> Bricks and mortar were blown in every direction and a string of two-story houses

---

*"Can Films Be Preserved for Posterity," Motography, vol. 13, no. 14, April 3, 1915, p. 1.
†"Federal Chemist Warns Against Improper Storage of Films," Motion Picture News, December 28, 1929, p. 22.

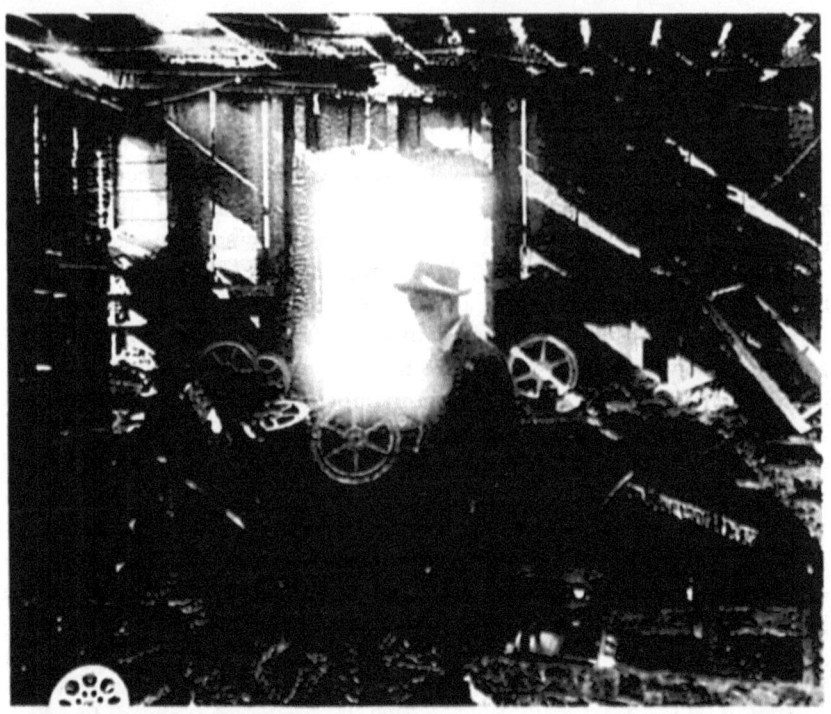

The aftermath of a nitrate fire in the 1920s. (Courtesy of the Academy of Motion Picture Arts and Sciences)

on the same street were badly damaged, some of them being practically destroyed. Rolls of burning film were showered everywhere and many of the adjoining frame buildings were set on fire. It was fire that injured the Italian boy who is not expected to recover; he was playing in the street near the vault at the time of the explosion and his clothes were ignited by a roll of film.

An examination of the files of *National Fire Protection Quarterly* reveals a number of nitrate-caused fires prior to the Second World War. Problems in the operation of projectors screening nitrate film caused fires in schools in Seattle, on May 14, 1920, in Sterling, Kansas, on November 1, 1921, and in Rochester, New York, on November 28, 1926. The Newcomb Theatre, New Orleans, was particularly prone to nitrate fires because of the poor repair of its Simplex projectors—it reported fires in its projection booth on November 9, 1917, and January 2, November 6, and November 8, 1920. On May 1, 1926, fifteen-year-old Louis Lelong, Jr., and his four-year-old sister Mary were fatally burned when a reel of nitrate film caught fire while being projected by the boy on a home movie machine. On November 17, 1922, a Puerto Rican family was watching a similar motion picture entertainment in their home. A lighted candle fell into the barrel of film, and nine children and two adults were killed.

Nitrate film catching in the gate of a film projector caused a potentially dangerous fire at sea on board the S.S. *Duilio* on March 14, 1928, three days before
its arrival in New York.

A film exchange on Commerce Street, Dallas, was totally destroyed on
December 10, 1921, by a fire and explosion causing a reported quarter-of-a-
million dollars in damage. A fire occurred in the inspection room of the Pathé
New York exchange on August 13, 1928. A nitrate fire at the Clawson Film
Laboratory in Salt Lake City, on October 23, 1929, took one life. A day later,
the Consolidated Film Industries laboratory in Hollywood was heavily damaged
as a result of a nitrate fire, and one employee was killed. In July 1930, 70 tons
of "scrap film" was destroyed in a spontaneous combustion fire at a Bound
Brook, New Jersey, laboratory.

On January 3, 1925, a seventy-year-old employee of the brush manufacturer, John F. Bowditch, picked up a bag of nitrate film scraps from the Famous
Players Exchange in Boston. He then boarded a subway car, placing the bag
under the seat next to a heater. The resultant explosion injured 50 passengers,
27 of whom were hospitalized. (The story brings to mind the plot of Alfred
Hitchcock's 1936 feature, *Sabotage,* in which a small boy carries a couple of
cans of nitrate film, in which is hidden a bomb, on board a London bus.)

About $100,000 in damage resulted from a fire at the United Film vault
on Charlotte Street, Kansas City, Missouri, on August 4, 1928. Hot tempera-
tures and the sun's rays shining directly on the nitrate film cans were given as
the cause of the fire. The most tragic of all American nitrate film fires in terms
of both loss of life and loss of America's film heritage occurred on July 9, 1937,
in a storage building rented by the Fox Film Corporation in Little Ferry, New
Jersey. Flames from the blast shot over 100 feet in the air and the same distance
horizontally over the ground. A thirteen-year-old boy living with his family in
a house immediately in front of the film storage vaults was killed while
shielding his mother from the blast, which destroyed 42 individual vaults, in
which the majority of silent films produced by Fox were stored. Following the
fire, 57 truckloads of burned nitrate film were salvaged for their silver content,
with each can of film ashes said to be worth approximately five cents.

Of course, the film danger from nitrate film can be helpful to archivists
in persuading companies and individuals to donate their nitrate holdings. On
July 29, 1980, an explosion took place at the Aladdin Theatre in the Norwegian
city of Kristiansand, severely injuring nine of the occupants. Initially, it was
assumed that someone had placed a bomb in the theatre, but two days later
it was revealed that the explosion was the result of self-combustion of a collection of nitrate films stored in the theatre's attic. Within weeks, the Norwegian
film archives, the Norsk Filminstitutt, had received three tons of nitrate film
from worried owners.

At the same time, archives have not been totally free of nitrate fires. Outside of the United States, perhaps the most spectacular archives fire took place

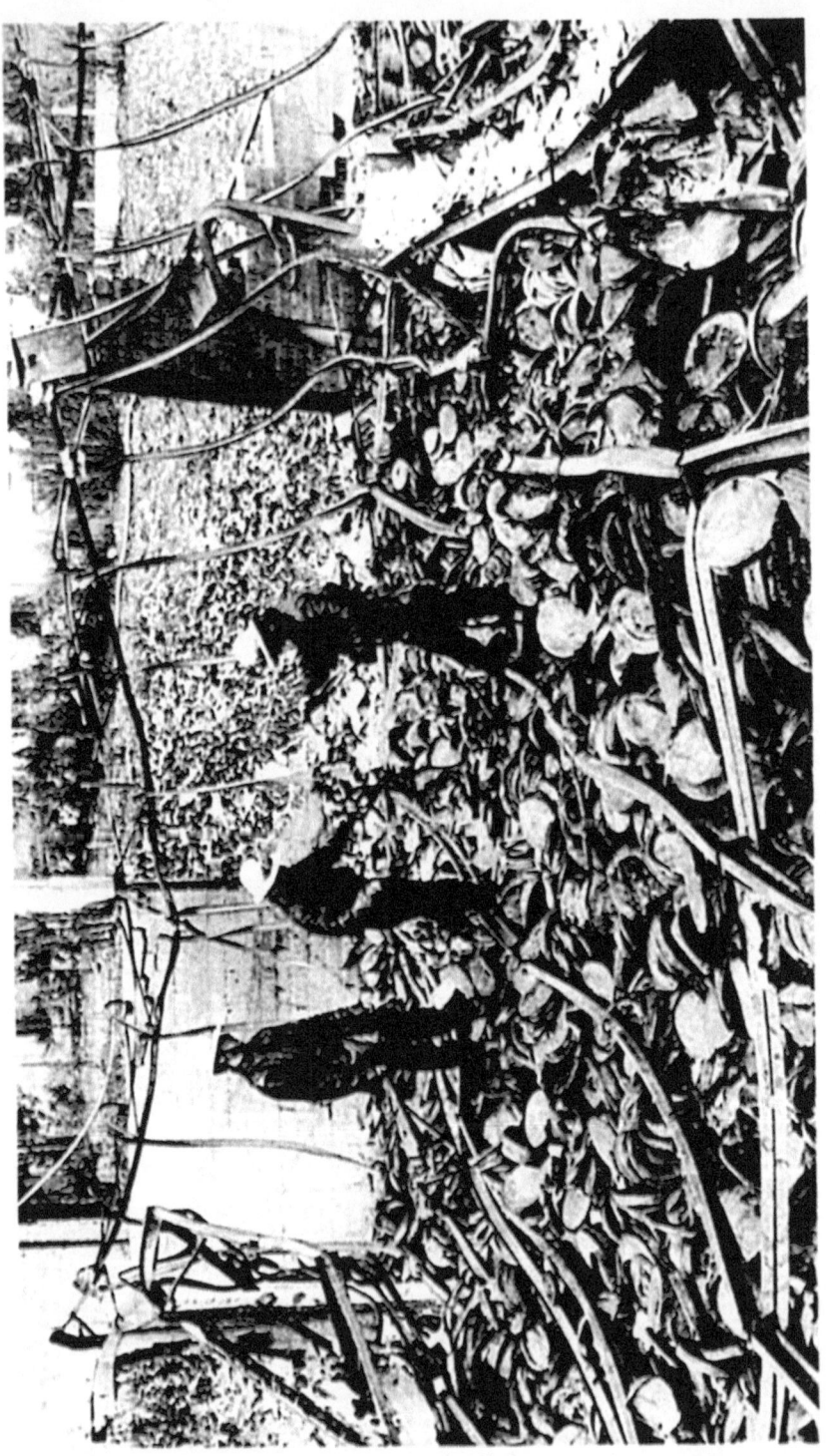

at the Cineteca Nacional in Mexico City, on March 24, 1982. The nitrate fire destroyed 6,506 films, of which 3,300 were Mexican features and short subjects (a substantial portion of Mexican film history). Also destroyed were the Cineteca's library, which included original notebooks and drawings by Sergei Eisenstein and artwork by Diego Rivera. The rehabilitated Cineteca Nacional was dedicated on February 8, 1984.

A major fire in 1967 at the National Film Board of Canada had a positive effect in that it resulted in the Board's arranging for the National Archives of Canada to archive its holdings. (Treasury Board funding for the establishment of a Canadian Film Archives became a reality in 1976, and the National Film, Television and Sound Archives, now the Moving Image and Sound Archives Division, was created.)

On August 3, 1980, a fire totally destroyed a warehouse of films belonging to the Cinémathèque Française at Rambouillet on the outskirts of Paris.

> It will never be known exactly what was lost in the disaster, because the fiercely independent-minded Cinémathèque refused at that time to publish a complete catalogue of its collection [commented *Le Monde*, April 19, 1990]. Officially, it claimed that only duplicate copies and out-takes were destroyed by the blaze.
>
> It has been estimated in some quarters that about 15,000 reels of film were lost, including a large number of original prints. Film buffs familiar with the Cinémathèque's collection point out that certain films shown before the fire have never been shown since, and that it can therefore only be assumed they formed a part of the Villiers-Saint-Frederic [warehouse] collection.

The Bundesarchiv in Koblenz reported a "minor" fire on January 26, 1988, but still it resulted in the loss of 1,860 reels of nitrate film.

In the United States, there have been rumors of small nitrate fires in at least two archives. The National Archives suffered two major nitrate fires in 1977 and 1978. On May 29, 1978, a spectacular blaze resulted from the spontaneous combustion of nitrate films stored in a concrete holding vault at the International Museum of Photography at George Eastman House. Total damage was estimated at $1.4 million, and the fire destroyed 516 M-G-M features and short subjects. Happily, duplicate copies of all the titles existed in the studio's own vaults.

In the summer of 1981, a fire at a Lyon storage vault in Hollywood destroyed 150 reels of film belonging to the Academy of Motion Picture Arts and Sciences, and, as a result of the blaze, the Academy arranged for the storage of all its other nitrate holdings in the vaults of the UCLA Film and Television Archive. The past attitute of the Academy towards its nitrate holdings is symptomatic of the problems that film archives have had for years in trying to persuade the film industry to preserve its output.

The Academy had accepted large collections of nitrate films, including the

Opposite: The aftermath of the fire at the Cinémathèque Française on August 3, 1980.

works of one of America's leading silent film directors, Lois Weber, and Will
Rogers. Unhappy with the Academy's attitude towards the Rogers films, the
comedian's son withdrew them from the Academy and arranged for their preservation by the Museum of Modern Art. There was no one to worry about Lois
Weber's work, and the bulk of her films were allowed to decompose. In 1970,
the American Film Institute arranged to preserve the Academy's nitrate holdings. Unfortunately, the program was suspended in 1974, when an over-
ambitious executive at the Academy decided that he wanted the organization
to function as a film archives. Further nitrate decomposed in the meantime,
and it was not until 1981 that Academy executives began to ponder the need
for a more professional attitude towards film preservation.

In April 1923, *Photoplay* took up the issue of the preservation not only
of films, but also film-related paper materials. Terry Ramsaye had been compiling his "The Romantic History of the Motion Picture" for serialization in
Photoplay, a historical survey of the American film industry which was first
published in book form in 1926 by Simon and Schuster, as *A Million and One
Nights: A History of the Motion Picture*. Ramsaye had already spent a year-
and-a-half in research, and he had become aware of the scattering of the
memorabilia of the industry's past across the American continent, as well as
noting the amount of unique data unprotected in private hands. In an editorial titled "Lest We Forget," he wrote in part:

> The motion picture needs a museum. Now is the time to establish it. An ap-
> preciative respect for the past and an obligation to the future of the art alike re-
> quire it. . . .
> The archives and relics of the early motion pictures and the beginnings of the
> art are scattered over all parts of America, and there are numerous documents and
> instruments of importance in various parts of England and the Continent.
> Nowhere and at no time has there been an effort to specially preserve these
> things, to hold them together for their sentimental and intrinsic values to the mo-
> tion picture and its public.
> It is a passing opportunity, available now. . . .
> It is still possible to see Edwin S. Porter's famous picture *The Great Train Rob-
> bery*, complete in its original form, just as it went on the screen to startle the world
> with the story telling powers of the motion picture two decades ago. There are per-
> haps a half a dozen copies of this classic in existence. Mr. Porter has in his ex-
> perimental workshop the machine with which he projected the shows of the Eden
> Musée in the dim dark days of ancient film history. In a basement bin and scattered
> about in old desks at the Biograph laboratories in uptown New York are memen-
> toes and relics of early Biograph days that are worth their weight in gold. There
> the curious searcher can find fascinating fragments that tell of the early efforts of
> Mary Pickford, the little girl star of *The Violin Maker of Cremona*, stills from the
> picture when young David Griffith worked as an extra. And farther back still,
> among the Mutoscope reels of Biograph's peep show days are the little card wheel
> pictures of Boxing Match at Canestota, the first product of the Biograph camera,
> the now famous Empire State Express, motion picture of William McKinley and

his young friend Theodore Roosevelt, in his wasp waisted days in the politician's frock coat of the nineties, Joe Jefferson in Rip Van Winkle, and half the contemporary history of the world.

The legal files of the Motion Picture Patents Company and the bookcases in the office of Henry Norton Marvin, where an old brass plate still bears the once mighty legend of the company, constitute a whole Alexandrian library of the screen.

A mutilated copy of the Gutenberg Bible, of the handiwork of the accredited father of the modern art of printing, today costs more money than would be required to bring all of the existing relics of early motion picture history together and give them adequate care while making them available to the public and today's makers of screen history.

America sends expeditions of learned men to dig in the dust of Egypt to seek out the gewgaws and bracelets where the Shepherd Kings buried their harems. Meanwhile, the beginnings of the one great art that is more nearly America's alone than any other are rapidly on their way to become at one with Nineveh and Tyre.

The endowment of a museum of the motion picture presents an opportunity for some of those so magically enriched by the screen to make graceful acknowledgment of their debt to Yesterday. By this means the motion picture's beginnings may be preserved to history and spared the sketchy inaccuracies of some future archaelogy.

Within a few years of Ramsaye's plea, at the end of the decade, two Los Angeles institutions, the University of Southern California and the newly-formed Academy of Motion Picture Arts and Sciences had both begun collecting film-related books, papers and still photographs. Even in the teens, there had been limited interest in the acquisition of paper items, notably books and scripts, relating to film history. Columbia University had introduced lectures on the motion picture as an art form as early as 1914, and had actively sought to acquire paper materials on the subject.

When the Famous Players Film Company was founded in the summer of 1912, it was approached by Branders Matthews of Columbia with an offer to retain and preserve one copy of each of the company's features. The offer was unconditionally accepted. "That this fact will be the strongest inducement to all the players of the American stage to impel them to consent to portraying their work for the screen needs no saying," commented *The Moving Picture World*. "James O'Neill was so pleased with Monte Cristo that he has decided to present a copy of the film to one of the clubs with which he is connected."* Of course, the reality is that none of the Famous Players productions survived at Columbia, and those that are still extant, including *The Count of Monte Cristo*, are available for study today only because paper print copies were deposited at the Library of Congress.

Despite the urgings of the trade press, film producers in the teens and twenties paid scant attention to the need to safeguard their films for either archival study or future commercial release. With an average of 6,000 feature

---

*Blaisdell, George, "Adolph Zukor Talks of Famous Players," The Moving Picture World, vol. 15, no. 2, January 11, 1913, p. 136.

films produced in each decade, there was little, if any, need to resurrect an old film for reissue. Audiences wanted to see the latest releases. Probably the only company which did reissue its films on a regular basis was the American Biograph Company, which added new titles to one-reel productions to double their length and even lengthened and retitled D.W. Griffith's four-reel *Judith of Bethulia* (1914) to make it the six-reel *Her Condoned Sin* (1917). American Biograph discovered that the fictional shorts it had produced between 1909 and 1913, directed by D.W. Griffith and featuring such members of his stock company as Mary Pickford, Lillian Gish, Robert Harron, Henry B. Walthall, and Blanche Sweet, had value once the individuals concerned had moved on elsewhere and received the screen fame denied to them during the anonymous years they were under contract to American Biograph.

It is perhaps exactly because these American Biograph productions had reissue value that they were cared for and survived, almost in their entirety, with the majority preserved today at the Museum of Modern Art. Indeed, an examination of lists of films from the nitrate era which have survived clearly indicates that those productions which saw later reissue are almost without exception the ones that eventually found their way into film archives for preservation. They might have suffered cuts along the way—*Lost Horizon* and *Becky Sharp*, for example, were in need of restoration because of their reissues—but they continued to live on, in one form or another, in the industry's vaults.

The serious work of film preservation in the United States can be dated from the founding of the Film Library of the Museum of Modern Art in 1935. As early as the summer of 1929, the Museum's first director, Alfred H. Barr, Jr., had suggested that film take its rightful place alongside the other modern arts represented there, but the trustees felt that the Museum must first establish itself before taking the then-revolutionary step of endorsing motion pictures as an art form. Barr again urged the trustees to support film in 1932, and that same year Iris Barry (1895–1969) joined the Museum as a librarian.

Iris Barry was the first of the colorful characters who lit up the archival film scene, and whose like will never be seen again in today's bureaucratic world of film preservation. "She was a tiny woman, extremely slim," recalled Ivor Montagu. "She was always strikingly and fittingly dressed on no money at all. She had a clear, but slightly sallow skin. Her blue eyes were searching and impressive. Her hair was black.... A lesser feminine creature of that day might have settled for an obscure fate. Iris did not."*

Born in Birmingham, England, she had helped form the London Film Society, the world's first such group, in 1925, and served as film critic for both *The Spectator* and the *Daily Mail*. In 1925, she published a witty and intelligent study of the cinema, titled *Let's Go to the Pictures*, which was published the following year in the United States as *Let's Go to the Movies*. (In

---

Montagu, Ivor, "Birmingham Sparrow," in Remembering Iris Barry, p. 5.

1940, she published one other film book, *D.W. Griffith: American Film Master;* and in 1938, she edited and translated Bardeche and Brasillach's *A History of the Motion Picture.*)

Following the break-up of her first marriage to Alan Porter, a member of the Oxford group of poets, she came to the United States, and began work at the Museum of Modern Art; she had earlier been a librarian at the University of London's School of Oriental Studies. On June 25, 1935, the formation of the Film Library was announced, with a founding grant from the Rockefeller Foundation. The department rented space in the Columbia Broadcasting Building at 485 Madison Avenue; Barry's second husband, John Abbott, was named director, and Iris Barry became the Library's first curator.

The Museum's November 1935 *Bulletin* announced, "The Museum of Modern Art Film Library has been established for the purpose of collecting and preserving outstanding motion pictures of all types and of making them available to colleges and museums, thus to render possible for the first time a considered study of the film as art." Initially, screenings were held for members at the Museum of Natural History, but on May 11, 1939, the Film Library commenced its first series of public screenings at the new Museum of Modern Art building at 11 West 53 Street. *The New York Times* (November 6, 1939) commented, "This is the first time that the illustrative programs of the Film Library have been open to the public, and should afford an excellent opportunity for interested persons to become acquainted with the background of motion pictures, as well as for others to see again some of the memorable pictures of the past." With these screenings, the Museum of Modern Art began the first continuous repertory presentation of classic and contemporary motion pictures, screenings which continue to the present, and which have become a model for all other institutions to follow.

Prior to these screenings, older films had generally been totally unavailable to the public. The Museum of Modern Art played an extremely significant role in consciousness-raising not only through screening early films, but also through the creation of a distribution library, making available such films in 16mm and 35mm for educational and institutional use.

With the Film Library's creation, Mary Pickford agreed to host a party at Pickfair in August 1935. All the major producers were represented. Recalled Barry,

> After an excellent dinner, the lights were lowered, and we ran a series of excerpts from outstanding American films. Oddly enough, the most recent proved the most affecting. It was the sequence showing the death of Louis Wolheim in *All Quiet on the Western Front.* Everyone suddenly realized that Wolheim himself, a major star, had died soon after — and now was almost forgotten. It was probably the first intimation of mortality.*

*Quoted in Knight, Arthur, "I Remember MOMA," The Hollywood Reporter, *April 21, 1978, p. 14.*

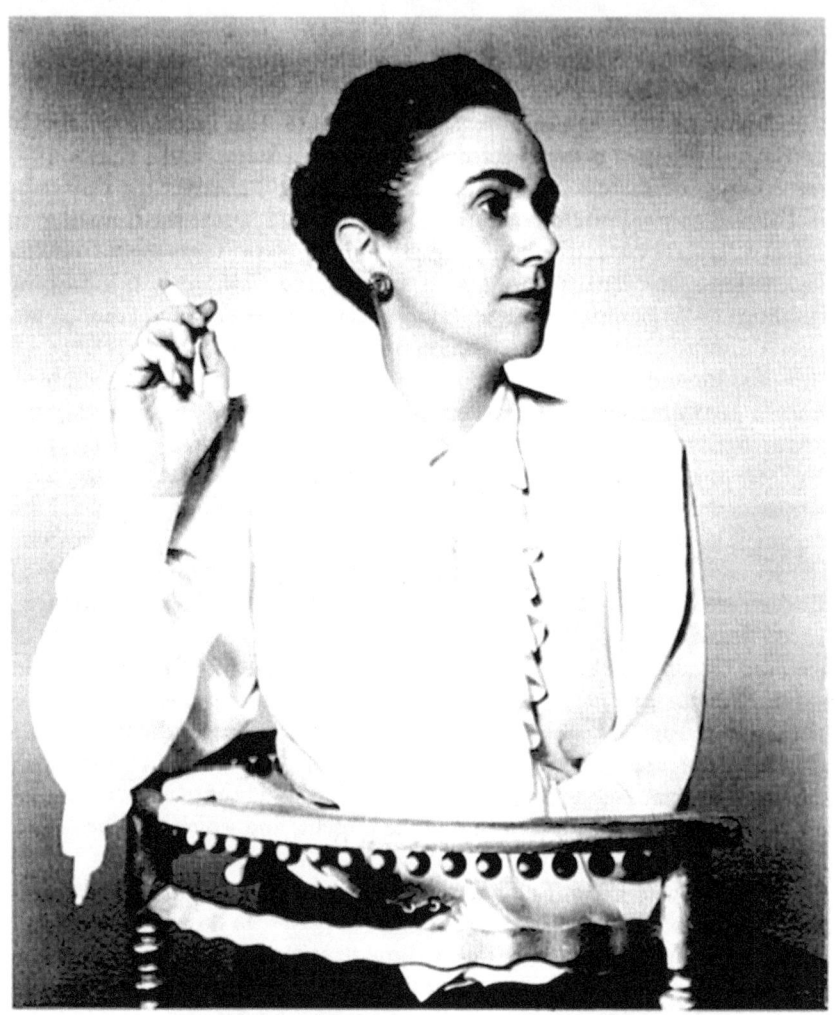

Iris Barry (courtesy of the Museum of Modern Art).

As a result of that presentation, the Museum of Modern Art received donations of 11 films from Harold Lloyd, 11 from Warner Bros., 7 from 20th Century–Fox, 2 from Goldwyn, and a package of early shorts from Walt Disney. The Film Library was well and truly established, helped the following year with a trip to Europe by Barry and Abbott, which resulted in their acquiring "100 miles of film" for the Library.

Further recognition for Barry's work came in 1938, when the Museum of Modern Art received a Special Award from the Academy of Motion Picture Arts and Sciences "for its significant work in collecting films dating from 1895 to the present, and for the first time making available to the public the means of studying the motion picture as one of the major arts." Forty years later, the Museum of Modern Art received a second Honorary Oscar from the Academy, "for the contribution it has made to the public's perception of movies as an art form."

By 1941, the Museum boasted a collection of 16 million feet of film in its vaults, including the personal film collections of D.W. Griffith and Douglas Fairbanks, Sr.

Aside from gathering films, Iris Barry was also gathering around her a small core of enthusiasts, Arthur Knight, Jay Leyda, Ezra Goodman, and Alistair Cooke, whose names were later to become synonymous with the study of film history. She also offered a temporary home at the Museum for such film figures as Billy Bitzer and Luis Buñuel.

Iris Barry also prospered. In 1939, John Abbott resigned as the Film Library's director to become an executive vice president of the Museum and, following a number of years during which the position was unfilled, Barry became the director of the Film Library in 1946—it was not renamed the Department of Film until 1966. In 1949, the French Government made her a Chevalier of the Légion d'Honneur. She retired in 1951, and lived in the south of France until her death.

Iris Barry's legacy is an archives, small, or at least medium-sized in comparison to some of the other film archives, but one which has preserved the majority of the great works of art produced by the motion picture industry. In what might be regarded as almost an arrogant manner, Iris Barry determined what films were important, what films should live and which should be allowed to die. But at least she collected them! Most film histories, certainly through the 1950s, are based on her philosophy and her choices as to what constitutes motion picture art. Even with the work of a director as important as D.W. Griffith, she decided that some of his minor films should not be preserved because they were precisely that—minor films in her determined opinion. In the 1970s, the Museum of Modern Art was able to acquire from Eastern Europe a print of Griffith's 1919 feature, *A Romance of Happy Valley*. Almost 30 years earlier, Iris Barry had turned down the opportunity to acquire the only surviving nitrate print of the film in the United States.

Happily, the Museum's attitude towards film has changed—it changed with Barry's successor, Richard Griffith, and continued with his successors, Willard Van Dyke, Margareta Akermark, Ted Perry, and Mary Lea Bandy—and today, the Museum is much more open to acquiring and preserving any film which has value as popular culture as much as art. In fact, the changes in staff and concomitant changes in selection policies and justifications for individual films have proved healthy for both the Museum and film preservation.

Certainly, in her day, Iris Barry was not without her detractors. In 1945, the Los Angeles critic Herb Sterne wrote a scathing denunciation of her:

Miss Barry's superficial realization of her responsibilities combined with her abysmal ignorance of the American film's worth and import, results in the Library's fragmentary collection which is but ill fitted to aid the student and aesthete in his quest for specific information. Personal reaction, or the lack thereof, seems by the results to be the only yardstick with which the curator is capable of evaluating values. This and the preposterous printed forewords with which the classics of the screen are defaced [a reference to the introductory titles to films in the library's circulating library] above Miss Barry's bold signature have rightly won her, in civilized circles, the title of "The Attila of the Films."

Entangled as is Miss Barry in the foreign films, she finds little time to understand or salvage many important aspects of the American motion picture. The serial, a salient and vastly popular attraction in this country from 1913 to 1920, is represented not at all. In a published statement, Miss Barry admits she recovered certain episodes of the Pathe-Pearl White week-to-weeker, *The Exploits of Elaine*, but she carefully adds that the Library will not circulate the exciters because she personally finds them "dull." It is hardly possible to believe the Metropolitan Museum of Art would own and not hang a Rosa Bonheur merely because of the brassy attitude of a member of its staff.*

Concurrent with the establishment of the Film Library of the Museum of Modern Art, film archives were also formed in England (the National Film Archive), France (Cinémathèque Française) and Germany (Reichsfilmarchiv). It was obvious that these archives would need to work together on matters of mutual concern, and to that end they decided to establish an International Federation of Film Archives. French director Georges Franju has claimed that the concept for such an organization came from director Germaine Dulac, who first broached the idea to representatives of the three archives.

While credit for the idea may be disputed, there is no question that the International Federation of Film Archives/Federation Internationale des Archives du Film (generally known by the acronym FIAF) was officially launched by John Hay Whitney in November 1938. He signed the Federation's charter in the screening room of the Museum of Modern Art, watched by a group which included Barry, Abbott, MOMA president A. Conger Goodyear, MOMA treasurer Nelson A. Rockfeller, and film historian Terry Ramsaye.

In a prepared statement, Whitney said,

This International Federation of Film Archives marks a great step forward in the task of preserving the important films of the world. It is a significant recognition of the international importance of the film as a record of contemporary times. As a result of the close cooperation made possible between the member organizations, the work of preserving for posterity this valuable new type of social and historical document will be assured. It will make possible the easier exchange of books, printed matter, still photographs, scenarios and other material pertinent to the world film, as well as insuring the preservation of the films themselves.

Film archives of other than the four signatory countries have already indicated

*Sterne, Herb, "Iris Barry: The Attila of Films," Rob Wagner's Script, vol. 31, no. 702, April 14, 1945, pp. 14–15.

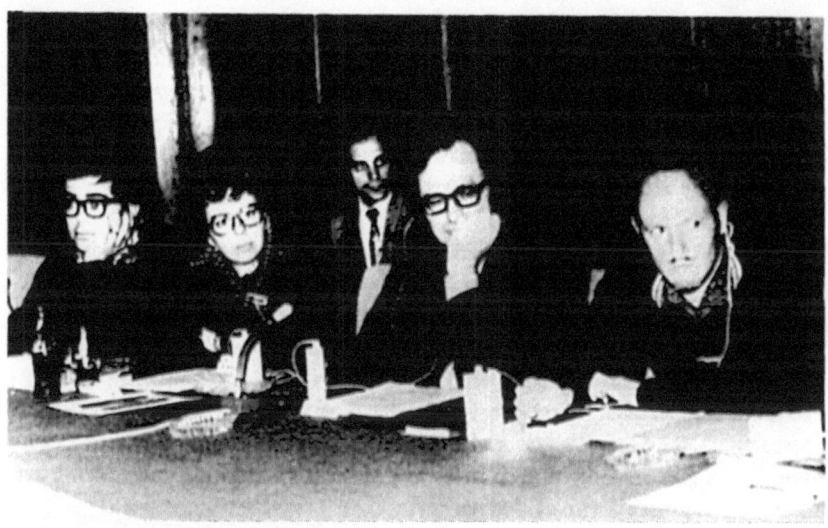

The excitement generated by a FIAF congress is evident in this photograph from the early 1970s. The participants left to right are Lawrence F. Karr, Kathy Karr (both American Film Institute), Clive Coultass (Imperial War Museum), unidentified. The subject under discussion is "Influence of Soviet Cinema on World Cinema."

their desire to join us as members of the International Federation. In times like these it is most encouraging to realize that nations, through the medium of the film, can get together in a strong cooperative movement that is practical and entirely non-commercial, that has no political motivation, but has for its object the better understanding, in a most enjoyable fashion, of the lives, customs, art and achievements of the citizens of every country.*

The four directors of the Federation were John Abbott, Henri Langlois of the Cinémathèque Française, Olwen Vaughan of the National Film Archive (then still called the National Film Library), and Frank Hensel of the Reichsfilmarchiv. The Federation's secretariat was located at the Palais Royale in Paris, with Georges Franju as its elected executive secretary. The first, exploratory, meeting of the Federation took place in May 1938 at the Musée du Jeu de Paume in Paris, and the first annual congress was held at the Museum of Modern Art in August 1939.

The Second World War curtailed the Federation's activities, and it was not reestablished until 1946, by which time the Reichsfilmarchiv had ceased to exist. The secretariat remained in Paris until 1969, when it was moved to Brussels.† While very much a closed organization, whose meetings and findings

---

*"Whitney Starts World Federation to Cooperate on Films' Archives," Motion Picture Herald, November 5, 1938, p. 31.
†The current address is FIAF Secrétariat, rue Franz Merjay 190, 1180 Brussels, Belgium.

remain restricted to public access, FIAF is less secretive than it was. Equally, while still a highly political group, there is less internal bickering than in the past, when the Cinémathèque Française quit in protest, followed by its close American sister institution, the International Museum of Photography at George Eastman House. (Both archives subsequently rejoined the organization, but only after the death and retirement of their respective heads, Henri Langlois and James Card.)

The FIAF is a highly bureaucratic organization, with its "Internal Rules" running to over 100 articles. The second of those articles delineates how an archives may become a member, with the would-be applicant required to have "Observer" status for at least one year, having to submit nine separate documents (15 copies of each), and finally, be visited by a member of FIAF's executive committee. Interestingly, Article 3 of FIAF's rules demand that archives which are part of larger institutions must have a certain, specified degree of autonomy. A reading of such rules would seem to indicate that at least two American member archives do not meet FIAF's rigid standards.

American archives have always had problems vis-à-vis the statutes definitions, and it might be argued that FIAF's disregard of such issues demonstrates not a rigid bureaucracy but a healthy flexibility.

Aside from its annual general assembly meetings in different countries, FIAF maintains three commissions, on Preservation, Cataloging, and Documentation, which meet as required. As far as the general public is concerned, the most visible of FIAF's activities is the compilation and publication of the *International Index to Film Periodicals* (which first appeared in 1972) and the *International Index to TV Periodicals* (first published in 1979).

2 NEWSREEL PRESERVATION AND THE NATIONAL ARCHIVES

On June 19, 1979, George Stevens, Jr., then director of the American Film Institute, and Lillian Gish appeared before the House Government Information and Individual Rights Subcommittee, urging Congress to fund the preservation of America's newsreels. Miss Gish spoke of this country's "powerful history," and the need to "preserve the living record of it." It was not an idle gesture, for while the features and shorts produced by the American film industry have been sought after and preserved, America's newsreels had generally been allowed to disappear through neglect and lack of funding.

One problem then and now is the sheer number of newsreels involved. They had been a staple of American moviegoing from 1911 to 1967. Shown on a weekly basis and each an average 1,000 feet in length, these shorts were produced by as many as half a dozen competing newsreel companies, each of which presented its own, often biased, view of the news; (further confusing the preservation situation, all often shared the same footage). In the 1940s, Howard Walls recalls that the Library of Congress regarded newsreels as major problems in its selection process as to what copyright deposits to keep and what to reject: "We wouldn't want to take all the newsreels, because they were substantially the same. So we thought it would be good to have *Fox Movietone* one year, *Paramount News* the next year, *Pathé* the next year, and so on. Each one would come around every five years."*

As far as preservation of the newsreels was concerned, it was not considered a major aspect of the work of American film archives. If any archives was to accept responsibility for newsreel preservation, it had to be the National Archives and Records Administration. The very valid reasoning behind this argument was that newsreels provided adequate coverage of events which either documented or helped clarify and explain government activities.

Interview with the author, October 7, 1990.

25

The National Archives and Records Service (NARS) was created by an act of Congress on June 19, 1934 (48 Stat. 1122) and was made "responsible for establishing policies and procedures for managing the records of the United States Government." In 1949, it became a service of the newly formed Government Services Administration (GSA). A successor agency, the National Archives and Records Administration, was established by an act of October 19, 1984 (44 U.S.C. 2101 et seq.).

To many, it is surprising that the National Archives was so late in being born. Equally surprising is that film should always have been considered so important a part of the holdings of the Archives, and that the agitation for a government-sponsored national film archives should have been so influential in the creation of the National Archives. As early as 1923, Will H. Hays, president of the Motion Picture Producers and Distributors of America, Inc., had discussed with President Warren G. Harding the need for a fireproof film vault in the basement of the White House. The vault, under the supervision of the President's secretary, was to house footage of events of national importance, such as President McKinley's inauguration and the burial of the unknown soldier in Arlington National Cemetery. President Harding died before Hays' proposal could become reality, but the latter continued to lobby for the idea. He was joined in his efforts by Sydney S. Cohen, president of the Motion Picture Theater Owners of America, who argued for "the location of a Government building in Washington for the proper storage and care of such motion picture film as has sufficient historic value."*

In September 1926, Congress appropriated $6,900,000 for a National Archives building, and Will H. Hays proposed the new building should contain 20 film vaults, each capable of holding 1,000 reels of film. On June 10, 1930, Hays' organization drew up a formal "Resolution for Industry Cooperation in Selecting and Preserving Film Records of Historical Events." However, a 1932 report by Louis Simon, the government's advisory architect, indicated that space for films in the National Archives should be limited to films already owned by the government or films produced by it. Political maneuvering by members of the film industry, President Franklin D. Roosevelt, and others eventually resulted in a bill, which stated in part: "The National Archives may also accept, store, and preserve motion-picture films and sound recordings pertaining to and illustrative of historical activities in the United States, and in connection therewith maintain a projecting room for showing such films and reproducing such sound recordings."

Credit for expanding the role of the National Archives beyond the storage and preservation of government films belongs to Representative Sol Bloom of

---

*"*Cohen Urges Hall of Film Records,*" Morning Telegraph, *March 2, 1924. This and other information relating to the origins of the National Archives is taken from an unpublished paper, "The Origin of Motion Picture and Sound Recording Collection Policy in the National Archives," by Marjorie Heins Ciarlante.*

New York, who introduced three bills into Congress to establish a National Archives, each of which referred to motion pictures, and to John G. Bradley, who was clerk of the House Committee on the Library in 1933–34. Bradley had a personal interest in ensuring that motion pictures should be an integral part of the National Archives. He evaluated the candidates for the position of the first Archivist of the United States. His choice was R.D.W. Connor, Kenan Professor of History at the University of North Carolina. From what we know of Washington politics today, it is not surprising that the first division to be organized in the National Archives was that of Motion Pictures and Sound Recordings, and as its chief, Connor appointed John G. Bradley.

Born in Jackson County, Illinois, on July 31, 1886 — Connor once referred to him as "an Illinois spoilsman"* — Bradley majored in science at Valparaiso University and spent three summers at the University of Chicago, pursuing graduate work in the liberal arts. His early career was varied, including employment as a sales executive, college instructor in English, speech and journalism, and research director for Capper Publications. He dubbed himself Captain Bradley, by virtue of his appointment as captain of the 5th Texas Cavalry, and entered the federal service in 1933 as clerk of the House Committee on the Library.

Howard Walls, with whom Bradley worked at the Library of Congress, recalls him as "a delightful person, witty and friendly. He was a kind of poseur. He knew very little about motion pictures, and, furthermore, he didn't give a damn. He liked the government because it paid him a good salary and he didn't have to do any work."†

One innovation for which Bradley does deserve credit is the development of water-seal storage cabinets for nitrate films. In a February 1949 "confidential" memorandum, the vaults are described thus: "The basic principle of the design is a diversion of heat from the storage area of the cabinet into a common flue and the introduction of water into the cabinet where it flows over, under and around each storage container as a means of carrying off the heat. The source of the water is an automatic sprinkler head."

The storage cabinets were patented under government auspices and tested, and approved, by the National Bureau of Standards. However, they are impractical for the storage of nitrate films in any volume. Currently, the National Archives stores its preservation materials in a climate-controlled facility, equipped with refrigerated vaults, in Alexandria, Virginia.

Bradley remained with the National Archives until July 1945, when he was appointed director of the newly created Motion Picture Division at the Library of Congress. He was well liked by his Library of Congress colleague Howard

---

*Quoted in Shelley, Fred, "The Interest of J. Franklin Jameson in the National Archives: 1908–1934," The American Archivist, vol. 12, p. 43.
†Telephone conversation with the author, December 5, 1990.

Walls, who found the new director supportive and happy to while away the time in his office playing a game of tossing pennies. After a final year as a motion picture consultant to the Library of Congress, Bradley retired from government service at the end of July 1948.

He moved to Colorado for a decade, returning to Washington, D.C., in 1959 to work for audiovisual equipment manufacturer Paul Brand and Sons. He retired again in 1966 and the following year moved to Rancho Bernardo, California. Bradley died in an Escondido, California, nursing home on October 12, 1974.

The film trade press was quick to acknowledge Bradley's appointment to the National Archives. *Motion Picture Herald* (February 9, 1935) reported, "The Motion Picture Producers and Distributors of America has informed the archivist that he will be offered prints of numerous company produced films of historic interest. In addition news and educational films will be collected."

Some of the first films received by the National Archives were of news footage of the First World War, produced by the U.S. Signal Corps, and for the "rehabilitation" of which, $35,000 was assigned in the budget. The Office of the Chief Signal Officer has provided the National Archives with its most substantial film collection, more than 22,000 items dating from 1909 to 1964.

Each government agency commenced, and continues today, to turn over film and video materials to what is now designated the Motion Picture, Sound and Video Branch of the National Archives. One of the earliest of such materials are films filed as plaintiff's exhibits in a copyright case brought by the American Mutoscope and Biograph Company vs. Siegmund Lubin in October 1903 before the U.S. Circuit Court for the Eastern District of Pennsylvania. However, government-related film generally dates from after 1913, when the Department of Agriculture established a motion picture unit.

Nongovernmental gifts to the National Archives are designated Records Group (RG) 200, and within this collection may be found the newsreel holdings, consisting primarily of *Paramount News* (1941–1957), *Fox Movietone News* (1957–1963), *News of the Day* (1963–1967), *Universal News* (1919–1967), *The March of Time* (1935–1951), and *Official War Review* (1917–1919). Also here are items donated by the Ford Motor Company, including *Ford Animated Weekly* (1914–1921) and *Ford Educational Weekly* (1916–1925). (In 1970, the National Archives published a *Guide to the Ford Film Collection in the National Archives*, compiled by Mayfield Bray, describing all 1,500 reels in that collection.)

Because all government-produced film footage is in the public domain, the National Archives quickly became a popular source for actuality footage, available for outside use at cost. In fact, the Archives operates, currently as part of the Motion Picture, Sound and Video Branch, a Stock Film Library, with more than 10,000 reels of film on file. The Stock Film Library contains trims and out-takes from U.S. government productions from the 1940s through the present, with the bulk of the footage originating with the National Aeronautics and Space Administration (NASA). In 1969, the National Archives began administration of the National Audiovisual Center, created as a central sales and distribution agency for current government films and the more popular of earlier titles.

Because of the amount of potential donations—a problem all film archives face—the National Archives has developed a "gift collection acquisition policy" (General Information Leaflet No. 34). Potential public acquisitions by the National Archives are governed by the following factors:

One. The research value of the audiovisual materials, including but not limited to the uniqueness, the quantity and quality of pictorial or aural information, the physical condition, and the relative age of the material.

Two. The relationship of the audiovisual materials to official records or to other gift materials in the National Archives.

Three. The donor's willingness to deed the donated physical property to the National Archives and to allow access to the gift materials for purposes of preservation, study, exhibit, and reproduction, consistent with the donor's applicable underlying rights or copyright interests and with the National Archives' mandate to make its holdings available.

Four. The total processing and preservation requirements. Large collections will not be accepted if it is beyond the means of the National Archives to provide archival processing and reference service within an acceptable period of time. Donor support, however, can be a mitigating factor in measuring the concomitant archival workload.

As of 1990, the National Archives priorities with regard to acquisitions were newsreels from the 1930s and earlier, daily television newscasts, unedited television news coverage, and cable television coverage of Congressional committee hearings. Perhaps it might seem strange that American archives are selective in their acquisitions of nitrate film, but this is a result not only of lack of funds and lack of storage space, but also, and this is perhaps more relevant, the high cost of preservation, management, and disposition of nitrate film elements. Disposal of nitrate film has become a costly exercise. The International Museum of Photography solved the problem by burying its decomposing nitrate film in the ground. Other archives are forced to arrange for salvage companies to remove the film at a cost of $800 or more per barrel, with each barrel containing not only reels of nitrate film, but also cans and sufficient water to cover the contents. Long gone are the days when salvage companies would pay for nitrate film in order to recover its silver content.

Inadequate public funding has long hampered the preservation work of the National Archives. Inadequate funding can also, arguably, be blamed for a disastrous fire which took place at the Suitland, Maryland, nitrate vaults of the National Archives on December 7, 1978. Built in 1948 as temporary storage facilities, the Suitland vaults did not meet contemporary archival standards for nitrate storage. On the day of the fire, unsupervised construction workers were using electric power tools within the vaults. Heat from the tools apparently set off a fire, which spread quickly because the vault doors had been left open while the workers were at lunch. Thirteen units from the Prince George County Fire Department arrived within seven minutes of the alarm being given, but instead of immediately tackling the fire, they began opening further vault doors in search of trapped workers, an exercise in dangerous futility in that all the workers had fled. The opening of additional vault doors further accelerated the fire.

The fire destroyed a total of 12,600,000 feet of film, including 70 percent of the out-takes from the *Universal Newsreel* footage, donated to the National Archives by MCA-Universal in 1974. An earlier fire at the National Archives vaults on August 29, 1977, had already destroyed one million feet of *March of Time* footage, donated by Time, Inc.

Two reports were prepared on the National Archives fires, the first in the summer of 1979 by W.H. Utterback of Amarillo, Texas, and titled "An Opinion on the Nitrate Film Fire, Suitland, Maryland," and the second, House Report No. 96-574, "National Archives Film Vault Fire," released on October 31, 1979, and prepared by a House of Representatives subcommittee chaired by Richardson Preyer.

In his "Washington Merry-Go-Round" column of April 24, 1979, Jack Anderson had denounced the National Archives for its "gross mismanagement and negligence," pointing out that not only was the Archives allowing its film holdings to decompose, but also its paper collections were in immediate danger. Anderson claimed that the Archives management had ignored a 1969 internal report warning of "the self-igniting potential" of nitrate film.

Anderson and the official reports all ignored the basic problem, a lack of funding. There seems little doubt that anyone involved in film preservation is fully aware of the potential danger from nitrate film decomposition, but without adequate funding, there is no way the situation can be improved. Hindsight is all very well and good for politicians and political commentators but only money can rectify harmful situations.

In 1976, William T. Murphy was appointed chief of the Motion Picture, Sound and Video Branch of the National Archives. Only three months prior to the Suitland fire, in December 1978, he he had circulated a draft proposal for "A National Program for the Preservation of American Newsreels," commissioned by the American Film Institute. In his report, Murphy noted that approximately half a million feet of news footage was decomposing each year, and that less than 25 percent of the newsreel footage from the 1920s was known to exist. At that time, Murphy estimated it would cost between 15 and 30 million dollars, over a 20-year period, to preserve America's surviving newsreels.

One of the problems which Murphy indicated had to be resolved as part of an inclusive newsreel preservation program was that many newsreels were in private ownership. John E. Allen, Inc., held *Telenews* (1948–1954) and an incomplete run from the 1920s and early 1930s of *Kinograms*. Sherman Grinberg Film Libraries, Inc., also had issues of *Kinograms*, as well as *Pathé News* from the early 1900s through 1956 and *Paramount News* (1927–1957). In 1977, Sherman Grinberg Film Libraries approached the Library of Congress, asking that it take over the company's rotting nitrate, but with long-term restrictions on its subsequent use.

Fox Movietone News held 49 million feet of nitrate and 24 million feet of safety film for both its edited newsreels and out-takes from 1919 to 1963. In 1976, Fox and the National Archives began a joint preservation program for the silent newsreels from 1919 to 1930. Safety fine-grain masters were made with funding by the National Archives. The masters were stored at the Archives, but rights to the footage were retained by Fox for a 50-year period. It was a sweetheart deal which did little for the American taxpayer, who was footing the bill, but was highly advantageous to Fox, which not only had its footage preserved at no cost, but also insisted that the work be done at its own laboratory!

In 1980, 20th Century–Fox, of which Fox Movietone News is a division, announced the donation of all the newsreel footage, including out-takes and paper records, to the Thomas Cooper Library at the University of South Carolina. According to *The New York Times* (March 29, 1980), "South Carolina received the library because it had pioneered in the audio-visual presentation of education programs and had the computer technology to handle the newsreel cataloguing, indexing and retrieval." Unfortunately, the University had neither the laboratory facilities nor adequate funding to preserve the footage, and much of the material remains uncopied onto safety film as of 1991. James Jackson, Jr. (1924–1990), had been a writer-producer on the PBS series *Lowell Thomas Remembers*, which made extensive use of the *Fox Movietone News* footage. He was largely responsible for arranging the donation to the University of South Carolina, and was director of the News Film Library there from 1980 until his retirement in 1988.

At the time William T. Murphy prepared his report, the other major, privately-held newsreel was Hearst Metrotone News, a division of King Features Syndicate, founded in 1914 by William Randolph Hearst and active in newsreel production through 1967. In December 1981, the Hearst Corporation announced the donation of the newsreel collection (excluding various programs derived from the footage) to the UCLA Film and Television Archive. Randolph A. Hearst, chairman of the Hearst Corporation, commented, "Over the past 75 years, my family has been privileged to be able to serve and contribute to the University of California in a number of ways. Our family is rooted in California and we are enormously pleased to know that the Film Library will be a valuable teaching and research source at the

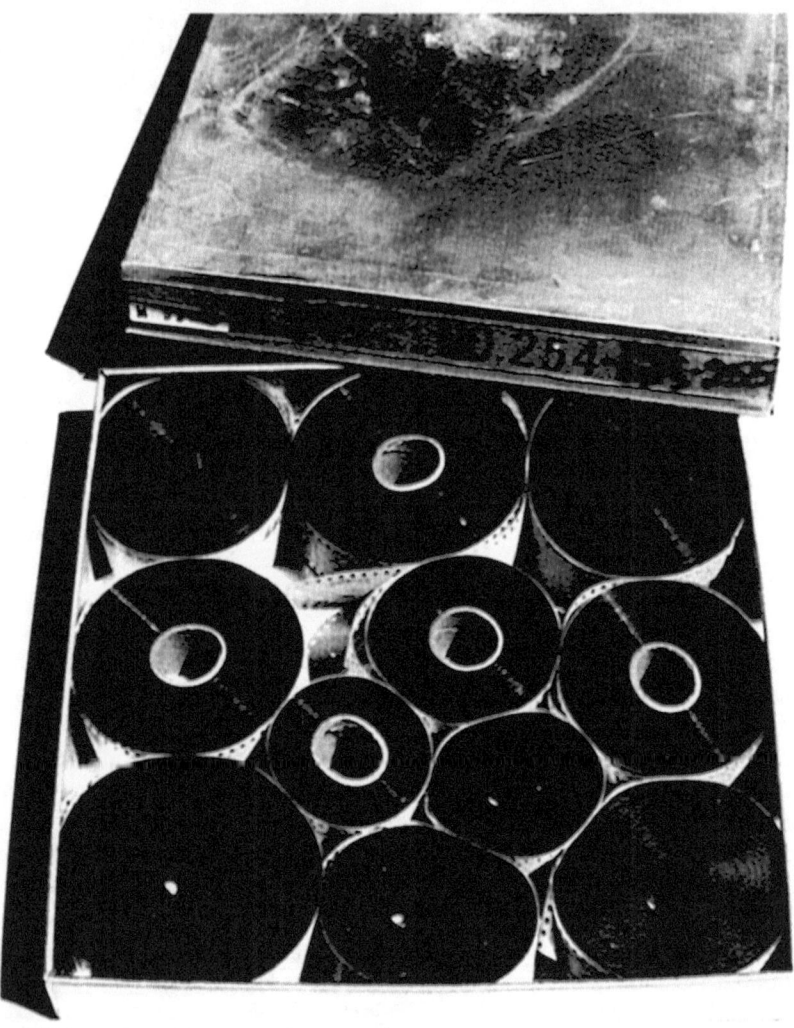

A can of Hearst Metrotone News footage as originally stored and donated to the UCLA Film and Television Archive (photograph by Blaine Bartell).

University."* The first batch of film arrived at the Archive in 1982, with the remainder of the 27 million feet arriving the following year. (Approximately half of the footage is safety film.)

Newsreel footage can consist of either the original newsreel story or stories (generally referred to as "cut picture") and the trims or out-takes, not utilized

*Quoted in Harwood, Jim, "Hearst Newsreel Footage Goes to UCLA Film Archive," Daily Variety, December 3, 1981, p. 1.

in the released version of the newsreel. The cut picture is obviously important as far as preservation is concerned, because it will consist of the best shots taken by the cameraman and will also indicate to the social or political historian a potential bias in the manner in which the narrator describes the news event. However, the trims and out-takes are equally important, sometimes for the same reason—they will show scenes which the newsreel management might not want the viewer to see.

The UCLA Film and Television Archive is lucky in that it has all the newsreel components, but the cut newsreels have, generally, not been stored as such. They have been cut into small rolls, by subject, wrapped around spindles, with a thousand foot reel of newsreel comprising six or eight such small rolls. For the earliest sound newsreels, 1929–1935, the Archive has only rolls of composite prints. From 1935 onwards, it has both the negative and the projection print, both of which also cut up into small rolls.

The rolls are stored in cans identified by the volume and issue number of each newsreel, and, in addition, the Archive has synopsis sheets listing the stories for all the newsreels. The policy of the UCLA Film and Television Archive is to preserve and restore the newsreels, issue by issue, in their entirety. Blaine Bartell has been responsible for UCLA's newsreel preservation program since April 1984. He explains the problems encountered in preserving newsreels as opposed to feature films and short subjects:

> Very few features have been cut up into 100 feet rolls, which have to be pieced back together. And in synching the sound track back up to the picture that you've pieced together, there is a good deal of voice-over narration which is not synchronized with the action. It can be deceptive as to whether or not you've got it actually in synch, especially if there are a lot of jump cuts. In the sense that newsreels were often used as stock footage, there are an excessive amount of jump cuts. In features, the sound track negative is basically stored to be matched to the picture negative. Whereas the newsreels were stored for an entirely different purpose.
>
> The other big difference would be that with features you have a professional film crew with controlled lighting, and the images were lit and blocked to match when the editor went to cut the picture together. In the newsreels, they took what they could get, and the image quality can vary wildly. It's a problem with timing. It can be a problem with developing as well. You can go from a very flat image to a very contrasty image in the same story. If you are going from a print, and you are going to make a duplicate negative from that, you have to find a point in the developing midway between to get the most out of both and still be compatible with the majority of the other shots. Sometimes, you'll have to ignore a particular shot—it's too flat or too contrasty to be retrievable. Ideally, you could go through the film and make a duplicate negative for every shot, and splice that together and then print up from that. But that would really be expensive.*

As with all preservation programs, the newsreel preservation at UCLA is hampered by lack of funds, with the two major sources for many years being

Interview with the author, November 8, 1990.

the National Endowment for the Humanities and the David and Lucile Packard Foundation. Half of the available funds go toward preserving the released
newsreels, and the remainder is used to preserve the trims and out-takes. Selection can be a problem, as Bartell points out:

> We try and do the earlier things first. At this point, just about everything silent
> is the top priority. Also, we emphasize American events. We've done a lot of
> things in the 1930s, particularly pertaining to strikes, political rallies, America
> First, anti-Hitler rallies, going off the gold standard.
> We're so understaffed. Ideally, we should be winding through the film, getting
> a better idea of what's there, inspecting it for deterioration. The time spent
> debating the merits of preserving one presidential election versus the other is not
> a good use of time. With people who are not aware of some of the problems in-
> volved with the film, you can really sound like you don't have standards. But that
> really isn't the case. There are a lot of problematic things with the collection which
> you can create for yourself — additional problems — if you aren't careful.
> The last year or two, an awful lot of what we've done has been dictated by what
> started to deteriorate. You can spend a lot of time just working the material over,
> deciding if it should be preserved or not, because a lot of the descriptions are
> misleading. You can waste an awful lot of time looking for something that is not
> there. Expediency is what matters. When you have something in your hand and
> you know it's valuable, then preserve it.*

While not a newsreel archives like the University of South Carolina or
UCLA, Iowa State University's American Archives of the Factual Film is a third
important nongovernmental source of actuality footage. Founded in 1975, the
Archives holds more than 8,000 nontheatrical films and related documentation. Among the sponsored 16mm films in its holdings are those produced by
American Telephone and Telegraph, the American Medical Association,
General Electric, International Harvester, Pan American Airways, and West-
inghouse. The earliest film in the collection is *Back to the Old Farm*, sponsored
in 1911 by International Harvester.†

In 1980, the American Archives of the Factual Film did receive a $3,910
grant from the AFI/NEA for the development of a preservation program, but
regrettably preservation is not a high priority with the Archives, as its curator
and founder, Stanley Yates notes:

> In the good old days when the American Archives of the Factual Film had a
> film archivist, there was a fledgling preservation/conservation program. As much
> as we would like to reinstitute such a program, the realities of the current situation
> are not favorable. Perhaps upon my retirement within the next year [1991], a film
> archivist will be hired and the AAFF can then go ahead with a preservation/conser-
> vation program. We can only hope (and do a little agitation).§

---

*Ibid.
†*For more information, see Perkins, Daniel J., "The American Archives of the Factual Film,"*
Historical Journal of Film, Radio and Television, *vol. 10, no. 1, 1990, pp. 71–80.*
§*Letter to the author, November 2, 1990.*

Funding for preservation of newsreel and actuality footage remains a continuing problem. In January 1986, the Smithsonian Institution's National Air and Space Museum urged the aerospace community to donate $550,000 for the preservation of 800,000 feet of Fox Movietone News footage on major aviators and aviation events.

In England, a group of private newsreel companies have got together to form the Nitrate 2000 Campaign. Pathé News Archive, Movietone News Archive, Scottish Film Archive, London Transport Museum, National Motor Museum, Sikorski Museum, Cannon Screen Entertainment, Austin Rover Car Co., Ray Hooley-Ruston Collection, Yorkshire Film Archive, and London Film Productions urged public funding to a total amount of $14.5 million, for the preservation of their collective holdings of 12 million feet of news film.*

*The address for Nitrate 2000 is 111 Wardour Street, London W1V 4AY, England. For more information, see "Nitrate Project 2000: A Race Against Time," Historical Journal of Film, Radio and Television, vol. 7, no. 3, 1987, pp. 325–334.

3 THE LIBRARY
OF CONGRESS

As Doug Herrick has written in his excellent historical survey of the film preservation program at the Library of Congress:

> The story of the national film collection at the Library of Congress is not a narrative involving the sweep and dramatic scope of a major government undertaking. Unlike the creation of the British Film Institute, the French Cinémathèque, or the National Film Board of Canada, there is no date that one can point to to observe the birth of the Motion Picture Collection at LC. Perhaps it occurred in 1893, when Thomas Edison's assistant W.K.L. Dickson registered several "Kineographic Records" for copyright protection at the LC. If so, it was an inauspicious beginning, for LC lost the materials.*

Because there was no provision under the copyright act for films to be registered as such, beginning in 1894, motion pictures were deposited at the Library of Congress on paper strips. These paper strips or prints came under the jurisdiction of the Division of Prints, established in 1897, which did nothing with the material except place it in storage. The earliest reference to the paper prints is in the 1902 Annual Report of the Librarian of Congress, which notes that the holdings of the Division of Prints consists of 118,980 "Photographs (including 38,781 stereoscopic views and 1413 kinetoscope films)."

In 1912, the Townsend Act was passed, recognizing motion pictures as entities in their own right for copyright purposes. In that the Print Division had no capability for the storage of nitrate film, an agreement was worked out whereby the Library of Congress would process copyright registrations within one day of the receipt of the films, which would then be returned. The Library would retain only supplemental material, such as scripts, posters, credit sheets, or synopses.

The year 1939 is often hailed as one of the most important in the history

*Herrick, Doug, "Toward a National Film Collection: Motion Pictures at the Library of Congress," Film Library Quarterly, vol. 13, no. 2/3, 1980, p. 5.

of the cinema, a year which saw the release of *Gone with the Wind*, *Stage-coach*, *The Wizard of Oz*, and countless other major Hollywood productions. It was also a crucial year for film preservation at the Library of Congress. It saw the retirement of Herbert Putnam (1861–1955) as Librarian of Congress. A renowned scholar and the first trained librarian to head the venerable institution, Putnam was the longest serving librarian in the history of the Library of Congress, having been appointed in 1899. Putnam had developed a new system of book classification and he had acquired a valuable collection of European incunabula, including a Gutenberg Bible, for the Library. He viewed libraries as repositories for books and papers; he did not consider film an appropriate Library asset.

Putnam's replacement was Archibald MacLeish (1892–1982), who was appointed by President Roosevelt over the objections of members of the House who viewed him as a fellow-traveler of the Communist Party. MacLeish had an intense interest in films; he had coproduced the 1937 documentary, *The Spanish Earth*, directed by Joris Ivens. He was a visionary rather than a librarian. Of him, Herbert Putnam commented:

> There is first the Scot in him — shrewd, austere, exacting, but humorous. There is the poet in him — whose stuff is not made of mere dreams but of realities. There is the humanist, keenly sympathetic to all that calls for social sympathy. The lawyer-trained to analysis through determination of exact issues. The soldier — pledged to duty under discipline. The athlete pledged to fair play. And finally there's the orator — capable of vivid and forceful speech.*

Also in 1939 a young man named Howard Walls, a graduate of the University of Michigan, was hired by the Library of Congress, on March 10. He was enthusiastic and anxious to find a niche for himself there. He recalls:

> I started out working in the reference division. Then I got into legislative research, in which you looked up material or did research for U.S. senators and congressmen, and prepared the material for them. I decided I'd like to work in the copyright office. I asked for it, got it, and they put me to work in what was called the Index Section. They were revamping all of the copyright files so that you could get at the materials easier and faster. So I became interested in which might have been deposited for copyrights in the way of motion pictures, not expecting to run into the pictures themselves. I wanted to get the literature they had sent in describing the stuff.
>
> There was an old vault in the main building, right under the main reading room. It hadn't been opened for 35 years. I went to Colonel [Clement Lincoln] Bouvé, the Register of Copyrights, and I told him, I suspect there's a lot of material in there that might be valuable, and that I'd like the key to look into. He said I'd have to get permission of the Librarian of Congress, Archibald MacLeish. He said, Of course. Bouvé handed me the key, and he said, "I'm afraid you're not going to find anything in there except a lot of paper junk." That one was for the ages! When we got over there, we couldn't get the lock open because

---

*Quoted in Current Biography, *1940, p. 541.*

it had rusted shut. So we got a maintenance man, and he sawed that lock off. Behind this great big iron door, I saw these Edison and Biographs stacked up from the wall all the way up to the ceiling.

There was a grating, with air coming in to the vault. That vault had been open to all kinds of weather, but the grating was over a shaft so it never rained in there, it never snowed in there. And the successive wrappings on these paper rolls protected them. Each time it was wrapped around, the picture underneath was protected. I walked over and looked at one end of the paper roll, and I remember it said Biograph on it. I knew right away we'd just hit the jackpot.*

What Walls had uncovered were the paper prints of motion picture films, deposited at the Library of Congress for copyright purposes prior to 1912, when there was no other legitimate way by which films could be copyrighted. In order to copyright their works, early producers had been forced to print the films onto rolls of paper, which could be copyrighted as photographic images. Despite the change in the copyright law in 1912, some producers continued to deposit paper prints as late as 1916.

For help in reconstituting the paper prints, Walls approached Carl Louis Gregory (1882–1951), a motion picture engineer with the National Archives. Gregory had been a pioneering cinematographer; he filmed the 1914 serial *The Million Dollar Mystery*. On the staff of the National Archives from 1936 to 1946, Gregory was also interested in the technological history of the cinema.†

> Some of the paper ribbons were perforated like film, but many of them had been printed by some continuous process on imperforate paper tape [reported Gregory]. It was obvious that none of these fragile paper ribbons could be run through any ordinary projector or printing machine and that, even if they could be so run, they could not be projected on account of the opaque paper base.§

For the restoration of the paper prints, Gregory modified a process optical printer with a special projection head with interchangeable sprockets and pull-down pins to take the paper without mutilating it. An adjustable aperture plate allowed for framing off-standard frame lines. Because the paper prints had been made on a continuous basis without adjustment for the varying densities of the original negative, Gregory arranged that the reflected light necessary to illuminate the surface of the paper prints for copying could be adjusted, intensifying and reducing the lighting dependent upon whether the scenes were light or dark. "The description may sound complicated," commented Gregory, "but it is in reality quite simple when compared to devices and processes which are in daily use in all the animation studios."**

This and other quoted remarks from Howard Walls are taken from an October 7, 1990, interview with the author.

†*One of Gregory's first articles on the history of motion picture technology was "The Early History of Wide Films" in* American Cinematographer, *January 1930, pp. 5, 29.*

§*Gregory, Carl Louis, "Resurrection of Early Motion Pictures,"* Journal of the Society of Motion Picture Engineers, *vol. 42, no. 3, March 1944, p. 164.*

**Ibid., p. 169.*

Daily Variety announced on June 7, 1943, "It won't be long before those first pictures may be making a comeback." In reality, the Second World War intervened, putting a halt to the work on the paper prints. There was some interest from commercial companies, and, in fact, RKO paid to have a 35mm dupe negative made of the 1904 paper print of the Vanderbilt Cup Race. RKO was supposed to return the negative to the Library of Congress after its use for a short subject, *Past Performances,* in the Sportscope series, but instead it cut the original negative into the film and failed to return the trims.

Other film-related activities were taking place at the Library of Congress. In 1942, Archibald MacLeish arranged for the Rockefeller Foundation to fund a program whereby the Museum of Modern Art would make a selection of films submitted for copyright registration which were to be retained by the Library. The selection process was completed in April 1945, with the Library's acquiring 603 reels of feature films, 188 reels of newsreel, 62 documentaries, and 118 reels of short subjects. This group had been selected from a total of 4,398 films by a committee of five: Norbert Lusk, Philip Hartung, Liane Richter, Barbara Deming, and Barbara Symmes. In his 1943 Annual Report of the Librarian of Congress, MacLeish wrote:

> For better than a quarter of a century the Library has been obliged to return copyright deposits of motion pictures because it had no vaults for the storage of inflammable films. The opportunity to build up a national collection of moving pictures has been lost, but not necessarily for good. Our magnificent collection of old moving pictures prior to 1912, the discovery of which in paper prints was reported last year, and the existence, in private hands, of collections of the most important materials of the period from 1912 to date, would make it possible, with the aid of generous collectors, to reconstitute what has been lost.*

In 1943, MacLeish appointed Howard Walls assistant in charge of the motion picture archives. Walls took over two study rooms on the upper tier of the Library's annex building, took down the partition to give himself more room, and decorated the walls with paper materials from the copyright deposit files. On January 28, 1944, Archibald MacLeish established the Motion Picture Collection, with Walls as its curator. On October 4, 1946, the Motion Picture Collection became the Motion Picture Division, with a staff of 17. Walls continued as curator, and John Bradley, from the National Archives, was named its director.

The first matter with which the new entity had to deal were the German, Japanese, and Italian films seized by the Alien Property Custodian. As Walls recalls:

> They didn't know what to do with them. MacLeish asked if we could handle it, and I said we could try. There was thirty million feet of film, stored in what was called a cooling tower in the Interior Department. Frank Capra had his office

Annual Report of the Librarian of Congress, 1943, p. 47.

in that cooling tower, and had all these films available at his fingertips. He had
a motion picture machine running day and night, with two operators, to make
synopses, so he could go over them to see if he wanted to use any material for
"Why We Fight."

That stuff was all nitrate and it was very hazardous. I told MacLeish, if that stuff
goes off down there, somebody's going to be guilty of murder, because it'll kill
a lot of people. He moved fast on that. He called up the Pentagon, and they made
available to us the old Civil War powder vaults at Fort Hunt, Virginia, just three
miles short of Mount Vernon. We put the films in there, but then we had the rainy
season, and the water came in the vaults. We fixed up some kind of chemical apparatus that was supposed to absorb the water in the vault, but there was too much
water. You couldn't possibly absorb it.

I wrote a memorandum to the files, copying Mr. MacLeish and the Alien Property Custodian that I was renouncing all responsibility for the damage that would
be done to these films. That did it! The Alien Property Custodian hired a lot of
vaults at Bonded Film Storage in New York, and we used their services while we
were building a big vault out in Suitland, Maryland.

About the time the Suitland vaults (which are still in use) were completed, the Army Pictorial Service contacted the Library to announce it had 75
million feet of seized German film on hold in New York. The film arrived from
Germany not in cans, but packed in sawdust inside crates. Three trucks transported the film from New York to Washington, D.C.

Here was our first building ready for film, and we had enough film here to fill
every single vault [recalls Walls]. The vault was made out of blocks cemented
together, and the cement had not yet dried. We had great fans standing at one
end of the building, blowing air through, and all the doors open to the vaults.
We hired enough people to clean the films and put them in cans, and we put them
in vaults and left the vault doors open. We didn't have any alternative. After we
got them all in, an airplane took off from Bowling Field, right next door, and
crashed twenty yards from the building! He didn't hit the roof, but there was some
real criticism about it—the Keeper of the Collections [Alvin W. Kremer] got the
blame.

In 1963, Public Laws 87-846 and 87-861 returned copyrights in the seized
German, Japanese, and Italian films to their original owners or successors, but
the Library of Congress and the National Archives were permitted to retain
custody of the films and make them available for screenings. In 1967, the
Library of Congress agreed to return the Japanese films to their country of
origin, but with the proviso that the Tokyo Museum of Modern Art make new
safety prints for the Library.

The first major nongovernmental film collection which the Library of
Congress set out to acquire was that of Mary Pickford. Ever the business-
woman, Pickford was disturbed at the bills she was paying for the storage of
her films, and rumor reached Howard Walls that she might be willing to
deposit the materials at the Library of Congress. Walls drafted a letter to Pickford for Archibald MacLeish's signature, and the latter confirmed that it had

been sent with a memorandum reading, "I have cast my net towards the broad and blue Pacific, and hope to catch some very large and silver fish."

By this time, Carl Louis Gregory had relocated to Van Nuys, California, and he was hired by the Library of Congress to inventory and examine the collection. In November 1946, he began winding through the films, and a month later he had an eight-page inventory listing not only all of Pickford's films, but also many non–Pickford titles in which the actress had a financial interest. Tragically, the Library of Congress was not to have the funds available to preserve the Pickford films. Some were copied, in 16mm, by the International Museum of Photography at George Eastman House. At her death in 1979, Pickford left her films to the Library of Congress. Since then, some effort has been made for their preservation. Matty Kemp, managing director of the Mary Pickford Company, has also restored some of the titles, and made arrangements for the preservation of some non–Pickford features, including *The Bat Whispers* (1930) and *The Gay Desperado* (1936), by the UCLA Film and Television Archive. The latter has also been able to preserve Pickford's 1920 feature, *The Love Light*, directed by Frances Marion.

Back at the Library of Congress, Archibald MacLeish resigned in December 1944, and he was succeeded in June 1945 by Luther Harris Evans (1902–1981), a longtime Library of Congress staff member. Evans was ambitious—he was later to become director general of UNESCO—but he was also less of a visionary than MacLeish. Like so many bureaucrats who were to enter the film preservation field in later years, Evans was not just interested in film preservation as an important job in its own right. He wanted more from the Motion Picture Division. He wanted the Library of Congress to become involved in the distribution of films, and he made a speech promoting that idea to the National Board of Review in New York.

Evans' proposal came at a time when the House Appropriations Committee was considering a $500,000 budget for the Motion Picture Division. The film industry, disturbed by what it viewed as an incursion into its territory, brought pressure to bear on the California representatives, and the Committee voted to cease funding the Division. The decision was upheld in the votes of the House and the Senate. On July 31, 1947, the Motion Picture Divison was formally closed and its entire staff dismissed. Howard Walls was invited by Evans to remain on at the Library of Congress, but he decided to cash in his pension—$1,200—and go to Los Angeles, in an effort to interest the film industry in keeping the paper print restoration project alive.

A mere $12,000 was allocated in the Library of Congress budget for the storage of films, which were placed under the control of the Keeper of the Collections. With no funding available for copying, the Keeper of the Collections had no alternative but to inspect the films on a casual basis and junk any reels showing signs of deterioration. Between 1949 and 1959, the Library of Congress halved its holdings of nitrate film.

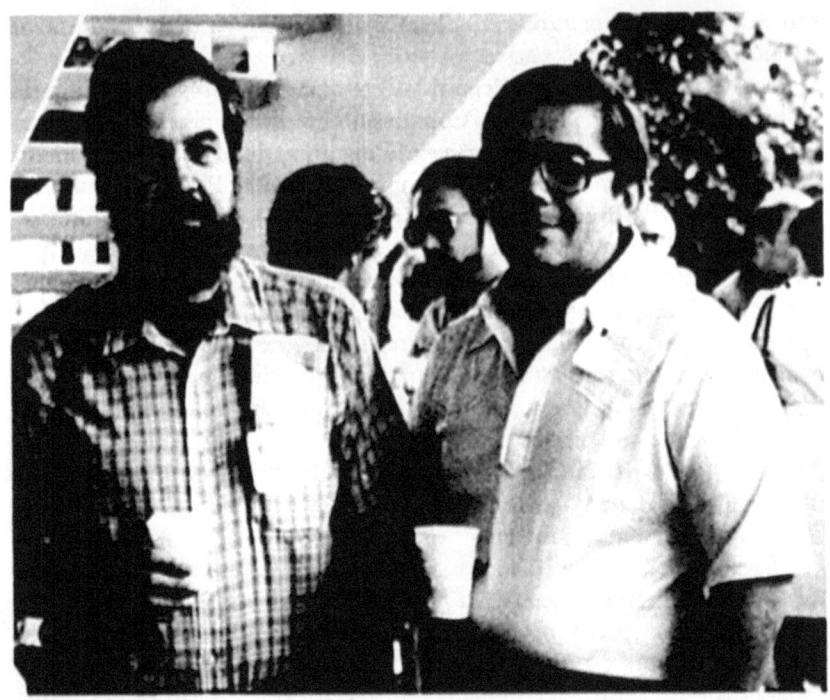

Paul Spehr (left) and Lawrence F. Karr at the 1982 FIAF Congress in Mexico City.

Film historian and industry observer Terry Ramsaye wrote to Howard Walls, "According to reports that I hear from Washington the Congressional Library's film project is not likely to recover its health for a long time. I am inclined to fear that the Library is becoming decidedly more of an institution of politics than of culture."*

On July 12, 1949, Bradley also wrote to Walls, "As yet Dr. Evans has not, so I am told, asked for a restoration of the motion picture program and I understand also, that no money was requested even for preserving the present collection. I am very sad about this."

In fiscal year 1951–1952, James Culver was appointed custodian of the Motion Picture Collection. He left the Library in June 1964, by which time the Motion Picture Section had been resuscitated. (The title change took place in fiscal year 1955–1956.)

In 1958, Congress once again began to appropriate funds for film preservation at the Library of Congress, thanks in large part to the efforts of California Senator Thomas Kuchel.

*Letter from Terry Ramsaye to Howard Walls, dated January 20, 1948, in the files of the Margaret Herrick Library of the Academy of Motion Picture Arts and Science.

In July 1965, John Kuiper (born 1928), a former film professor from Iowa State Univeristy, was appointed head of the Motion Picture Section, and he more than any other individual revived the Library's film preservation activities. Kuiper initiated the microfilming of the copyright records relating to film, and he actively encouraged producers to deposit their films with the Library as part of the preservation process. The founding of the American Film Institute in 1967 further enhanced the work of the Motion Picture Section in that the Library was charged with the storage and preservation of films gathered by the new organization. Further, in its early years, the Institute provided funding for much of the work of the Motion Picture Section.

In 1969, the libraries of negatives and other preprint materials of both RKO and United Artists were deposited with the Library of Congress. A year later, the Library established its own in-house preservation film laboratory in the basement of the Thomas Jefferson Building, with an initial staff of two. By 1977, the laboratory was handling some six million feet of film a year. Quality control of the Library's preservation work was a problem for a number of years. While its preservation work has now reached acceptable standards, the same cannot be said of the prints and negatives which the Library provides under its public access policy. Individuals ordering material from the Library often find themselves paying for shoddy laboratory work, reminiscent of earlier days in film history when it was assumed that it was impossible to obtain good quality prints of old films.

The activities of the Motion Picture Section had expanded to such an extent in 1972 that it was necessary to move its operations from the main Library building to the Thomas Jefferson annex. In 1973, Alan M. Fern became chief of the Prints and Photographs Division, of which the Motion Picture Section was a part, and he was an enthusiastic and diligent promoter of the work of the Section, sometimes finding it necessary to emphasize that it was the Motion Picture Section which was preserving America's film heritage rather than the publicity-hungry American Film Institute.

The handling of nitrate film on the premises of the Library of Congress was discontinued in 1979 as a direct result of the National Archives vault fire. Librarian of Congress Daniel Boorstin insisted that all of the Library's nitrate holdings had to be disposed of as soon as practical, and that its acquisition of nitrate should be on a far more selective basis. Further, nitrate film could no longer be made available for outside screenings. The Library's in-house film laboratory was moved to Wright Patterson Air Force Base in Dayton, Ohio, and became operational there in the fall of 1981. Jokes circulated around the film preservation community that the Library's policy was changed for fear of a nitrate fire taking the lives of politicians on Capitol Hill. It was OK to handle nitrate in Ohio, because the lives of the inhabitants of that state were expendable.

In 1980, the Motion Picture Section was upgraded to become the Motion

Picture, Broadcasting and Recorded Sound Division, independent and equal
to its former parent, the Prints and Photographs Division. (The title change
indicated a new concern for preservation in the area of television.)

When John Kuiper left the Library of Congress in 1977, to become director of the Department of Film at the International Museum of Photography
at George Eastman House (a position which he held until 1987), Erik Barnouw
was appointed chief of the Division on July 31, 1978. Barnouw's appointment,
and that of his successor Robert Saudek, indicated a desire on the part of the
Librarian of Congress to appoint figureheads from the world of broadcasting
rather than what might be described as the old-fashioned type of hands-on
film archivists and preservationists such as John Kuiper and the Division's long-
time assistant chief, Paul C. Spehr.

(Dr. Kuiper was asked to comment on this chapter but declined, describing it as "full of holes, omissions and distortions." He also wondered "how you
can identify, understand and consequently express the generative mechanisms
behind the events at LC, for example, the lack of movement then sudden and
abrupt actions, without having been in federal service."*)

Back in 1947, Luther Evans had envisioned the Library's organizing a per-
manent film exhibition program. His dream became a reality on May 10, 1983,
when the 64-seat Mary Pickford Theatre was dedicated in the Library's new
James Madison Memorial Buildings, thanks to a $500,000 donation from the
Mary Pickford Foundation. The Motion Picture, Broadcasting and Recorded
Sound Division also made a move to the new building.

*Letter to the author, February 24, 1991.

4 THANKS TO
THE FILM COLLECTORS

The relationship between film collectors and film archives has always been an uneasy one. The former tend to view archives as bureaucratic strongholds which horde films and deny access to their holdings to people who genuinely "love" film (that is, collectors). Film archives must at least make a show of recognizing copyright laws. Such laws are generally ignored by collectors, who argue, with some reason, that the laws are far from clear in terms of the rights of individuals to own and enjoy, in the privacy of their own homes, copyrighted films.

If a collector is to permit an archives to own or have access to his films, then the collector expects something in return, and often that something is a copy of the borrowed film. Archivists are placed in the difficult position of not only having to spend a portion of their limited budget to make a print for the collector, but also having to deal with a copyright law which they perceive as denying individuals the right to own copies of copyrighted films.

A feeling of mutual suspicion developed between collectors and archivists. The situation changed somewhat with the establishment of the American Film Institute and the appointment of David Shepard as its acquisitions manager from 1969 to 1971. Shepard was himself a film collector, and he understood the collector mentality. While other archivists shied away from collectors, Shepard went out and talked to them about ways in which their films might be made available for preservation. Another AFI archivists, Lawrence F. Karr, explained the Institute's philosophy regarding private collectors:

> When we find caches of old films, we usually try to strike a bargain with the owner. We offer to put his name on the collection, or, if possible, promise him prints of the films when they've been copied. If he's got a lot of old nitrate film in the attic, it's not generally too difficult to persuade him. The stuff is a fire hazard, it's dangerous to put through a projector. Basically, we explain, it's not doing anyone any good.*

*Ward, Alex, "Gone with the Nitrate," NEA Cultural Post, May/June 1977, p. 9.

Two of the first major collections of nitrate films acquired from individuals by David Shepard for the American Film Institute came from George
Marshall and George Post. Marshall had an automobile repair shop in Vine-
land, New Jersey, outside of which he had a sign, "Old Films Bought and
Sold." Film historian George Mitchell recalls visiting him:

> He was a cripple, terribly crippled, he had to walk with crutches. The man had
> built himself a 35mm reduction printer, and he could reduce 35mm to 16mm.
> Of course, anyone who is a good carburetor repair man can fix just about every-
> thing—they get top dollar and they're hard to come by. Everything was neat and
> clean as a pin. He had copied a hell of a lot of film.
> At the New Yorker Theatre on Sundays [William K.] Everson would run silent
> pictures, 35mm stuff. He used to go down to Lloyd's Film Storage—he had some
> sort of connection with Lloyd's Film Storage—and he would come up with 35mm
> stuff you just can't believe. The last time I saw George Marshall, Everson had a
> trailer for *Ben-Hur* [1926] in Color, and he loaned this guy the trailer. And the
> guy just looked like he'd been bestowed on a hunk of gold. Hobbling over to his
> car, to go back to Vineland, New Jersey, he told me, "I'm going to print this one
> in color." He was a dedicated film preservationist.*

George Post had escaped from his native Russia, through Manchuria, at
the end of the First World War. He settled in San Francisco, and became a pro-
jectionist at art theatres screening foreign-language films. David Shepard recalled:

> The most interesting part of his collection was an accumulation of over 15,000
> feet of newsreel stories on the history of San Francisco, beginning back before the
> earthquake and going up through 1934. This is one of the finest deposits we found
> in any one spot on the history of a particular urban center and the way it
> developed. He also had a very large number of two-reel comedies and feature films
> which he had acquired mostly in the late 1920s. He never liked talking pictures
> because of his trouble understanding English. He thought that for ethnic markets
> such as his own silent films would always be popular. He began buying out old
> exchanges with the idea of operating a rental library of these films when everyone
> else had converted over to talkies, a plan which never materialized but which
> helped save a great many pictures.†

The bulk of the film in the Post Collection was purchased by the American
Film Institute in the summer of 1970. Many years later, some additional titles
from the Post Collection were deposited with the UCLA Film and Television
Archive.

The list of film collectors who have helped the American Film Institute
in its acquisition and preservation efforts is considerable. In 1972, the collection of Don Nichol was purchased; it included 74 feature films (among which
were *Traffic in Souls* and *The Red Kimono*), 56 two-reel shorts, four serials (one
of which was *The Woman in Grey* with Arline Pretty), and 17 newsreels. That

---

Interview with the author, May 31, 1990.
†Shepard, David, "The Search of Lost Films," Film Comment, Winter 1971-72, p. 62.*

same year, L.P. Kirkland of San Diego donated the Maurice Tourneur feature, *A Girl's Folly* (1917); I.K. Meginnis, who lived just outside of Washington, D.C., in Maryland, donated four reels of *The Italian* (1915) and the 1921 Mary Miles Minter feature, *The Little Clown;* and Jerome Kraemer gave a substantial donation of prints. In 1973, the estate of collector Maurice Rony donated 500,000 feet of nitrate film, dating from 1917 through the early 1940s. In 1978, the film collection of director Irvin Willat came to the AFI, and included nitrate negatives on four features which he had made in 1920 and 1921. In 1979, Victor and Walter Cromwell donated 150 reels of nitrate film. An exciting donation in 1982 was the 16mm home movie collection of illustrator Ralph Barton, given by his family, and including unique footage on Charlie Chaplin, Sinclair Lewis, H.L. Mencken, Ferenc Molnar, and others.

Not exactly gifts from collectors but similar in nature were donations to the American Film Institute from personalities in the film industries or their heirs. One of the earliest such donations came in the summer of 1970, when the Institute completed negotiations with Thomas H. Ince, Jr., and Mrs. Thomas Ince, and acquired a collection of original negatives, fine grains and prints on 55 feature films produced by the legendary silent filmmaker, Thomas Harper Ince, between 1916 and 1924. Unfortunately the availability of these films for scholarly study diminished Ince's reputation rather than enhancing it. Also in 1970, Winifred Bryson Baxter Manger donated to the AFI five features in which her former husband, Warner Baxter, had starred, along with a number of home movies.

Somewhat appropriately, Christine Jorgenson helped the AFI, in the spring of 1972, to acquire two sex education films from the 1920s, along with an early drama dealing with drug addiction, *The Devil's Needle* (1916). That same year, Bette Davis donated 35mm prints of two of her features, *Bad Sister* (1931) and *Of Human Bondage* (1934), together with 16mm copies of several television shows in which she had appeared.

A 1934 short by Orson Welles, *Hearts of Age,* was discovered at the Greenwich (Connecticut) Public Library in December 1969, and donated to the Institute. In 1971, Colleen Moore donated negatives on two of her features, *Irene* (1926) and *Lilac Time* (1928). In 1982, Elizabeth Taylor donated 70 boxes of preprint material from third husband, Mike Todd's 1956 feature, *Around the World in 80 Days.*

Collectors, of course, could also cause archives problems, playing one against the other in an effort to obtain a better "deal" for the donation of a film. When a collector found the only surviving print of the 1915 Raoul Walsh feature, *Regeneration,* in Montana in 1975, he tried to have the AFI, the Museum of Modern Art, Blackhawk Films, and the feature's producer, Fox, bid against each other for the title. In the end, Blackhawk purchased the film, but turned it over to the Museum of Modern Art for preservation, as the Museum had the largest extant collection of Raoul Walsh silent films.

Beginning in 1974, the F.B.I. began an all-out campaign against film piracy, which meant, in effect, the harassment of innocent film collectors. Among the well-publicized F.B.I. raids were those on Roddy McDowall, Ray Atherton, Woodrow (Woody) Wise, and Los Angeles–based Budget Films. Many of the charges were eventually dropped, and those that were not were often rejected by the courts. For a number of years thereafter, the F.B.I. remained relatively quiet on the film collector–film piracy front. However, other law enforcement agencies were coming on the scene, notably the Los Angeles District Attorney's Entertainment Industry Task Force.

In August 1983, the Task Force raided the vaults of a private collector, Merle Ray Harlin, at E-Z Storage in Burbank, California. Six hundred sixty-one films were seized, including original nitrate prints on the two-color Technicolor features, *Doctor X* (1932) and *The Mystery of the Wax Musuem* (1933). The latter had been preserved by the American Film Institute through Don Malkames' making a 35mm Eastman Color negative in the early 1970s; 16mm prints were around as well, the film having been duped when loaned by Warner Bros. to an Orange County, California, college for a tribute to its director, Michael Curtiz. Also found at E-Z Storage was material on the "Lose That Long Face" number from *A Star Is Born* (1956), which had just been restored minus that song. The two Technicolor features were subsequently preserved by Turner Entertainment and the UCLA Film and Television Archive, and "Lose That Long Face" was restored to *A Star Is Born*.

Harlin had been a stock footage librarian at Columbia, which shared the Burbank Studios lot with Warner Bros. The latter had, according to Harlin, thrown the films into the trash — a not unreasonable proposition in view of the lack of interest at that time by studios in film preservation. With much hoopla — and a publication of the complete list of films, now confiscated, in *Daily Variety* (April 6, 1984) — the Merle Ray Harlin collection was returned to its "rightful" owners. Harlin was fired by Columbia, but quietly rehired by Lorimar, where he remained, as a stock footage librarian, until his retirement in 1989.

One quasi-film collector and entrepreneur who has given film archivists a number of headaches through the years is Raymond Rohauer (1924–1987). Rohauer's specialty was the acquisition of often dubious rights to vintage films, with his claims to such films based on loopholes in the American copyright law. He would contact widows and executors of apparently worthless estates of once-prominent names in the film community, and negotiate representation of the estate's rights in films, to which quite often the estates had no claims. Forming associations with a varied group of personalities, including Buster Keaton, Douglas Fairbanks, Jr., and Jay Ward, Rohauer began a ruthless campaign in the 1960s to force archives to surrender their holdings on films in which he claimed an interest.

One of Rohauer's first attacks on the Museum of Modern Art came in 1966, when he claimed the Museum had been duping and renting prints of the French silent classic, *Un Chien Andalou* (1928), to which he claimed ownership. Ironically, the film's director, Luis Buñuel, had been given employment at the Museum of Modern Art during the Second World War. Rohauer took advantage of a FIAF Congress at the Museum of Modern Art in 1969 to serve notices on a number of archivists, including Ernest Lindgren of the British National Film Archive. Rohauer's action seriously jeopardized the National Film Archive's restoration of *The Black Pirate* and forced Lindgren to order the withdrawal of *The Birth of a Nation* from distribution by the rental library of the British Film Institute. There are even those who claim that Rohauer's legalistic antagonism towards Lindgren eventually led to the curator's death.

Raymond Rohauer was one of the principals in a lengthy court battle over the rights to D.W. Griffith's 1915 masterpiece *The Birth of a Nation*, a battle which began in May 1969 when Epoch Producing Corporation (formed after the production of the film) filed suit against the Museum of Modern Art and Paul Killiam, as successor to the estate of D.W. Griffith. The case was settled on August 13, 1975, with the U.S. Circuit Court of Appeals, 2nd Circuit, ruling that Griffith was the creator and legal "author" of the film. The ruling was upheld by the U.S. Supreme Court, and, in practical terms, meant that *The Birth of a Nation* was in the public domain.

In 1969, the American Film Institute acquired 90 cans of original negative trims and out-takes on *The Birth of a Nation* from the Academy of Motion Picture Arts and Sciences. Two years later, Paul Killiam agreed to put up half the purchase cost of $5,000 for between 32 and 36 cans of original negative materials and preprint on *The Birth of a Nation*, owned by a private collector and discovered by David Shepard. The footage was handed over to, and copied by the Library of Congress, with Paul Killiam controlling access.

Epoch filed a copyright infringement suit against the American Film Institute in 1973, and sent federal marshals, with a seizure warrant, to the Motion Picture Section of the Library of Congress. Technical Officer David Parker was the highest ranking staff member in the Section when the marshals arrived. He was able to contact John Kominski, the Library's chief legal counsel, and Kominski ordered the Library's guards to eject the federal marshals from the premises. Later that same year, federal marshals were able to seize and seal the cans, but they remained in the physical custody of the Library of Congress. The cans were "sealed" by the attachment of a notice of such "sealing" to the cans and the shelves on which they were stored; because of the dangers in sealing cans of nitrate film, they were not physically sealed.

Further complicating the issue, and unbeknownst to Rohauer or the Epoch lawyers, the American Film Institute had been approached in 1974 by a private collector with what appeared to be the most complete nitrate print of *The Birth of a Nation*. Legal problems prevented the Institute's accepting the film, and an arrangement was worked out whereby a film dealer in Los Angeles named Tom Dunnahoo would have his company, Thunderbird Films, acquire the nitrate from the collector. Dunnahoo copied and surreptitiously released 16mm prints of the film. At the same time, he deposited the nitrate with the UCLA Film and Television Archive, on the understanding that it would be transferred to the Library of Congress on resolution of the various legal issues raised by Rohauer and Epoch.

Such legal problems were not finally resolved until November 6, 1979, when American Film Institute archivist Lawrence F. Karr was able to persuade Rohauer and Paul Killiam to sign a confidential settlement.*

Two of the best known collectors, with the largest holdings of 16mm film in private hands, are William K. Everson in New York and David Bradley in Los Angeles. In May 1969, the American Film Institute purchased at laboratory cost 16mm fine grains and reference prints on 16 silent features, made from Bradley's negatives, for deposit with the Library of Congress. Everson served as a consultant to the American Film Institute Archives for a number of years, and has also permitted a number of 16mm prints in his collection to be copied for preservation. He had no substantive consultant involvement with the archives program after 1972.

One such print, which the American Film Institute was able to copy and preserve in 1974, was an incomplete version of Frank Borzage's 1929 feature, *The River*. The original nitrate on the film had been in the vaults of 20th Century–Fox. A former employee there, who has received considerable attention, not least of all from William K. Everson, for his self-proclaimed preservation of the Fox films,† decided that as the feature was incomplete, it was not worth being kept and passed on to the Museum of Modern Art for preservation. (The major Fox and 20th Century–Fox titles were preserved by the Museum of Modern Art; the so-called "lesser" features were deposited with the UCLA Film and Television Archive, and a number have been preserved by that institution.§) Prior to junking *The River*, a 16mm reduction print was made for

---

Much of the information relating to The Birth of a Nation *is taken from a confidential memorandum from Larry Karr to the File, dated December 3, 1979.*

†*For example, see Everson, William K., "Film Treasure Trove: The Film Preservation Program at 20th Century–Fox," Films in Review, vol. 25, no. 10, December 1974, pp. 595–610.*

§*Among the Fox titles preserved by the UCLA Film and Television Archive are* After Tomorrow *(1932),* Almost Married *(1932),* Always Goodbye *(1931),* Bachelor of Arts *(1934),* Bachelor's Affairs *(1932),* Best of Enemies *(1933),* The Black Sheep *(1935),* Blue Skies *(1929),* Captain Lash *(1929),* Cheaters at Play *(1932),* Cheer Up and Smile *(1930),* Dance Team *(1932),* Disorderly Conduct *(1932),* Double Cross Roads *(1930),* East Lynne *(1931),* The First Year *(1932),* The Gay Caballero *(1932),* Goldie *(1931),* Good Intentions *(1930),* Hush Money *(1931),* I Believed in You *(1934),* The Infernal Machine *(1933),* Lilliom *(1930),* Man Trouble *(1930),* Men on Call *(1930),* Movietone Follies of 1930 *(1930),* Murder in Trinidad *(1934),* My Lips Betray *(1933),* My Weakness *(1933),* Not Exactly Gentlemen *(1931),* On Your Back *(1930),* Once a Sinner *(1930),* The Painted Woman *(1932),* Part Time Wife *(1930),* Servant's Entrance *(1934),* Sharp Shooters *(1928),* She Wanted a Millionaire *(1932),* Six Cylinder Love *(1931),* The Sky Hawk *(1929),* Three Girls Lost *(1931),* 365 Nights in Hollywood *(1934),* Under Suspicion *(1930),* Weekends Only *(1932),* The White Parade *(1934),* Women Everywhere *(1930),* Women of All Nations *(1931),* and *Young America *(1932).*

Everson, and that was all that survived on the film, and could be copied for archival safeguarding. The incident underlines a basic problem in the relationship between collectors and archivists. The latter believe, quite rightly, that films should be preserved in the format in which they were shot, 35mm, and that preservation is the first priority. Collectors are more interested in 16mm prints for presentation purposes, and in the minds of many of them "preservation" amounts to their having a 16mm print in their collection.

Film collectors can, and do, benefit archives, but there was also a time when at least one archives, unknowingly, benefited collectors. In 1956, three major New York film collectors, whose names must remain anonymous, contacted one of the vault custodians at the Museum of Modern Art. The Museum employee was a gambling addict, and agreed to accept what the collectors laughingly called a "stud fee" of $200 for each negative he would remove from the Museum's vaults and loan to the collectors for printing. A collector involved in a peripheral way recalls, "It was a very modest thing, really no harm was done. They were only getting a few things, like a Fairbanks feature, a Harold Lloyd short, nothing big—only little things which they were interested in personally. It blew apart when, like a lot of these things, they got greedy. And they began to bring the stuff out like it was Ali Baba and the Forty Thieves. Open Sesame and grab all the jewels. I don't know the details of how this fell apart, but it did in the end. The guy was not caught, but finally it got to the point it got dangerous."

One of the earliest known film collectors was actor George (André) Beranger (1893–1973), who began collecting 28mm films in the late teens. His collection was rich in one-reel American Biograph and Pathé Frères subjects, and a favorite leisure activity for many Hollywood stars of the 1920s was an evening at the Hollywood Athletic Club, viewing Beranger's films. By 1928, he had amassed a collection of 128 reels, which he offered for sale at $3,500, with the price also including projection equipment and a screen.* There were no takers, and Beranger held on to the films until 1942, when he decided to return to his native Australia. Beranger offered the films to cinematographer Charles G. Clarke for a mere $500.† Clarke was not interested, but he did arrange for the films to be acquired by the Academy of Motion Picture Arts and Sciences.

Beranger has not been the only actor who collected films. Roddy McDowall and Rock Hudson are two other examples. John Griggs was never a well-known actor, but his voice was heard on more than 5,000 radio programs, notably as Roger Elliott on Mutual's *The House of Mystery* (1945–1949). Not only did Griggs collect films, but also he copied many of the rare items in his collection, selling prints of them under the company name of Griggs-Moviedrome. At the

---

*Advertisement in The Film Spectator, July 9, 1927, p. 4.
†Letter from Beranger to Clarke, November 26, 1942, in the files of the Margaret Herrick Library of the Academy of Motion Picture Arts and Sciences.

time of his death, on February 25, 1967, John Griggs had a son in the graduate
program at Yale University. A group, "The Friends of Film at Yale," was
created by Chester LaRoche, with support from Frederick W. Beinecke II and
Richard Fuller, and it raised the necessary funds for the university to acquire
the bulk of Griggs' 16mm film collection. The John Griggs Collection became
the basis for the Yale Film Study Center. The price tag for the collection was
determined independently by film historian Herman W. Weinberg and
Griggs' fellow film collector, Robert E. Lee.

Robert E. (Bob) Lee operates one of the oldest film societies in the country, the Essex Film Club, founded in 1939 and still presenting vintage films on
a regular basis in Nutley, New Jersey. Lee joined the production department
at Mutual's WOR radio station in the 1940s. He recalls,

> One of my many jobs in New York's WOR was to put together so-called soap
> operas and on some of these I was able to work with most of the top actors in the
> New York area, and one of these was John Griggs. In WOR, we had about 20
> studios that were operating, as we also fed the coast-to-coast Mutual network. I
> could monitor any of these studios to find what activity was going on. My ears
> caught an interview with a popular commentator, Bessie Beatty, her subject was
> John Griggs, talking about his favorite hobby, his movie collection. I promptly
> went up to the studio, waiting for him to come off the air, and introduced myself,
> although we had worked together many times on radio. It was then a bond was
> formed between John and myself that was to increase and increase to many years
> up to the time of his death.*

In 1938, cameraman Don Malkames began building a collection of films
and early equipment, housed in his Tuckahoe, New York, home. In 1954, it
was described by *The New York Times* as "one of the most outstanding in private hands."†

The largest private collection of film amassed in the United States belonged
to John E. Allen. He had extraordinary luck not only in finding films but also
paper materials. At one time, Allen picked up 1½ tons of paper items, scripts,
still photographs, production data, and the like relating to the Triangle Company, a distribution agent for the films of D.W. Griffith, Thomas H. Ince, and
Mack Sennett, active from 1915 to 1917. The bulk of the collection was eventually acquired by the Cinémathèque Française, but a considerable volume was
offered for sale to collectors in the 1950s and 1960s at prices which today seem
ludicrously low.

Film historian George J. Mitchell has vivid recollections of Allen:

> When I first met him, he lived in Bergen County, New Jersey. This man was
> a one-man film archive. He had a wreck of car, and he would go out in this car,
> looking to buy old film. And he'd always be wearing dirty, ragged-looking clothes.
> Allen himself was an imposing-looking man, a great big fellow, a solid fellow,

---

Letter to the author, November 20, 1990.
†Godbout, Oscar, "Cinema Collectors Close-Up," The New York Times, February 21, 1954.

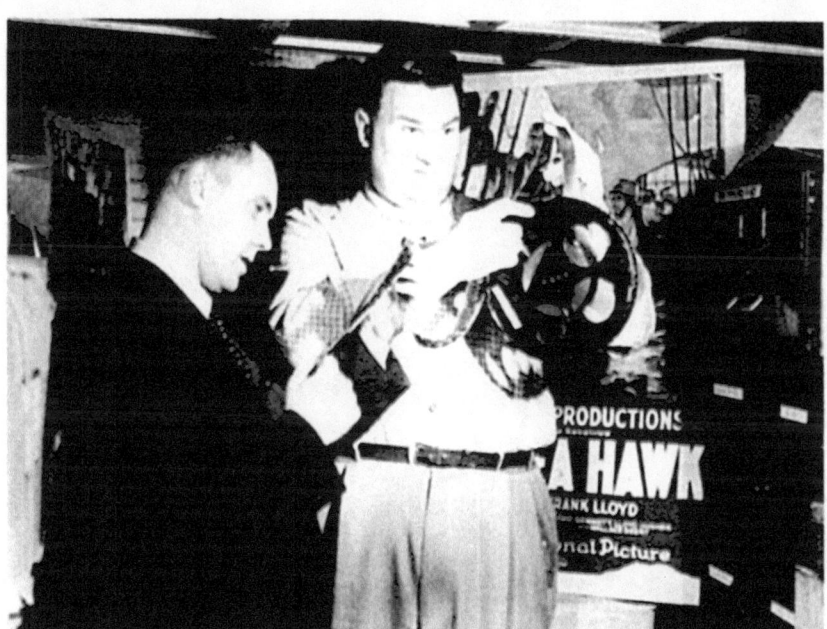

John E. Allen (right) with William K. Everson in 1953 (courtesy of George J. Mitchell).

probably six feet, three, 300 pounds, with no real fat on him. Good natured and pleasant. I remember he told me his first wife committed the most heinous crime of all, she threw his films out in the middle of the street—he left her after that!

He said, why don't you spend the night up here—I'm going to see this friend of mine, Don Malkames, over in Yonkers. It was in the wintertime, probably around November or December, 1952. Anyway, we got ready to go and see Malkames. He takes a big flashlight, and we go out back behind his house into this little wooded area. I see these piles of heavy tarpaulin over stuff. And he had nitrate film there! He had a pad underneath them of wood upon bricks, and then he had the film piled on top of that, covered with tarps.

When I came back ten years later, Allen had moved. He was still in Bergen County, but had moved up the road ten or twelve miles, and he had a lot larger place. He had built out in the back, out of brick and concrete, some very nice film vaults. Now he was strictly in business—he was really in the stock shot business. His wife, a very attractive woman, was very shrewd—shrewder than Allen—and later she began running the business. I never asked him where he got his films— it's like asking an intelligence officer or a policeman who his informants are.*

John E. Allen died in 1975, and his company continued under the direction of his son, John E. Allen, Jr. It boasted a collection of 28 million feet of film, dating from the 1890s through the 1960s. Also, it consists of a full-service film and video laboratory, which handled much of the preservation work for

*Interview with the author, May 31, 1990.

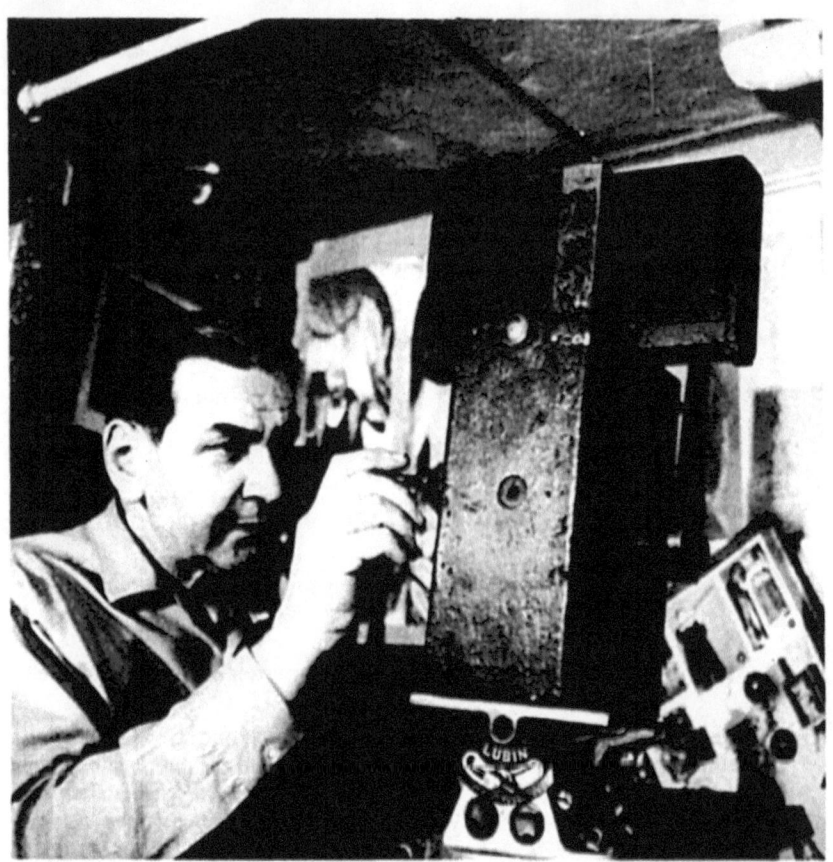

Don Malkames with an original Lubin camera (courtesy of George J. Mitchell).

the Museum of Modern Art and the International Museum of Photography at George Eastman House. In 1990, two of the younger Allen's employees left the company, to found their own film laboratory specializing in preservation work, Cinetech, in Southern California.

John E. Allen was noted for his generosity towards many film collectors, and he was equally generous in his early dealings with film archives. In 1945, he agreed to donate some 700 reels of nitrate film, which he had stored in the RKO vaults on Eye Street in Washington, D.C., to the Library of Congress. Unfortunately, the Library was slow in responding to the gift, and only 100 reels were eventually turned over.*

Allen also worked closely with the new film archives created as part of what

*According to Howard Walls in a letter, March 11, 1949, to Alvin W. Kremer at the Library of Congress.

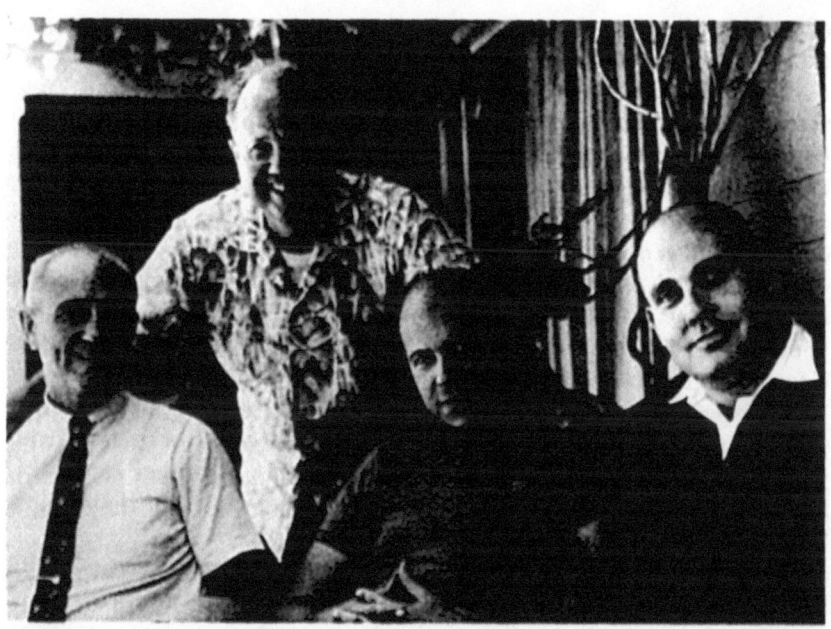

A group of prominent film collectors; from left to right: Ed Finney, George J. Mitchell, David Bradley, and William K. Everson (courtesy of George J. Mitchell).

was then called simply George Eastman House, and is now known by the some-what pompous title of the International Museum of Photography at George Eastman House. Allen was a close friend of James Card, and both donated films to George Eastman House and helped the film archives there locate titles.

James Card (born 1915) is the only film collector in the United States to have founded a film archives. A man dedicated to film acquisition and preser-vation in the manner of Henri Langlois, of whom he was a close friend, James Card was noted for his quick temper and his possessiveness towards the collec-tion which he built up at George Eastman House. He did not suffer fools or bureaucrats gladly, and was often openly critical of the more foolish actions of the American Film Institute. Paperwork held little interest for him, and he would often boast to his fellow archivists that six months or more had elapsed since last he wrote a letter.

Born in Shaker Heights, Ohio, Card graduated from Western Reserve University and spent a year studying at the University of Heidelberg. He had a close affinity to Germany and to German films. Unlike many of his col-leagues, he also had a sense of humor about himself and his work. In a reference to the French serials of the silent era, featuring Judex and Fantômas, Card once described himself as "Cardex, the Fantomas of the Film who dreams of world domination of film knowledge through the most complete record of extant films in existence."*

Following the Second World War, Card moved to Rochester, New York, accepting an appointment as a director and cameraman for the Informational Films Division of Eastman Kodak. He had started film collecting in the early 1930s, with his first acquisition being a print of Dr. James Sibley Watson's 1929 experimental short, *The Fall of the House of Usher*. Watson (1894–1982) produced a number of landmark experimental films, including *Lot in Sodom*. He designed an early optical printer, which was subsequently donated to George Eastman House, and was also innovative in the field of X-ray motion picture photography. He and his wife, Nancy, were generous financial supporters of George Eastman House for many years.

In November 1948, Card was invited to join the staff of the newly formed George Eastman House, with the initial title of "assistant to the curator" (who was Beaumont Newhall). Card's collection of 850 film titles came along with him, but they were not officially acquired by George Eastman House until 1957.

As its present name, the International Museum of Photography at George Eastman House, suggests, the institution is primarily concerned with the study and preservation of still photographs. It is located in Rochester, New York, in the home of Eastman Kodak founder, George Eastman, which he built for himself and his mother in 1905. Following Eastman's suicide in March 1932, the house was bequeathed to the University of Rochester as a home for its presidents. In 1947, the University and the Eastman Kodak Company agreed to work together to turn the house into a permanent memorial to George Eastman, and a nonprofit, educational corporation, chartered by the New York State Board of Regents, was formed.

George Eastman House opened to the public in November 1949, at which time it had few film items in its collection. Card wrote to Howard Walls on November 19 of that year:

> The films now available comprise three collections: the Eastman Historical Photographic Collection which includes twenty Edison films all made before 1897 (in perfect condition); the [Francis] Doublier Collection which was purchased along with his excellent store of early cameras and projectors; and the Card Collection. . . . I have charge of the motion picture end of things which as you can imagine is somewhat the country cousin in this essentially photographic institution.

The creation of the film collection began in earnest in 1950, under Card's direction, and with the full support of Eastman House curator Beaumont Newhall and its director, General Oscar Solbert. In that year, the cornerstone was

---

*Letter to Howard Walls, January 20, 1948, in the files of the Margaret Herrick Library of the Academy of Motion Picture Arts and Sciences.

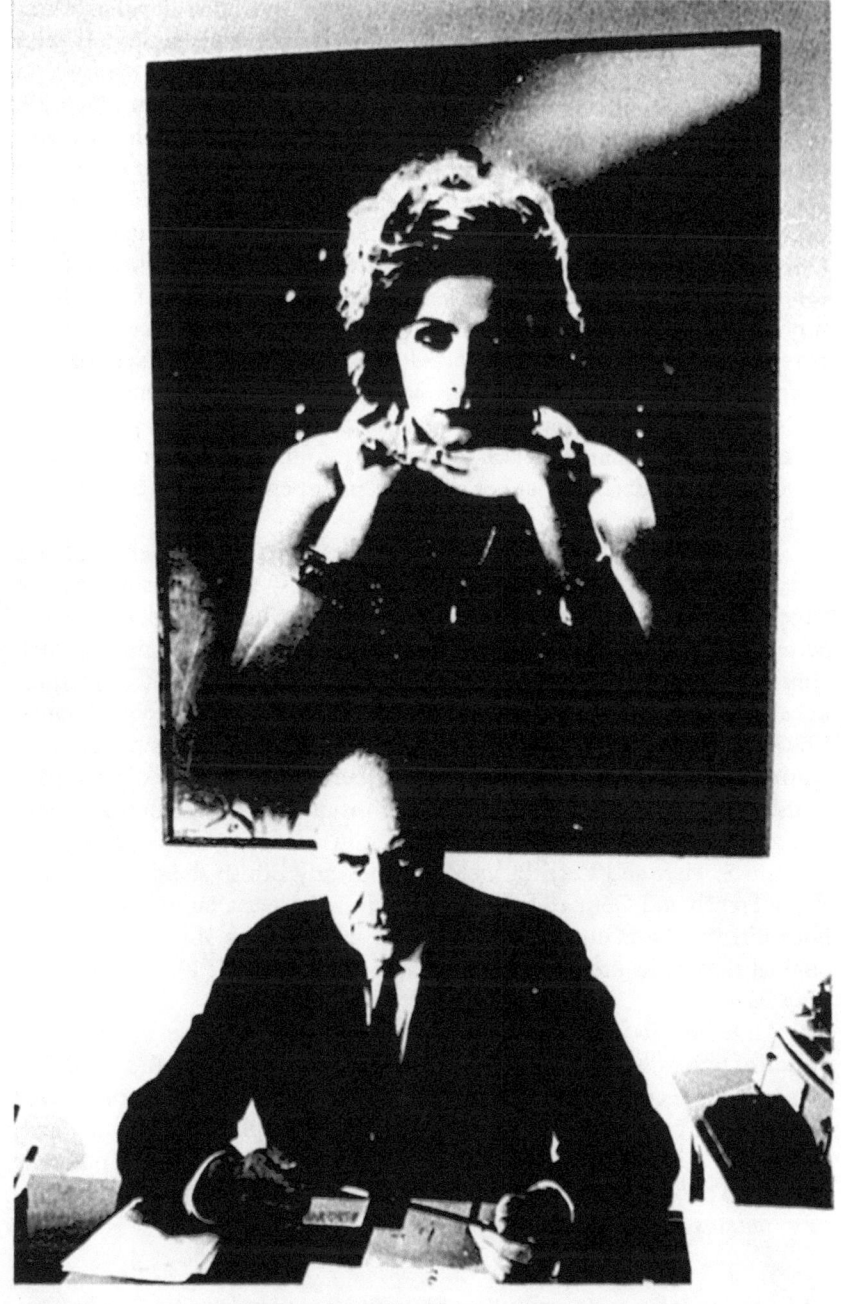

James Card, first curator of the Motion Picture Collection at the International Museum of Photography at George Eastman House.

laid for the Dryden Theatre, funded by George and Ellen Dryden, which opened the following year, and has been presenting regular seasons of films ever since.

In 1952, L. Corrin Strong, a Washington, D.C., resident, donated $100,000 to George Eastman House, with the money to be used to acquire and preserve films. Of that amount, $30,000 was used to build the first nitrate vaults at George Eastman House, and the remainder was used for film preservation. It was agreed at the time of the gift that the film collection at George Eastman House would be renamed "The Henry A. Strong Collection of Historical Motion Pictures." The Strong funds were the first monies George Eastman House received for film preservation, and the institution did not receive similar preservation funding of such magnitude until 1972, when the National Endowment for the Arts began making money available. During the 1950s and 1960s, George Eastman House was budgeting as little as $10,000 a year for film preservation. It is ironic that lack of funding for film preservation resulted in the loss, through deterioration, of one of its most personal films, the newsreel of the 1949 opening.

Because George Eastman House had so little nitrate film when the vaults were completed, an arrangement was made for it to store many items from the Museum of Modern Art collection, an arrangement which was not totally supported by Richard Griffith and his staff at the Museum, who did not like their films being stored albeit temporarily, outside of their control. Although there was a natural rivalry between the Museum of Modern Art and George Eastman House, it was (and is) a friendly one, and James Card initiated a policy of acquiring and preserving titles which the Museum of Modern Art did not have in its collection. George Eastman House's major archival holdings are silent and sound titles from M-G-M; it is also rich in the films of Thomas H. Ince, William S. Hart and Cecil B. DeMille, and early British short subjects and classic French and German titles. The archives also has a number of productions directed by Maurice Tourneur, and, in 1990, was able to restore the original tints to its preservation materials on the director's 1918 feature, *The Blue Bird*.

Aside from its film holdings, George Eastman House has an extensive collection of film stills (including more than a million from Warner Bros. and First National productions), an extensive research library, and what is considered one of the world's finest collections of cinematographic equipment. Since January 1952, it has published the occasional journal, *Image,* which is primarily devoted to photography, but has contained some important articles on film history, notably by George C. Pratt.*

---

*A collection of film-related articles from Image has been gathered together as Deutelbaum, Marshall, editor, "Image" on the Art and Evolution of the Film (New York: Dover Publications, 1979).

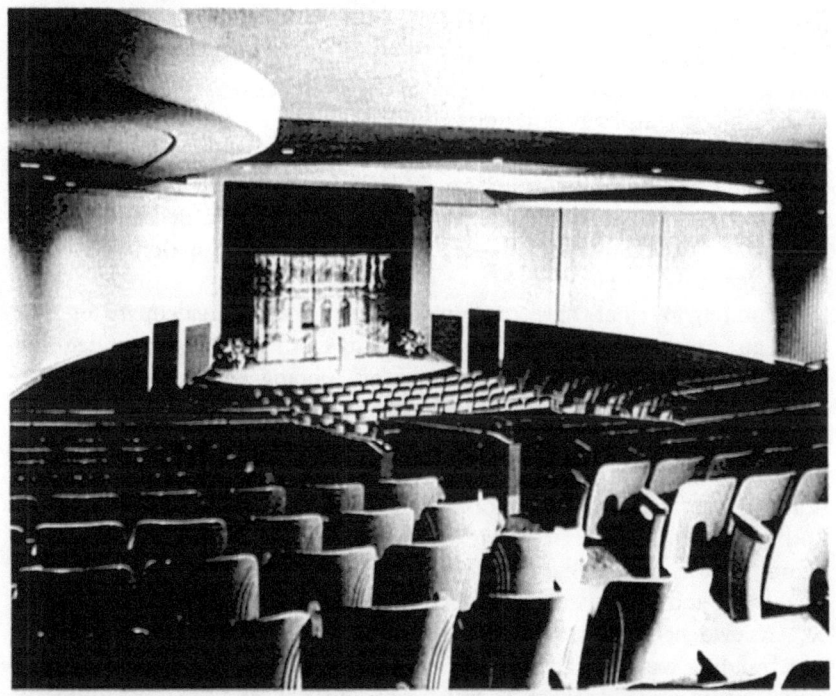

The Dryden Theatre at George Eastman House, which opened in 1951.

Writing in 1959, James Card described the film study collection as designed to enable a student to:

(1) examine each film which constitutes a major development in technique or style of filmmaking;

(2) observe the manner in which changing social problems affected the motion picture and how they were in turn affected by the public's reaction to popular films;

(3) trace career of leading motion-picture artists;

(4) learn the major steps in the development and use of motion pictures, specialized in their purpose;

(5) refer to newsreels and documentaries as source material in the study of specific events, or to obtain authentic details of dress and architecture; and

(6) compare the several versions of identical stories many of which have been repeated at intervals spanning most of the history of motion pictures.*

James Card retired in 1977, and he was replaced, as director of the film department, that same year by John Kuiper, who remained in the position

*Card, James, "The Historical Motion-Picture Collections at George Eastman House," Journal of the SMPTE, vol. 68, no. 3, March 1959, p. 143.

until 1987. There can be little argument that Card was somewhat autocratic in his administration of the film department. Film viewings by outside scholars and students were all too often based on the director's personal like or dislike of the applicant. Kuiper democratized the running of the film department, trying to administer it along the same lines that he had handled the Motion Picture Division at the Library of Congress. Unfortunately, Kuiper discovered that there was less time available to devote to running the film department, and more time required to deal with the increasingly political situation developing at George Eastman House.

Funding for all of the institution's activities had been inadequate for some time, and in the summer of 1984, the board of trustees recommended that George Eastman House's collection of films, photographs, equipment, and books be merged with that of the National Museum of American History at the Smithsonian Institution, with the resultant collection being named the National Photographic Collection and Research Center. The recommendation created a storm of controversy, and a local citizens group, Photo-Archives Belong in Rochester (PABIR), was created to fight the proposal. As a result of PABIR's efforts, the Eastman Kodak Company offered a 16 million dollar Endowment Challenge, and the Board of Trustees was persuaded to reconsider.

As evidence of the upswing in the fortunes of George Eastman House, a new building was dedicated in 1989, housing three new state-of-the-art film vaults, a film study center, a 25-seat screening room, and the 80-seat Edward Peck Curtis Theater. George Eastman House's name had been officially changed to the International Museum of Photography at George Eastman House in 1975 by then-director Robert Doherty. Film historian Jan-Christopher Horak, who had joined George Eastman House as an associate curator in 1984, was named head of the film department following John Kuiper's resignation in 1987; he now holds the title of senior curator, film collections.

While its film collection may be small in comparison to those in many other archives, the International Museum of Photogrpahy at George Eastman House does maintain a prestigious assemblage of titles, arguably equal in importance to the holdings of the Museum of Modern Art. It is a lasting memorial to its first curator, James Card, who was the last link in the American archival film field between the old and the new generation of film archivists. As he pointed out in a 1977 interview:

> I think in a general way, those of us who were pioneers really served our purpose in getting everybody upset about this problem and moving people to do something about it. And now it's the time to consolidate what has been brought together and save it on a very, very careful plan and [a] good, reasonable unemotional basis. Then when the next generation come on, it will be up to them to analyze and really make use of it. So each group seems ultimately to have its own function.*

*Reynolds, Herbert, "'What Can You Do for Us, Barney?' Four Decades of Film Collecting: An Interview with James Card," Image, vol. 20, no. 2, June 1977, p. 29.

5 THE FIFTIES AND SIXTIES

The final years of Iris Barry at the Museum of Modern Art were not particularly happy ones. She had begun to drink to excess, and felt that she was being mistreated by the Museum hierarchy. Only after her retirement in 1951 and her move to the South of France, where she ended her days, did she seem really relaxed and happy to her friends.

With her departure from the Museum, Iris Barry's position was split in two. Margareta Akermark was named executive secretary for administrative affairs, and Barry's hand-picked successor, Richard Griffith, was appointed curator of the Film Library. Richard Griffith (1912–1969) had graduated from Harvard in 1935 and first come to the Museum in 1937–1938, undertaking research on a Rockefeller Foundation fellowship. In 1940, he managed the Little Theater of the Science and Education Building at the New York World's Fair, and during the Second World War, he worked as a film editor at the Photographic Center of the Army Signal Corps, working on the *Why We Fight* series and other films. While serving as assistant to the curator of the Film Library at the Museum of Modern Art, he also found time, from 1946–1949, to act as executive director of the National Board of Review of Motion Pictures.

Richard Griffith was a film critic and a prolific writer on film history. His best-known work is, undoubtedly the sumptuous picture book, *The Movies,* coauthored with Arthur Mayer, and first published by Simon and Schuster in 1957. Griffith revised Paul Rotha's classic text, *The Film Till Now,* in 1950, and also coauthored with Rotha, and Sinclair Reed, *Documentary Film* in 1952. Earlier, in 1947, he had edited *Grierson on Documentary.* Other books and pamphlets by Griffith are *The World of Robert Flaherty* (1953), *Samuel Goldwyn: The Producer and His Films* (1956), *Fred Zinnemann* (1957), *Anatomy of a Motion Picture* (1959), *The Cinema of Gene Kelly* (1962), and *The Talkies: Articles and Illustrations from a Great Fan Magazine* (1971). The last was published by Dover, and was intended as one in a series of reprints and anthologies, to be edited or introduced by Griffith.

Perhaps the lesser title to which Griffith was named by the Museum proves the point of film historian, Lewis Jacobs, who comments, "He was not in the same league as Iris Barry." Jacobs continues, "I think Iris Barry was a very literate person. She knew all the literary figures and was a part of that circle in England in the twenties, before she came here. Certainly, she was more politically astute than Griffith. I think her standards were higher. I don't think he had the same social ambiance."* While that is undoubtedly true, Griffith's differing social outlook was important to the Museum's film collecting policy. He had a much more popular approach towards the cinema. Griffith understood the art of the film, but also he had almost a film buff's love of the medium. Silent film star Blanche Sweet would often recall her visits to the Museum of Modern Art during the Richard Griffith era. In one of her first talkies, she had performed a somewhat maudlin number titled "There's a Tear for Every Smile in Hollywood." Whenever Richard Griffith met the actress, he would always sing the song to her.

Richard Griffith is held in high regard by his ultimate successor, Eileen Bowser (born 1928), who joined the Museum's staff in 1954 as Griffith's secretary. One of the first projects upon which he set her to work was to read *The Moving Picture World* and document all references to Samuel Goldwyn, in connection with a series tribute to and pamphlet on the producer.

> I have the most extraordinary admiration and respect for Richard Griffith [states Bowser]. He really taught me everything that I know about film history. There was nobody more dedicated to film preservation—and the means at hand were so slight in those early years. When triacetate film came along in the early fifties, it seemed to give hope for the first time that nitrate film could be saved. He told me he could not sleep at nights thinking he had become curator of a collection that was going to disappear under his care. I don't know if he was the greatest fund raiser in the world or not. There was a time when it was very difficult to get anyone to take this seriously. We did fund raisers and did pamphlets, but the amounts of money we were able to raise were always so small. In the beginning, we could save only one or two films a year by copying them. I think if he could see what we have achieved, he would be overwhelmed. He wouldn't believe it would have been possible to achieve what we have done. I know there was nobody who cared more than he did.†

A very even-tempered, always pleasant individual, Griffith had one serious problem—he was an alcoholic. In 1965, he was forced to resign from the Museum. Eileen Bowser is satisfied that, in time, he was completely recovered. The irony is that he was killed in a car crash near Winchester, Virginia, on October 17, 1969, while on his way to a meeting of Alcoholic Anonymous.

Meanwhile, on the West Coast, Howard Walls was hard at work promoting restoration of the paper prints. He had arrived in Los Angeles in September 1947, and that same month met with Margaret Herrick, executive director of the Academy of Motion Picture Arts and Sciences, together with Jean

---

*Interview with author, January 27, 1991.
†Interview with the author, February 4, 1991.

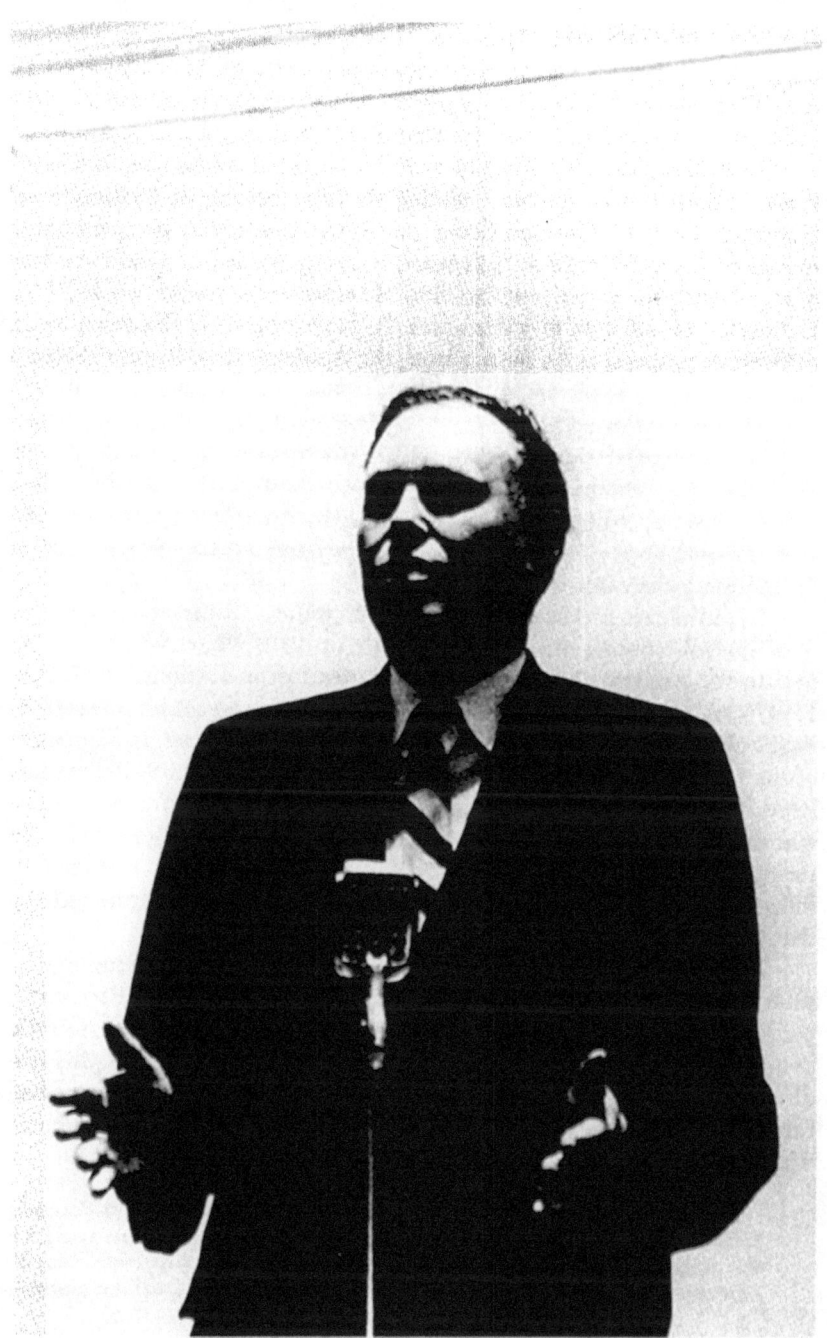

Richard Griffith, photographed in 1959 (courtesy of the Museum of Modern Art).

Hersholt, Walter Wanger, Donald M. Nelson, and Mary McCarthy. At a meeting at Romanoff's Restaurant, these representatives of the Academy agreed to hire Walls and to activate the organization's nonprofit wing, the Academy Foundation, to raise the funds for transfer of the paper prints to film.

Enthusiastically, Walls set to work. A technical committee, headed by Farciot Edouart, was formed, holding its first meeting at Paramount on November 10, 1947. Linwood Dunn, one of the most highly regarded optical special effects technicians in Hollywood, was approached to handle the work of transferring the paper prints to film. He estimated it would cost $6,782.16 to transfer 24,000 feet to 35mm film. In November 1947, Eastman Kodak pledged its support, and a month later, the Academy Foundation received its first donation, a check for $1,000 from Thomas A. Edison, Inc. The *Los Angeles Times* donated $4,000 on the understanding that it might be allowed to make commercial use of the paper prints. The Association of Motion Picture Producers gave another $4,000, and the American Society of Cinematographers came up with $500. Unfortunately, the Rockefeller, Carnegie, and Hearst foundations all reported they were unwilling to make money available for motion picture–related activities.

In addition to promoting the paper print project, Walls was also building up a film collection at the Academy. In August 1950, Walter Wanger turned over to the Academy prints of all his independent productions. In October 1950, Mary Astor's husband, Thomas Wheelock, donated a 35mm print of *The Beggar Maid*, the 1921 short which had started the actress' career. In September of the same year, John Shanks donated a 35mm print of the 1941 Alexander Korda feature, *Lady Hamilton / That Hamilton Woman*. The Academy's assistant director Sam Brown was able to tell Shanks, "The Academy is slowly, but steadily, building up what will one day be the most complete collection of films, stills, books and clippings in the world, and will become the archives that future students of our art form will find most valuable."*

Unfortunately, Howard Walls was discovering that the Academy was not what he had imagined it might be. No sooner had he fought off a decision by the Library of Congress in October 1948 to donate the paper prints to UCLA than he was contending with the eccentricities of Margaret Herrick, who had divorced two husbands, Donald Gledhill (whose job at the Academy she had been able to take over during the Second World War) and Philip A. Herrick. Walls recalls:

> Margaret had me up in the library one of the first days I was there. She was going to dump Sam Brown and put me in his place. She was making a pass at me. She was going to put me in, we were going to get married, and then we'd run the Academy. That's what she wanted! This was the beginning of all the trouble. I

*Letter from Sam Brown to John Shanks, September 18, 1950, in the files of the Margaret Herrick Library of the Academy of Motion Picture Arts and Sciences.

told her, Sam had been so nice to me, I'd never had a better friend in all my life. She was asking me to double-cross him. So I told her, I can't do that. She said, he had been a produce man. I said, that doesn't mean he still is. That's when she turned against me—from that point on.*

The Academy was already hurting for funds, and Mrs. Herrick was able to ensure that none came to Howard Walls for the film program. He was required to keep a record of the cost of every long distance telephone call which he made, and to justify its necessity. He received offers of films for sale from collectors William Donnachie, John E. Allen, and Raymond Rohauer, but had to reject them all. In desperation, Walls tried to interest commercial entities in the paper prints. In 1951, he was unsuccessful in persuading M-G-M to produce a series of short subjects based on material in the paper prints. Television producers Philip Krasne, Jack DeWitt, and Jack Gross did form a company, Linda Lee Enterprises, to exploit the paper prints, but nothing appears to have come of the idea.†

In May 1948, Howard Walls had reported to the Society of Motion Picture Engineers, at its Santa Monica convention, "We have only a shoestring and a lot of ambition."§ Yet Walls was able to accomplish a great deal in the years he was at the Academy, from 1947–1953. He created the nucleus of its film collection and established what is probably the first oral history program devoted to the motion picture industry. Walls interviewed at least two early pioneers, J. Searle Dawley and Albert E. Smith, and would undoubtedly have done more had he received adequate support from the management. During his years at the Academy, Walls also found time to take a leave of absence to return to the Library of Congress and compiled the first volume of its motion picture copyright records: *Motion Pictures 1894–1912 Identified from the Records of the United States Copyright Office* (published in 1953).

Walls' employment with the Academy ended with Margaret Herrick's padlocking his office door. Mrs. Herrick died in 1976; her body was cremated and her ashes scattered over the Pacific Ocean. As this writer sat talking with Howard Walls at his Santa Barbara, California, home, he looked out of the window and commented, "You know she's floating out here in the ocean right now. We must be drinking some of her!"

The paper print restoration project was revived some time during 1952 or 1953 by Kemp Niver, the individual with which it is most closely associated. Kemp Niver (born 1912), who was described by one writer as physically resembling Fred MacMurray** and by one of his colleagues as "very aggressive

---

Interview with the author, October 7, 1990.

†According to The Hollywood Reporter, *October 24, 1951, the paper prints were to be used in the pilot of an unidentified television series.*

§Walls, Howard Lamarr, *"Film-Collection Program,"* Journal of the SMPE, *vol. 52, no. 1, January 1949, p. 8.*

**Scheuer, Philip K., *"Restorer of Old Films Finds Producers Help Even in 1900,"* Los Angeles Times, *Part IV, May 15, 1955, p. 2.*

and irrascible,"* had a strange if interesting career prior to becoming involved with the paper prints. He had maintained an interest in industrial photography while spending time as a Los Angeles policeman, as a sheriff's deputy and, in the late 1940s, handling what he once described as "quiet muscle work" for legendary film producer Howard Hughes.† Niver first learned of the paper prints in 1952, when, as an investigator for the Los Angeles District Attorney's Office, he was assigned to locate some of the prints, which had gone astray. They were thought stolen, but were only mislaid. How either the Library of Congress or the Academy of Motion Picture Arts and Sciences were able to mislay such bulky items as the paper prints no one is able to explain.

With the encouragement of Margaret Herrick, he formed a company to specialize in film restoration and preservation, the Renovare Film Company (from the Latin, "to restore"), and devised a machine to reprint the paper prints on film. The Academy awarded Niver a contract for the work later in 1953, and funded the project through 1956, at which time private funding began. Beginning in 1958, the work was supported through funds appropriated by Congress for the overall preservation program of the Library of Congress.

In 1955, Kemp Niver received an Honorary Academy Award "for the development of the Renovare Process which had made possible the restoration of the Library of Congress Paper Film Collection." At that time, only 60,000 or 70,000 feet of paper prints had been copied, and two million feet remained for transfer. Niver copied the paper prints on to 16mm reversal film. He made a dupe negative for the Library of Congress, and retained the 16mm original master. From today's viewpoint, it is curious that the Library did not insist on 35mm copying or on turning over to its control the 16mm master.

While it would be wrong to denigrate Niver's work in any way, it is arguable that the copying of the paper prints was a complicated problem. William Ault joined Niver in May 1958 to operate one of the two machines used in the process, and he points out,

> It wasn't complicated to copy the paper prints. It's been made out to be complicated, but it's really a simple copying process. No great skill is involved. It requires patience and concentration. It's very simple in one sense and very complicated in another, because it's boring.
>
> The requirements are rather basic—to keep the film from drifting from left to right, and holding the frame line steady. Niver had a Bolex and a T-square, and he used the T-square to run the film along one side as a guide—just used the straight edge to keep the film from drifting. The camera is overhead and there are two lights down—it's just glorified microfilming.§

*William Ault in interview with the author, January 24, 1991.
†Niver to Joseph McBride in "Library of Congress' Paper Print Film Collection Proves Gold Mine for Pic Historian Kemp Niver," Daily Variety, November 11, 1974, p. 9.
§This and other quotes from William Ault are taken from an interview with the author, January 24, 1991.

The chief problems faced by Niver and his staff concerned the paper itself. According to Ault,

> When they first got some of the paper, it had been lying around at the Library all those years. It did not unroll very well, and it would not go through the machine easily. What they did was simply a photographic process, like taking a black-and-white print and putting it into water with a little pako solution, and then it can be run on a drum paper dryer. If you run it face down, you get a glossy image, if you run it face up you get a flat. That was done only when the paper was in quite bad condition. It has to do with the quality of the paper, and the conditions under which the paper prints were made. They were just slapped off in a hurry and air dried by the people who made the films.
> With the majority of the Keystones, the splices were a crude stapling device or just plain straight pins while the paper was wet. That way it maintained continuity, but when we tried copying it, there was a problem. We had to take it apart and put it back together. In the Biographs, with plain glue splices, the glue would dissolve, but if you'd number your paper on one side of the cut or the other, you'd match it and put it back together. Or you'd tape it underneath with transparent tape.*

Kemp Niver was an individual who liked to dominate any situation, sometimes with delightful results. At one point, he was visited by Raymond Rohauer, who had heard that Niver was holding a print of the Mack Sennett feature *Molly O'* on behalf of the Academy of Motion Picture Arts and Sciences. Rohauer claimed ownership of the film through control of the Mack Sennett estate. Rohauer sat across the desk from Niver and demanded that he hand the film over. Niver reached into a drawer, pulled out a gun and laid it down on the desk, asking Rohauer, "Do you want to leave now or later?" Rohauer left immediately.

There were many who found Niver difficult or even impossible, but as Ault points out, "Niver pushed the damned thing through—give the guy credit for being persistent." Within a few years of his beginning work restoring the paper prints, Niver gained a reputation as an archivist and film historian. Between 1962 and 1964, he was administrative curator of the Hollywood Museum, and in 1964, he was named associate curator of the Museum of the American Society of Cinematographers, of which he was elected an associate member.

Aside from restoring the paper prints to film, Niver also set about documenting them. Working with Bebe Bergsten, who joined his staff in the early 1960s, Niver was able to catalog and cross-reference the films, with director William Beaudine helping in the task of identifying the players in the American Biograph shorts. The result of Niver's researches was *Motion Pictures from the Library of Congress Paper Print Collection, 1894–1912*, published in 1967

---

*Niver's own description of the restoration process can be found in Niver, Kemp R., "From Film to Paper to Film," The Quarterly Journal of the Library of Congress, vol. 21, no. 4, October 1964, pp. 248–264.

by the University of California Press. In the fall of 1964, Niver formed the
Locare Research Group, which published a series of books, prepared by him,
with editorial assistance from Bebe Bergsten: *The First Twenty Years: A Seg-
ment of Film History* (1968), *Mary Pickford, Comedienne* (1969), *Biograph
Bulletins, 1896–1908* (1971), *D.W. Griffith: His Biograph Films in Perspective*
(1974), and *Klaw and Erlanger Present Famous Plays in Pictures* (1976).

In 1967, Niver gave one of his copying machines to the Motion Picture
Department at Ohio State University. William Ault went back to Ohio with
the machine, helping to set it up. In January 1982, Kemp Niver decided to
retire. He donated his other machine to the UCLA Film and Television Archive, on the understanding that Ault would be hired to work with it. The
paper print restoration project continues at UCLA, but with 35mm rather than
16mm copying. In August 1989, Niver donated his collection of books,
periodicals, and documents on early film history to the Academy of Motion
Picture Arts and Sciences. Appropriately, they are housed in the library named
after Margaret Herrick, Niver's original sponsor on the paper print project.

As it proudly boasts, the UCLA Film and Television Archive is the largest
film archives west of the Rockies, and, after the Library of Congress, the largest
film archives in the United States. It has over 200,000 titles of films, television
productions, and radio programs in its collection, together with approximately
27 million feet of newsreel footage. Through the years, it has undergone
various incarnations, sometimes calling itself the UCLA Film, Television and
Radio Archives. The present name dates from 1990, when the radio archivist
Ron Staley was laid off, supposedly because of budget cuts, and Radio was
quietly dropped from the Archive's title.

It is both a strange and yet impressive archives. Its work area is located not
on the UCLA campus in Westwood, but at the former plant of the Technicolor
Company in Hollywood. The complex has a derelict, rundown atmosphere,
and UCLA's section of it lacks the glamorous or efficient appearance of virtually
every other film archives in the world. There is no heating or air conditioning.
The working conditions probably fail to meet the standards set by both the
state and federal governments, yet here a dedicated and generally young staff
accomplish far more than their counterparts at many other institutions.

In some respects the physical appearance of the UCLA Film and Television
Archive is appropriate for its haphazard and relaxed beginnings. It was founded
as a result of a chance attendance by a former chairman of the Theatre Arts
Department at UCLA, Colin Young (who was later to head England's National
Film School)* at a FIAF conference. He mentioned to various attendees that
UCLA had a number of films, donated over the years and much of it decaying
in a Bekins storage facility, and that it might be appropriate for the University

*It was Colin Young who published the first call for the establishment of an American Film In-
stitute, with "An American Film Institute: A Proposal," Film Quarterly, summer 1961, pp. 37–50.

to organize a film archives. Los Angeles was the filmmaking capital of the world, and there should be a film archives in the city. And so, in 1965, Los Angeles acquired a film archives — at least on paper. A UCLA lecturer, Bob Epstein, was enthusiastic about the project, and he began acquiring a few film titles, and he also began to examine the nitrate film in storage at Bekins. No effort was made by UCLA to preserve or retain any of the unique footage there. Anything worth preserving was handed over to the newly-formed American Film Institute.

Occasionally, Epstein would find nitrate film in private hands. He would take it home, store it in his garage, and examine the footage using a pair of portable rewinds. Again anything worth preserving was passed on to the American Film Institute and the Library of Congress. Because the film came from Epstein's garage, it was designated by the Library of Congress as the Bob Epstein Garage Collection. (One of the items found by Epstein was a 35mm workprint of the 1921 feature *The Blot*, directed by Lois Weber, later restored by Robert Gitt while at the AFI.)

As Epstein remembers it, the Archive began to expand its operations in 1969–1970:

> The big breakthrough was Paramount, which, having had a couple of very big years, was looking for tax write-offs, and decided to give away some of their assets. These were titles over which they no longer had control, because they had sold them to MCA back in the late fifties. Paramount approached the Academy and said, we got scripts, we got still books and we've got prints. Initially, the Academy was going to take the whole caboodle, then somebody said, nitrate prints, we don't want them. And word got out to us that Paramount was looking for a home for these prints — about 740 titles [of films produced between 1928 and 1948]. So I went to Colin Young, and he held a kind of a meeting of people who were interested. Howard Suber [a UCLA professor] volunteered to put a lot of time into it, and at that time Ralph Sargent [who later founded the specialist preservation laboratory, Film Technology] was still on staff at UCLA, and he expressed interest.
>
> So very naively we started to court Paramount. And it was very complicated because it was a three-way deal between Paramount, MCA, which was the copyright owner, and the University. Around this time, Colin left to take up the job in England and Ralph left to start Film Technology, so Howard and I really had to do the work on this. Howard did the work with the University, getting the contract approved, and it was. An angel was found to pay for the vaults — we found decrepit old film vaults down at Washington and Vermont, on the old Film Row. There was no investment from the University. The University didn't know what was going on, except for the legal department up in Berkeley which has approved the contract. There was very little interest in the Theatre Art Department. It was a kind of freak thing we started. We had a feeling that once we got the confidence of one of the studios, the others seeing that would follow.*

Howard Suber was able to raise funds for additional vault space and to try to pay part-time employees. The Archive's first staff person was Charles

These and other remarks are taken from an interview with the author, December 21, 1990.

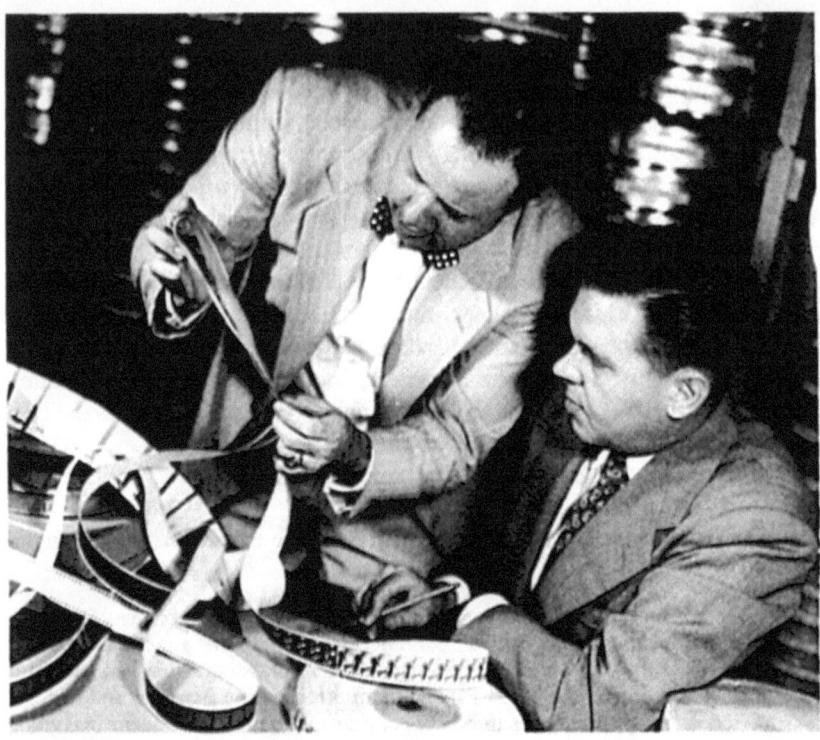

George J. Mitchell (standing) and James H. Culver (custodian of the Motion Picture Collection at the Library of Congress) examine a paper print (courtesy of George J. Mitchell).

Hopkins, hired in 1971 and now the motion picture archivist. As a result of the Paramount donation, 20th Century–Fox decided to deposit its nitrate prints with UCLA. Later, Warner Bros. would deposit nitrate prints of its features and shorts from the 1930s and 1940s, and an Animated Study Collection was received from the Professional, Technical and Clerical Employees Union, Local 986.

However, the first major acquisition, following the 20th Century–Fox deposit came from National Telefilm Associates, which was later to rename itself Republic Pictures in recognition of its best known asset. Harry Arends of the UCLA staff approached National Telefilm Associates, not realizing he was offering them a major boon in offering to house its nitrate holdings. The company had not only the Republic films but many other features and shorts in storage in Fort Lee, New Jersey. Furthermore they were paying storage costs and access was hampered by the distance involved. To save money, National Telefilm Associates hired refrigerated produce vans, which had delivered produce to the East Coast but were now returning empty to California, to transport the nitrate. Epstein recalls:

We couldn't get any more space down at Vermont and Washington, and it was not a good place to store film. In the meantime, Technicolor had vacated their space in Hollywood, and one of the things were film vaults. We were trying to talk the University into springing for the cost of one three-story vault building, but they were dragging their feet. And I had stuff coming from Fort Lee and no place to put it. It's the middle of summer. A truck arrives. Where do we deliver? I had them come out to the University campus, where there was a conference class-room not in use for the summer. The building was air-conditioned. We unloaded the whole truck of nitrate film into this classroom, and locked the door. I went to the department chairman and told him what I had done. The department chairman went to the dean. Nobody wanted to have responsibility for it. We had the Technicolor building within three days. That's what it took. That's how we operated in those days. It grew like Topsy.

Meanwhile, Howard Suber had bowed out of the Archive, disillusioned because a promised major grant from the Louis B. Mayer Foundation failed to materialize. Epstein did not want to function as an administrator, and the university agreed to make funds available for a full-time director. The first choice was James Card, who was on the verge of retiring from his position at the International Museum of Photography at George Eastman House. As he puts it, Epstein "did not feel comfortable" with Card, particularly after the lat-ter insisted on flying out first class for an interview. Finally, in 1974 UCLA film professor Robert (Bob) Rosen was appointed director, a position which he holds to the present. After almost 20 years with the Archive, Epstein resigned in 1981: "I felt I was doing a job with any sense of completion getting further and further away rather than closer and closer. It just wore me down."

For many years, the UCLA Film and Television Archive had shied away from preservation; it had assured the AFI and the Museum of Modern Art that it had no interest in that area. Then, as Epstein remembers,

There was a whole half-a-vault of stuff at 20th Century–Fox that wasn't being released to us—late twenties and early thirties titles that were going to the Museum of Modern Art. A year later, the stuff was still there. So somebody at Fox said, come and take this off our hands. Why didn't it go to the Museum? Because they were log-jammed. The AFI and the Library of Congress were log-jammed. They didn't want us to preserve films initially, because they thought there was only so much in the pie, and they were each getting so much out of the pie in grant money. They saw us as competition, but what they didn't realize was they needed help. Because, as you know, the job is undoable.

The first approach for preservation funds was made by Rosen in a 1976 let-ter to the AFI, in which he wrote, "Now we feel that the UCLA Film Archives has come of age. We are ready and anxious to assume our full share of the responsibility for preserving our film heritage."* The other archives were a lit-tle more uncertain. At a meeting in Rochester, New York, on July 14, 1976, they considered the possibility that UCLA might be "a handmaiden of the

*Letter, Robert Rosen to Win Sharples, Jr., May 8, 1976.

industry" and "the difficulty for a preservation-minded archives to control duping of its films in a university climate." Eventually, the attitude of the other
archives was summed up by James Card with the comment, "Say to NEA that
we are in favor, but not at our own expense."* UCLA would get its funding
for film preservation from the National Endowment for the Arts, but funding
for the other archives would remain intact.

The preservation program at UCLA can be dated from Robert Gitt's advent in 1977. It received national attention in 1984 with Gitt's restoration of
the first full-color Technicolor feature, *Becky Sharp*. Since 1988, the UCLA
Film and Television Archive has presented a Festival of Preservation, highlight-
ing the preservation achievements of the past year. By 1990, the preservation
staff had grown to five, with Eric Aijala, William (Bill) Ault, Blaine Bartell and
Yuell Newsome joining Gitt. That same year, the Festival of Preservation expanded to include examples of preservation work from the National Film Archive (which was represented at the Festival by its curator, Clyde Jeavons) and
the Los Angeles premiere of the Museum of Modern Art's restoration of D.W.
Griffith's *Intolerance*.

If nothing else, UCLA's Festivals of Preservation have helped to make the
public aware that funding of archival preservation does not come solely from
the National Endowment for the Arts, but also includes (at least as far as UCLA
is concerned) grants from the Cecil B. DeMille Foundation, the Stanford
Theater Foundation, Turner Entertainment Co., Republic Pictures, the Mary
Pickford Foundation, and, especially, the David and Lucile Packard Foundation.

Preservation efforts were further enhanced through a tribute by the
Museum of Modern Art in July 1988. The Archive was also a major contributor
of restored and preserved films to the 1989 "Dawn of Sound" tribute, organized
by Mary Lea Bandy, director of the Museum's Department of Film, with funding from AT&T. Robert Gitt collaborated with the Museum on the restoration
of *The Divine Lady* (1929), preserved many Vitaphone short subjects and also
some of the Vitaphone features, including *The First Auto* (1927) and *Noah's
Ark* (1928).†

In the mid-1970s, the archive was known simply as the UCLA Film Archive. It added television to its title in the late 1970s, when it took over administration of what was originally the NATAS-UCLA Television Collection
(later the ATAS-UCLA Collection). Through the efforts since May 1980 of Edwin (Ed) Reitan, Jr., the Archive has also been building up a collection of
equipment demonstrating the history of television technology and design. It
covers all areas of television technology, including black-and-white and color

---

Minutes of the Archives Advisory Committee, July 14, 1976, p. 2.
†*For further information, see Bandy, Mary Lea, editor, The Dawn of Sound (New York:
Museum of Modern Art, 1989).*

systems, live studio and field cameras, post-production and signal processing equipment, studio monitors and home receivers, and video recording systems.*

The growth of the UCLA Film and Television Archive is remarkable. In 1972, it was described by Bob Epstein as "a nice home for old films."† Less than two decades later, it is one of America's leading film archives. One can only hope that further growth will not lead it into becoming a bureaucratic monster, and that it will retain many, if not all, of its earlier ideals and philosophy.

*For further information, see Reitan, Edwin Howard, Jr., "Preserving the History of Television at UCLA," IEEE Transactions on Consumer Electronics, vol. CE-30, no. 2, May 1984.

†Quoted in Thomas, Kevin, "A Good Home for Old Films at UCLA Archive," Los Angeles Times, Part IV, March 1, 1972, p. 1.

6   THINGS ARE SELDOM WHAT THEY SEEM

There is a song from the Gilbert and Sullivan operetta *H.M.S. Pinafore* entitled "Things Are Seldom What They Seem." It would be an appropriate theme song for the American Film Institute and its much vaunted preservation program. In its more than 20-year history, the Institute has promoted film preservation as a major — at times its most important — priority. Yet, through the years, the amount of money devoted to film preservation in the Institute's budget has dwindled, and far too often the organization has chosen to embrace the preservation projects of other institutions as its own, often neglecting to acknowledge the often extremely complex work of the non–AFI individuals responsible for the work. Because National Endowment for the Arts preservation funding is channeled through the American Film Institute rather than given directly to the archives active in the preservation field, the Institute is able to claim some credit for projects in which it has had no involvement.

In 1990, the National Center for Film and Video Preservation at the American Film Institute published a bright and glossy brochure, "The Perils of Preservation." Among the "Preservation Success Stories" listed in the brochure, and by implication the Institute's success stories, were the restoration of *Lawrence of Arabia* (1962), which was funded by Columbia Pictures, and with which the American Film Institute was uninvolved, and the Fred Astaire television specials, restored through the efforts of the UCLA Film and Television Archive. Also listed was the restoration of *Lost Horizon* (1937), which was an AFI project, but unmentioned were the two individuals, Lawrence F. Karr and Robert Gitt, who had worked long, and often unpaid, hours to see the project to fruition.*

In June 1983, Insitute director Jean Firstenberg gave a talk on preservation to the National Association of Media Arts Centers. As part of her talk,

---

*The other two items included in the "Preservation Success Stories" section, on page 3, of this 6-page pamphlet are preservation of a 1924 Black feature, Birthright, directed by Oscar Micheaux, and the donation of television materials from NBC to the Library of Congress, and ABC to the UCLA Film and Television Archive.

74

Firstenberg screened the trailer for *Becky Sharp* (1935), the restoration of which she described as undertaken "with the coordination of the American Film Institute and the International Federation of Film Archives."* What such coordination consisted of, no one seems to know.

There can be no argument that the American Film Institute was created by a sincere group of men and women with high, almost visionary ideals. The Institute's establishment was announced by Roger L. Stevens, as chairman of the National Council on the Arts, on June 5, 1967. Actor Gregory Peck was its acting chairman, and George Stevens, Jr., the son of the distinguished Hollywood director, was named the Institute's director and chief executive officer. (Stevens, unrelated to Roger L. Stevens, was the former director of the Motion Picture and Television Service at the United States Information Agency.) Among the 22 members of the AFI's original board were Francis Ford Coppola, Arthur Knight, Sidney Poitier, Jack Valenti, and Fred Zinnemann.† Initial funding included $2.6 million from the National Endowment for the Arts and the Ford Foundation, and $1.3 million from the seven member companies of the Motion Picture Association of America.

President Lyndon B. Johnson endorsed the Institute, writing,

> I think your organizational approach is a sound one. Operating as a private nonprofit, nongovernmental corporation supported by funds from the National Endowment for the Arts, and private monies, the American Film Institute will have the necessary support as well as the essential freedom of action which a creative venture of this kind requires.§

The press announcement of the Institute's founding listed five areas of endeavor for the new organization: Filmmaker Training, Film Education, Film Production, Preservation and Cataloging of Films, and Publications. The release continued:

> Preservation and cataloguing of films is a task which lies at the heart of the Film Institute's purpose. It is as important to conserve as to create, and the founders wish emphatically to bring attention, as others have before, to the necessity of preserving this Nation's film heritage. This is a complete task and the American Film Institute expects to serve as a focal point for coordination and leadership, and will work with several organizations which are already involved in the field and will seek the cooperation of America's eminent archivists. The American Film Institute does not expect to create its own archives; rather, it will be prepared to coordinate and stimulate the activities of regional and private institutions.**

---

*Page 6 of the typed speech.

†The other original members of the board of trustees were Elizabeth Ashley, Charles Benton, Sherrill Corwin, the Rev. John Culkin, Bruce Herschensohn, Francis Keppel, Richard Leacock, Donald H. McGannon, David Mallery, William L. Pereira, Arnold Picker, Arthur Schlesinger, Jr., George Seaton, Danial Taradash, and Richard F. Walsh.

§Letter to Roger L. Stevens, May 24, 1967.

**Press announcement from the National Foundation on the Arts and Humanities, for release after 5 p.m., June 5, 1967, p. 4.

The "founding father" of the American Film Institute was Richard Kahlenberg. A former member of the foreign service, Kahlenberg had first met the
American Film Institute's founding director, George Stevens, Jr., while still in
his early twenties on a visit to the United States Information Agency, planned
to enable foreign service personnel to become more familiar with its work.
Stevens, who was head of the Agency's Motion Picture and Television Service
from 1962 to 1967, was impressed by Kahlenberg and briefly hired him away
from the foreign service. Later, Kahlenberg attended the University of London, studying film under Thorold Dickinson, and also embarked on a doctoral
program at Northwestern University, which involved his preparing a disserta-
tion on the British Film Institute. In the summer of 1967, Kahlenberg was
hired as a consultant to help formulate plans for the new Institute, primarily its
archival program. Kahlenberg recalls that Stevens

> and I walked into a small office across the street from the White House. And
> there was one room and one table and one chair, and George. I think he was sit-
> ting on the chair and I sat on the table, and then he got up and paced around
> and sat on the table, and I sat on the chair. That went on for a few weeks until
> we got another table and another chair in the same room. There we designed the
> program for the archives. George understood the minute I outlined the program.
> Just sitting looking at him, I knew he knew what was going on. He had a kind
> of nonverbal instinct. I can articulate things, and he just nods, but it is not a casual
> response.*

The archival program which Kahlenberg devised was not one of bricks-
and-mortar, as he is quick to point out, but one involving operations. It was
created as a collaborative effort with the Library of Congress. The Library would
store and preserve the films. The American Film Institute would go out and
acquire them on loan or deposit, raise funds for their preservation, and then
work in cooperation with other extant archives. "The linkage with the Library
of Congress made sense," says Kahlenberg. "No whim of the public or the
movie business was going to get rid of the Library of Congress. And we had
connections in Hollywood to get things for the library. We had the credibility,
I guess you would call it, and the other institutions didn't."

The first agreement between the American Film Institute and the Library
of Congress was signed on June 13, 1968. At that time, there were only five
positions in the Library's Motion Picture Section. Thanks to the Institute's
efforts, five further positions were created with money appropriated by Congress, and seven new positions were funded by the American Film Institute.
The Library acquired its first technical officer in David Lambert Parker, who
joined the Motion Picture Section in 1969. Most important of all, the Institute
designated one third of its budget for film preservation, with much of that
money going to the Library's preservation program.

*This and other quoted remarks from Richard Kahlenberg are taken from an interview with the
author, January 25, 1991.*

The collection at the Library of Congress was designated the National Film Collection, embracing the concept of a comprehensive collection of significant American films. First priority was given to films from the period 1912–1942, when the Library was not retaining copyright prints. Largely because it took away from publicity for the Institute's archival activities, in November 1969, it was agreed that the term National Film Collection would be dropped in favor of the American Film Institute Collection at the Library of Congress. In fact, the Institute's relationship with the Library sometimes hurt its own credibility. In 1969, it was forced to withdraw its application for membership in FIAF on a technicality, while the Motion Picture Section of the Library of Congress was welcomed to provisional membership. (It was not until May of the following year, at the annual congress in Lyon, France, that the Institute was finally accepted as a provisional member of FIAF.)

As archives coordinator, Kahlenberg's first task was to hire Sam Kula, who had been deputy curator of the National Film Archive and was at that time working as a lecturer in the Department of Instructional Technology at USC, as the Institute's first archivist. Kula served as archivist from September 1968 through August 1973, also holding the title of assistant director from 1970 to his resignation (and return to his native Canada). Kahlenberg's second appointment was David Shepard, who was the archive's acquisitions manager from January 1969 through December 1971. "David Shepard was to the film collectors what George and I were to the industry and government," says Kahlenberg. "The industry trusted George and me, and David's charismatic activities made sense to the collectors. And all of us were saying the same thing, may we borrow your films for copying, or hold them on your behalf. And we put them in the Library of Congress."

There could not have been a better group of people working in a better time to create a national film preservation program. As Kahlenberg puts it, "George had the good sense to hire me, and I had the good sense to hire these other people." Their activities served as an impetus for the other archives. Soon after the Institute's creation, in 1969 the trustees of the Museum of Modern Art allocated $600,000 out of capital funds towards the preservation of the Museum's film holdings. It was a decision undoubtedly spurred by the work of the Institute and the new funding opportunities provided by the National Endowment for the Arts (which had embraced film preservation thanks in no small part to the efforts of Nancy Hanks and Chloe Aaron).

One of the first positive steps taken by the Institute was publication, in December 1967, of a "rescue list"* of 250 American films believed to be lost or in imminent danger of decay, compiled by Arthur Knight, Willard Van Dyke, John Kuiper, and William K. Everson. The first major acquisition by the American Film Institute came in January 1969, when the entire RKO feature

*The complete list is given at the end of this chapter, beginning on page 87.

film library was deposited with the Library of Congress by Compagnie d'Entreprises et de Gestion (which controlled all theatrical and television rights to the films outside of the United States). Other important donations followed. A collection of Paramount films, primarily silent features, was made available to the Institute in March 1970, although not formally donated to the Library of Congress until 1978. In May 1970, the Institute, on behalf of the Library of Congress, received a donation of master elements and negatives on over 500 short subjects and 30 feature films produced by Hal Roach. In July of the same year, Mary Pickford donated 50 American Biograph films produced between 1909 and 1913 along with five features starring either brother Jack or sister Lottie. The next major studio donation came from United Artists and consisted of master elements of the pre–1948 Warner Bros. features and short subjects which the company had acquired. The donation was directly to the Library of Congress, and the United Artists management emphatically did not wish their films to be described as part of the AFI Collection. This attitude was in part due to fear of compromising the company's legal position vis-à-vis the IRS in what seemed to be never-ending litigation over the value of the tax deduction associated with the gift. As a result of the intractability of United Artists, when the Institute published a catalog of its acquisitions in 1978, it was forced to title it *Catalog of Holdings: The American Film Institute Collection and the United Artists Collection at the Library of Congress.*

Recognition for the Institute's work in particular and for the need for film preservation in general came in September 1969, when the New York Film Festival programmed a series of rediscovered films from the American Film Institute. The Institute was also trying to gain public interest in film preservation through a series of presentations hosted by various department stores around the country. On October 23, 1974, it organized the first National Film Day, on which more than 4,000 movie theatres donated half of their box office receipts to the Institute for the specific purpose of "preserving old films." Neither gimmick was particularly successful, and both were quietly dropped.

In the late 1960s and early 1970s, while there might be some antagonism and jealousy from other archives, there was little to fault in the AFI's archival program. In 1970, Sam Kula was able to report,

> Within two years the fruitful collaboration between the Institute and the Library has evolved a film preservation program that measures its success in millions of feet of film. At the end of two more years the Library expects to present an ongoing program that can end the state of emergency in nitrate preservation, a program for which Congress will accept full responsibility and adequately fund through direct appropriation.*

Richard Kahlenberg points out that "the film archive consists basically of people," and in the early 1970s those people at the American Film Institute

---

Report on the Library of Congress Film Preservation Program, January 16, 1970, p. 4.

archives changed. Kahlenberg had departed in September 1968 to set up the Institute's Center for Advanced Film Studies on the West Coast. David Shepard moved on in December 1971, taking over the programming of the Institute's new film theatre at the John F. Kennedy Center for the Performing Arts in Washington, D.C., and also running the film program at the Los Angeles County Museum of Art. Sam Kula resigned in August 1973, to return to his native Canada, where he headed the National Film Archives of Canada.

Only one individual represented stability for the archives program, and that was Lawrence F. (Larry) Karr, who had joined the Institute as associate archivist in October 1971 and was to remain there until August 1983. Karr's wife, Kathleen, was briefly with the archives program as an assistant archivist in 1971 and 1972, and is credited with introducing the phrase "moving image" rather than film to the Institute's work. It was an important change in terms of the Institute's later involvement with television. Larry Karr was more devoted to preservation than he was to the American Film Institute. He placed the archives program and its relationship with the other archives and the Library of Congress above the often petty politics of the Institute. It was not an attitude which went over well with the Institute's administration.

With Kula's departure, Karr was named acting archivist, and one of his first decisions was to hire this writer as assistant (later associate) archivist in September 1973. Karr also deserves credit for introducing Robert Gitt to film preservation and restoration by hiring him as a part-time technical officer in July 1973. Karr was demoted to motion picture archivist in August 1974, and Daniel A. Rose was appointed archivist. When Rose left the Institute in January 1976, Win Sharples, Jr., was appointed with the title "Administrator: Preservation and Documentation." When he departed in April 1978, Karr was back as "Acting Administrator: Preservation," eventually appointed "Administrator: Preservation" in July 1978, and finally "Director, Preservation" in July 1980. He remained at the Institute until August 1983, when he joined the computer consulting firm which had, in 1983, designed a computer system for the *AFI Catalog*. (Since then, he has formed Karr Associates, which specializes in analyzing the requirements and providing appropriate data processing systems for archives, libraries, and museums.)

The Institute's failure to understand the need for a person such as Larry Karr to head its archives is evident from its appointment of two men with neither reputation nor prior experience in preservation. In fact, Daniel A. Rose's résumé, as released by the AFI, shows him to be exclusively involved in television production and programming. This writer has reason for remembering Rose's appointment with chagrin. As a result of his appointment, I learned on June 11, 1974, that I was to be fired. The dismissal was rescinded by George Stevens, Jr., once he learned of it, but not before Karr and Gitt had privately agreed to resign in protest, and John Kuiper at the Library of Congress and Chloe Aaron at the National Endowment for the Arts had promised action.

Larry Karr offers a different version of what took place:

> My memory is of working after 6:30 one evening and then being backed against
> the corner in my corner area by [deputy director Richard] Carlton and George
> Stevens, Jr., being told that you were to be fired to provide the money to pay for
> Kahlenberg's $1,000 (or whatever) per week consultancy on television. Obviously
> my chagrin is not quite as bad as yours, but television and money were the issue.
> The AFI relented when they were told by NEA that they couldn't spend film
> preservation contract money on television. There were other things I was doing
> behind the scenes, needless to say.

One of the reasons why the AFI administration was uneasy with Karr may
have been that the archives program was not receiving adequate publicity. It
appeared to be doing less in comparison with the activities of the Museum of
Modern Art and the International Museum of Photography at George Eastman
House. Yet the reality was that there was less to be done by what was, after
all, primarily a service organization.

The number of films acquired by the Institute for the Library of Congress
was bound to, and did, diminish, as the years went by. As of May 1971, the
Institute had acquired 5,000 titles. A further 3,000 were added in 1971, and
1,500 in 1972. From that year onwards, the figures were never more than 1,000
a year: 500 in 1973; 1,000 in 1975; 337 in 1975-1976; 800 in 1976-1977; 700
in 1978-1979; 617 in 1979-1980; and 719 in 1980-1981.

Much of Karr's time was spent in cleaning up the paperwork left over from
the Kula-Shepard days. Films that had earlier been acquired without documentation were officially added to the collection, such as the 70 feature films
starring Marion Davies produced between 1916 and 1936, copied by Richard
Simonton, Jr., in the early 1970s, but not officially acquired until 1975. Karr
also continued and developed the good relationship which the archives program had with various small 8mm and 16mm film distributors, always an important source of films.

The primary dealers with whom the AFI dealt were Blackhawk Films,
Thunderbird Films, Glenn Photo, and Dennis Atkinson (whose companies
were called Spectra Pictures and Standard Film Service). Some dealers with
whom the Institute was involved provided only one item, but it could be an
important film, such as the 1926 *M-G-M Studio Tour*, the original and only
known 35mm nitrate print of which came from Niles Film Products of South
Bend, Indiana. Blackhawk Films was probably the most cooperative and
legitimate of the various dealers, thanks to the integrity of its owner, Kent D.
Eastin. When the Institute had to raise $12,000 to purchase the Don Nichol
Collection, Blawkhawk advanced $3,000 against copying privileges on the col-
lection. When the Institute needed 16mm prints of its restoration of *Foolish
Wives*, it was Blackhawk which supplied six such prints in return for access to
the preservation negative. Blackhawk also helped finance the restoration of
Oliver Twist (1922), in return for exclusive access to the restoration on a royalty

basis. *Oliver Twist* is one of those nearly forgotten, yet important restorations. Initiated by David Shepard, the restoration involved the acquisition of the only known material on the film from Yugoslavia and the restoration of the titles back into English by the film's producer, Sol Lesser, and star, Jackie Coogan.

Just as Karr was overseeing fewer acquisitions, he was also having to deal with smaller amounts of money available for preservation, both in the Institute's own budget and from the National Endowment for the Arts. Information is not readily available as to how much the AFI currently budgets for film preservation, aside from the funds which it administers on behalf of the National Endowment for the Arts. It is known that in the mid- through late 1970s, the amount was little more than $100,000, with less than two-thirds of that used for film preservation as opposed to administration. Compare this to the period 1967–1972, when the Institute spent $633,054 of its own funds to maintain the preservation program, and granted the Library of Congress $345,225 of its own fund to finance its preservation activities.*

Despite such decreases in preservation support, the Institute was able to maintain a public front as a major contributor. Typical of the Institute's thinking on the subject is the following extract from a memorandum from Win Sharples, Jr., to AFI Deputy Director Richard Carlton, dated March 9, 1976:

> This year, the funding level of AFI-administered grants to the Library of Congress, George Eastman House and the Museum of Modern Art [i.e. those funds received directly from the National Endowment for the Arts and not raised by the Institute] has risen to $455,000. With this amount doubled by matching grant provisions at these institutions, we can now say that over one million dollars per year are being spent by the American Film Institute and its three sister preservation programs.†

Under contract to the National Endowment for the Arts, the Institute was in the enviable position of administering funds for the entire preservation program in the United States, although it must be pointed out that the disposition of the grants was, and continues to be, recommended by the Archives Advisory Committee. The granting of these funds placed the Institute in the position of overseeing the work of other archives, and was a continuing source of friction in the archival community. In the mid-1970s, the Institute was criticized by the Archives Advisory Committee, consisting of representatives from the Museum of Modern Art, the International Museum of Photography at George Eastman House and the Library of Congress, for its insensitivity, its interference in the internal affairs of other archives, and its appointment of non-archivists as archivists. At a meeting on October 16, 1975, at George Eastman House, the problem came out into the open, when James Card accused the AFI

---

*AFI Memorandum, Larry Karr to Marcia Johnston, August 31, 1978.
†"Report on Preservation Program to AFI Board," AFI Memorandum, Win Sharples, Jr., to Richard Carlton, March 9, 1976.

of "attempting to act as chairman of the group, setting forth agendas, state-ments, proposals, and determining what preservation activity will be ac-cepted." He went on to state that "the Committee is becoming a bureaucratic structure responding primarily to fiscal conditions" and that "the archives on the Committee have been preserving films for many years and can appropriately determine what is proper archival activity without outside supervision." The National Endowment for the Arts, through its representative Nancy Raine, rebuffed attempts by the member archives to deal directly with the NEA. She insisted that the AFI was contracted to administer the funds, and had a respon-sibility for resolving the resultant difficulties.

The relationship between the AFI and its sister archives never fully recovered from the open comments by James Card, even with his later retire-ment. Perhaps the AFI learned the need for a little more diplomacy in its handling of archival coordination, but beneath the surface, carefully obscured by politics, the simmering resentment of the AFI by its sister institutions remains.

Typical of the Institute's heavy-handedness and subsequent backlash from fellow organizations was its decision to become involved in television pre-servation. At its December 1972 board of trustees meeting, a decision was made to embrace television preservation as well as film preservation. In a memorandum to the AFI staff, George Stevens, Jr., explained:

> It has been our concept from the beginning that "film" refers to the moving image and, therefore, the intent and the goals of The American Film Institute fully encompass television....
>
> It is time also to re-examine what the AFI's responsibility should be in the area of television archives. Initially, we determined that the nitrate film preservation task was so enormous for a new and young organization that it would be necessary to defer any involvement with the equally difficult task of television archives. However, with our motion pictures archives program proceeding well, I think now is the time to re-examine the question of whether AFI should prepare to deal with television in much the same fashion and with much the same energy as we dealt with the nitrate picture problem.*

On February 4, 1972, Sam Kula reported to Stevens that there had been various tentative efforts by others to introduce a television archives program, "but they have not succeeded in establishing a substantial collection.... UCLA makes a lot of noise about its TV archive ... but there is not much tape or film in the collection." The area was obviously ripe for exploitation by the AFI, and in the fall of 1973, Richard Kahlenberg was invited back to the Institute to formulate a proposal for a television archives program. As he now sum-marizes his efforts, "I organized the same coalition of people who had been involved in the cinema, got the same suspects together plus the television

---

*AFI Memorandum, "Television and Its Place within the American Film Institute," George Stevens, Jr., to the AFI Staff, January 25, 1972, p. 1.

networks plus the television archives. And they hired somebody to carry on, but he was no Kula. And it didn't go."

While, in principle, Kahlenberg is correct, the process was somewhat more complicated, and the lack of success may be blamed as much on a lack of finesse by the Institute's senior executives as much as its new archivist, Daniel A. Rose. The first problem arose when Richard Carlton, AFI deputy director for operations, asked permission of the National Endowment for the Arts to use some of the funds granted for nitrate preservation to finance initial development of a television archives program. The request was denied in March 1974.

Undaunted, the Institute went ahead with the proposal. Kahlenberg's plan was to have the AFI act in the role of coordinator, working with the Library of Congress to acquire entertainment television programming and the National Archives to obtain retrospective news material. Any duplicate material acquired would be passed on to the Academy of Television Arts and Sciences, presumably for deposit at the UCLA Film and Television Archive, "thus making the TV Academy a western branch of the Library of Congress."*

In theory, it was a worthwhile idea, but it did not take into account the various television archives already in existence and the reality that such organizations were long aware of the need for television preservation as well as the problems involved. On March 8, 1974, the AFI hosted a meeting in Washington, D.C., of representatives from the Library of Congress, the Broadcast Pioneers Library, the William S. Paley Foundation, the National Academy of Television Arts and Sciences, the National Archives, the Broadcast Education Association, and Vanderbilt Television News Archives. A press release was already prepared announcing formation of the National Coordinatng Committee of Television Archivists when letters arrived from Ruth Schwartz, director of the NATAS-UCLA Television Library, James E. O'Neill, deputy archivist of the United States, L. Quincy Mumford, Librarian of Congress, and John Eger, acting director, Office of Telecommunications Policy of the President. All stated basically the same point, the Institute's proposal was premature and might interfere with ongoing activities.

Undeterred, the AFI continued to press the matter. Perhaps the biggest mistake it made was to have George Stevens, Jr., address the annual meeting of the Popular Culture Association, in St. Louis, Missouri, on March 21, 1975. As reported by Les Brown in *The New York Times* on March 22, 1975, the speech was critical of what had been accomplished to date.† In fact, quite a bit had been happening, including support from the Ford Foundation, which

*AFI Memorandum, "Hidden Agenda," Richard Kahlenberg to George Stevens, Jr., and Richard Carlton, April 25, 1974, p. 1.

†Despite the evidence of an AFI press release and a New York Times story, it appears that the speech was prepared by Stevens, but he did not attend the meeting, and the speech was delivered by Daniel A. Rose.

had three subcommittees at work on the problem. "We have a long list of priorities so if you or any other member of the ad hoc committee feel that this project is not worthwhile, I will be happy to recommend to my superiors that we cease our activities in this field," wrote Ford Program Officer Stuart F. Sucherman to Stevens.*

The speech was also adapted for an April 12, 1975, *Washington Post* article, which evoked additional anger from Dr. Alan Fern, chief, Reference Department, Prints and Photographs Division, at the Library of Congress, of whose division the Motion Picture Section was a part. In a letter published in the *Post*, and also sent directly to Stevens, Fern commented,

> Mr. Stevens calls for a reordering of priorities which seems to indicate that one job slips into second place, while another assumes a higher importance. Considering that, until recently, the American Film Institute spent much of its time and effort encouraging the Library of Congress, the Museum of Modern Art, George Eastman House, and other archives to accelerate their film preservation programs, it is disconcerting to read that these efforts, which are far from completed, should now be turned aside.†

The work to create a nationwide television preservation program did continue, but basically through the efforts of organizations other than the American Film Institute. On February 13-14, 1977, the Library of Congress hosted a meeting of television archives, "to explore questions of mutual interest and ways to further cooperation."§ The AFI's deputy director, Richard Carlton, was "surprised (perhaps annoyed, more to the point)" to first learn of the Library's plans through a letter of invitation from Erik Barnouw.** It was not until 1979 that the AFI organized its own meeting, a Television Archives Advisory Committee Meeting, on January 18-19, which approved creation of the group commonly referred to as TAAC (Television Archives Advisory Committee), modeled after the Film Archives Advisory Committee (FAAC). Its purpose, as "approved by nodding of heads" on January 18, 1979, was as

> an advisory consortium of institutions concerned with the archival management and preservation of television materials. Its purpose is to encourage cooperation among television archives through the sharing of experience and information. The TAAC as an organization does not take stands on issues or make binding decisions, although its meetings may at times serve as a forum within which institutions in their own names may choose to act in concert.

Having spent half of the 1970s decade worrying about television preservation without accomplishing a great deal, it was time for the American Film Institute to return to the problem of nitrate preservation, which, of course, still

---

Stuart F. Sucherman to George Stevens, Jr., April 4, 1975, p. 1.
†*Alan Fern to the editor*, The Washington Post, *April 18, 1975, p. 1.*
§*Erik Barnouw to Win Sharples, Jr., December 29, 1977, p. 1.*
**AFI Memorandum, *"Television Preservation Conference," Richard Carlton to Win Sharples, Jr., February 7, 1978.*

remained largely unsolved, thanks to continuing lack of funding and inadequate money raising efforts.

In 1980, the Institute unveiled its list of the "Ten Most Wanted" films for archival preservation. They were: *Frankenstein* (1910), *Cleopatra* (1917), *The Kaiser, the Beast of Berlin* (1918), *Little Red Riding Hood* (1922), *Greed* (1923), *That Royle Girl* (1926), *London After Midnight* (1927), *Camille* (1927), *The Divine Woman* (1928), and *Rogue Song* (1930). It was an eclectic list, including works by such prominent filmmakers as Walt Disney (*Little Red Riding Hood*), Erich von Stroheim (*Greed*, in its complete form of course), and D.W. Griffith (*That Royle Girl*), as well as starring vehicles for Theda Bara (*Cleopatra*), Lon Chaney (*London After Midnight*), Norma Talmadge (*Camille*), and Greta Garbo (*The Divine Woman*). Surprisingly missing were two major features of 1928: Ernst Lubitsch's *The Patriot* and F.W. Murnau's *Four Devils*.

There was, perhaps, a hidden agenda behind the chosen list. The Institute always maintained good relations with the Walt Disney Archives, and the inclusion of Disney's *Little Red Riding Hood* was probably at the latter's request. The archives staff knew that a print of *Frankenstein* survived in the hands of a collector named Aloïs (Al) F. Detlaff, Sr., of Cudahy, Wisconsin. He had been collecting film since 1928 and claimed to own one million feet, in various formats. A few feet of *Cleopatra* had been found by this writer in 1974, and was handed over to James Card at George Eastman House. I can still see the look of excitement on his face as he took the little clip—it was the smile of a true worshipper.

According to Larry Karr,

> The 10 most wanted list was a publicity stunt. Our hope was to dramatize the problem by citing namebrand films of either actor or filmmaker or title. *Camille* was my private tweak of Raymond Rohauer, since I knew he had something on the title—he later tweaked me on this, but never came across with the film. I believe he had four to six rotting reels. I picked the Disney for the Disney name. They weren't asked, other than to verify they didn't have it. They didn't request its inclusion. There were easily another fifty contenders including the two you cite. I privately regarded the actual titles selected as a MacGuffin.

In 1981, a 2½ minute clip from *Rogue Song* was found at Keene State College, New Hampshire, by Lawrence Benaquist, and handed over to the AFI for preservation. As of 1974, M-G-M had the nitrate picture negative of reel four of the film, but it appears to have decomposed. Turner Entertainment, as successor to M-G-M, does have the complete soundtrack to *Rogue Song* on disc. (The original elements are on deposit with the UCLA Film and Television Archive.)

For reasons which are still unclear but which possibly indicate a worsening in the relationships between AFI and the National Endowment for the Arts, the two organizations created the National Center for Film and Video Preservation in September 1983. It began operations in January 1984, with Robert Rosen as its first director. Described at its formation as "a significant new departure in the effort to safeguard our nation's film and television heritage,"* the Center simply continued the activities of the AFI archives program. Located at the Institute's West Coast headquarters, but with its archivist headquartered in Washington, D.C., the Center is partially independent of the Institute, and has its own director and own board of advisors. Aside from handling the preservation activities of the Institute, it took over responsibility for the *American Film Institute Catalog* project (a definitive filmography of the American cinema) and created the National Moving Image Data Base (providing information on the holdings of America's archives and production and distribution companies). The National Endowment for the Arts preservation grants, averaging $500,000 a year, are administered through the Center. The grants are, however, designated as the AFI/NEA rather than the NCFVP/NEA Film Preservation Program.

One particularly worthwhile activity of the Center was the expansion of the two groups, FAAC and TAAC. They were merged into one, F/TAAC, consisting of four groups of archives: the major U.S. archives belonging to FIAF, local television news archives (also designated news and documentary archives), the avant-garde and independent group, and the subject-oriented archives. As the Center's former deputy director, Michael Friend, points out the Center helped "to build bridges between these archives and the NEA."† At a meeting, held in Portland, Oregon, from October 30 to November 3, 1990, F/TAAC decided to change its name to the Association of Moving Image Archivists (AMIA), open for membership to individuals rather than institutions. This decision appears to indicate a move away from the Center.

One area in which the Center has been unproductive is fund raising. The only major grant raised by the Center was $100,000 from Hiram Walker, importers of Canadian Club Classic, given in 1984 for the preservation of 12 classic films by the Center's member archives: *City Streets, Dark Command, Death Takes a Holiday, Irene, Portrait of Jennie, Rebecca, Folies Bergere, Kitty Foyle, A Midsummer Night's Dream, Once Upon a Honeymoon, Road to Rio,* and *Skippy.* (It was subsequently discovered there were insufficient funds to preserve the last title.)

The Center inherited a major publicity gimmick from the American Film Institute, the Decade of Preservation. Despite the fact that a number of film archives had been actively involved in film preservation for a couple of decades, the Institute decided to take upon itself the privilege of naming 1983–1993 as "The Decade of Preservation." The announcement was made at a dinner at the Beverly Hilton Hotel on June 21, 1983, with Bette Davis, Jessica Lange, and

---

Center Factsheet, undated, p. 1.
†*Telephone conversation with the author, May 8, 1990.*

James Caan in attendance. A five-minute film on preservation, produced and directed by Jon N. Bloom and narrated by Jack Lemmon, received its premiere, and RKO, which helped sponsor the event, pledged to donate $200,000 to preservation. Missing from the evening were the individuals at America's archives who were physically responsible for preserving this nation's film heritage. They were not invited.

Halfway through the Decade of Preservation, the Institute threw another star-studded bash, the First Film Preservation Ball, which drew a crowd of 700, including President Ronald Reagan, and raised $175,000 for film preservation — or at least for the administration necessary for film preservation to succeed.

It would be unfair to dismiss the AFI's film preservation efforts as more a public relations effort than a substantive program. A lot of good came from the AFI, particularly in the early years, but a lot of money and a lot of effort was certainly wasted, in large part because of a lack of dedication from the higher levels of the Institute's administration. A philosophical Richard Kahlenberg comments,

> It's one thing to design a phenomenon that will last. It's another to deal with the fact that it may be there, that it may even be strong, but is it any good any more? I am challenged by the work of designing a phenomenon that will even survive a change in personnel, as has the American Constitution. That's a phenomenon that was well thought out. They designed a way of rejuvenating it — mid-course correction perhaps.

It is interesting that when George Stevens, Jr., was interviewed by *Variety* (February 13, 1980), and asked to name the four major landmarks in the development of the American Film Institute, he replied the Center for Advanced Film Studies, the creation of the AFI Life Achievement Awards, the establishment of a film theatre at the Kennedy Center in Washington, D.C., and the Congressional defeat of the Institute's attempt to seek federal appropriations in December 1974. Notably, he did not mention the AFI's archival or preservation program.

The following is a complete list of films on the AFI "rescue list," dated December 11, 1967:

The Air Circus *(1928)*	The Battle Cry of Peace	Blind Bargain *(1922)*
Alone *(1932)*	*(1915)*	Body and Soul *(1927)*
Alone in the Wilderness	The Battle of Gettysburg	Broadway *(1929)*
(1912)	*(1913)*	Camille *(1921)*
Amateur Gentleman *(1926)*	Battle of the Century *(1927)*	Captain Blood *(1924)*
American Madness *(1932)*	Beau Brummel *(1924)*	The Captive God *(1915)*
Anna Christie *(1923)*	Beggar on Horseback *(1925)*	The Case of Lena Smith
Around the World in 80	Bella Donna *(1923)*	*(1929)*
Minutes *(1931)*	Betrayal *(1929)*	The Cave Man *(1925)*
The Aryan *(1916)*	Beyond the Rocks *(1922)*	The Cheat *(1923)*
The Bat *(1926)*	Bits of Life *(1921)*	Children in the House *(1916)*

Children of Eve *(1915)*
Cimarron *(1932)*
Cleopatra *(1917)*
Confessions of a Queen *(1925)*
A Connecticut Yankee in King Arthur's Court *(1931)*
The Count of Monte Cristo *(1922)*
The Cradle Snatchers *(1927)*
Dance of Life *(1929)*
A Daughter of the Gods *(1914)*
David Harum *(1915)*
The Devil's Passkey *(1920)*
The Dictator *(1922)*
The Divine Woman *(1928)*
Don Q *(1925)*
Down on the Farm *(1920)*
The Drag Net *(1928)*
Du Barry *(1917)*
The Enchanted Cottage *(1924)*
The Enchanted Cottage *(1945)*
The Enemy *(1928)*
The Escape *(1914)*
Eternal Love *(1917)*
Evangeline *(1919)*
Excuse My Dust *(1920)*
The Exquisite Sinner *(1926)*
Fazil *(1928)*
Fire Fighting Zouaves *(1913)*
Foolish Wives *(1922)*
Fools for Luck *(1928)*
Forever *(1922)*
The Front Page *(1931)*
The Garden of Allah *(1927)*
Ghost of Old Morro *(1917)*
The Girl from Montmartre *(1926)*
The Girl Glory *(1917)*
Greed *(1924)*
Hats Off *(1927)*
Hawthorne of the U.S.A. *(1919)*
The Hayseed *(1919)*

Her Husband's Trademark *(1921)*
Her Love Story *(1924)*
Hollywood *(1923)*
The Hoodlum *(1919)*
The Hunchback of Notre Dame *(1922)*
Isle of Lost Ships *(1923)*
Journey's End *(1930)*
Kentucky *(1925)*
Kid Boots *(1926)*
Kiss for Cinderella *(1926)*
A Knight for the Road *(1911)*
Lady Windermere's Fan *(1925)*
Last Moment *(1928)*
The Letter *(1929)*
Lightnin' *(1925)*
Little Man, What Now? *(1934)*
London After Midnight *(1927)*
Lost Horizon *(1937)*
The Lotus Eater *(1923)*
Madame Sans-Gêne *(1928)*
The Man from Blankley's *(1930)*
Man, Woman and Sin *(1927)*
Mare Nostrum *(1926)*
Men *(1924)*
Merton of the Movies *(1924)*
Miss Lulu Bett *(1921)*
Mockery *(1927)*
Nell Gwyn *(1926)*
Neptune's Daughter *(1917)*
The Old Army Game *(1926)*
The Old Dark House *(1932)*
Oliver Twist *(1922)*
The Patriot *(1928)*
The Penalty *(1920)*
The Potters *(1927)*
The Private Life of Don Juan *(1934)*
The Racket *(1928)*
Ramona *(1928)*
Reaching for the Moon *(1931)*
The River *(1928)*

River Woman *(1928)*
The Road to Glory *(1926)*
Mr. Robinson Crusoe *(1932)*
Rogue Song *(1930)*
Romola *(1924)*
Rosita *(1923)*
Running Wild *(1927)*
Sadie Thompson *(1928)*
The Salvation Hunters *(1925)*
Scarlet Days *(1919)*
Scarface *(1932)*
The Show *(1927)*
The Sky Pilot *(1921)*
So Big *(1925)*
So's Your Old Man *(1925)*
The Squaw Man *(1914)*
Stagecoach *(1939)*
Station Content *(1918)*
Straight Shooting *(1917)*
Street Angel *(1928)*
The Student Prince *(1927)*
Sweet and Twenty *(1909)*
Tell It to the Marines *(1927)*
Thais *(1918)*
The Third Degree *(1927)*
Three Bad Men *(1926)*
Tillie's Punctured Romance *(1928)*
To Save Her Soul *(1909)*
The Tower of Lies *(1925)*
Trent's Last Case *(1929)*
Twenty Thousand Leagues Under the Sea *(1916)*
Two Flaming Youths *(1928)*
Typhoon *(1914)*
The Unknown *(1927)*
Upstream *(1927)*
Washington Merry-Go-Round *(1932)*
What Price Glory *(1926)*
White Gold *(1927)*
The White Moth *(1924)*
Wild Oranges *(1924)*
The Winning of Barbara Worth *(1926)*
A Woman of Paris *(1923)*
Zoo in Budapest *(1933)*

7 SPECIALIZATION
IN THE SEVENTIES

The concept of specialization in the archival and preservation fields began in the 1970s, as new institutions were created and older archives began to consider genres in American film history which they had ignored.

"The preservation options for the independent filmmaker are very few," wrote Ted Perry in 1978.

> He can hardly afford to make the expensive black-and-white separation masters. As to cold storage, even if there were ample space, many of the independent filmmakers would probably not turn their life's work over to some institution, preferring to keep the films nearby, in home-made storage facilities, however inadequate. The results are sometimes disastrous — floods, fires, snowstorms, dehumidifiers that were not turned on it time. And the death of an important independent filmmaker quickly reveals even more overwhelming problems, for the materials are often in great disarray.*

Despite a plea by the well known independent filmmaker Stan Brakhage to George Stevens, Jr., director of the American Film Institute, it was obvious that both the Institute and the Library of Congress had higher preservation priorities than saving the works of America's experimental and avant-garde filmmakers, whose films were, after all, shot on safety film (either 8mm or 16mm) and with their inflated egos could often provide more problems than solutions.

The impetus for the preservation of experimental film would have to come from someone associated with the genre, and that someone was Jonas Mekas, who established the Anthology Film Archives in 1970. Located initially at Joseph Papp's Public Theater, at 425 Lafayette Street, New York, Anthology Film Archives moved in 1975 to 80 Wooster Street, and, in 1979, acquired the 2nd Street and Second Avenue Courthouse building as a permanent home.

After being closed for six years, Anthology Film Archives opened its doors at the new location on October 12, 1988. The new building includes offices,

---

*Perry, Ted, "Will Experimental Film Disappear?" American Film, vol. 3, no. 10, September 1978, p. 6.

storage vaults, a library, a 66-seat theatre (named in honor of filmmaker Maya
Deren), and a 200-seat auditorium.*

Although it lacks the prestige and the reputation of the archives of the
American film establishment, Anthology Film Archives has been able to build
up a reference library, a screening program, a publications program in cooperation with New York University Press, and a core collection of films, including
such "classics" of the American avant-garde as Joseph Cornell's *Rose Hobart*
(1939), Kenneth Anger's *Fireworks* (1947), and Robert Frank's *Pull My Daisy*
(1959).† In 1989, Anthology Film Archives began awarding the annual Jay
Leyda prize in Cinema Studies, named in honor of the film archivist and
scholar (1910–1988) who had produced seminal works on the Soviet and
Chinese cinemas. The first year, the $2,000 cash award went to Richard Abel
for his book, *French Film Theory and Criticism*.

In cooperation with the Museum of Modern Arts and Pacific Film Archive,
Anthology Film Archives began preservation work in 1974. As of November
1976, it had copied 200 black-and-white films, 30 color films and the entire
footage from the Maya Deren Haitian project. Guidelines for the archival work
were intitially set by an advisory committee, consisting of Jay Leyda, Amos
Vogel, Donald Richie, Sheldon Renan, and Lewis Jacobs.

Films preserved by Anthology Film Archives are generally in the 16mm
or 8mm formats. The preservation work is relatively simple, as indicated in a
1978 report:

> When a film is selected for preservation, it is inspected for damage and shrink-
> age. Any necessary repairs are made before the film is "prepared for duping" at
> either International Filmtreat or FilmLife. In this process, scratches are removed
> and the film rejuvenated.
> When the original material is ready for printing, at least two pieces of preserva-
> tion materials are struck, one positive and one negative image. Corresponding op-
> tical sound tracks are struck if necessary. If release prints are to be made, it is decided
> whether to use the original or, should it be too badly damaged or shrunken, a
> printing master is struck in addition to the two pieces of preservation material.§

Anthology Film Archives began a commitment to video as well as film in
1973, and by 1990 had an annual operating budget of $700,000. In an effort
to provide the Archives with a more professional image, in keeping with its
new building, Jonas Mekas accepted the title of artistic director, and in May
1988, Jane Safer became Anthology's new executive director.

The films of Andy Warhol, such as *Flesh* (1968) and *Heat* (1972), which

*For more information, see Haller, Robert A., "The Return of Anthology Film Archives,"
Media Arts, vol. 2, no. 5/6, winter/spring 1990, p. 8.

†A complete listing of its holdings was published in Sitney, P. Adams, editor, The Essential
Cinema: Essays on the Films in the Collection of Anthology Film Archives (New York: New York
University Press, 1975).

§Report on the Independent Film Preservation Program at Anthology Film Archives, July 20,
1978, p. 1.

were, in reality, directed by Paul Morrissey and only "produced" by Warhol, are major, semicommercial features that are hard to accept as part of America's independent film movement. The same applies to the "experimental" films which Warhol did direct between 1963 and 1968, a group of which includes such titles as *Sleep, Empire, Blow Job, The Chelsea Girls,* and *Lonesome Cowboys.* In a collaborative effort between the Whitney Museum of American Art and the Museum of Modern Art, and as evidence of Warhol's status within the artistic community, 13 of those early films have been preserved, with circulating copies available from the Museum of Modern Art.*

A year after Mekas established Anthology Film Archives in New York, Sheldan Renan created the Pacific Film Archive (PFA) as a San Francisco–based exhibition program, modeled after that of the Cinémathèque Française in Paris. Despite its name, Pacific Film Archive is more a screening facility than an archives. Those of its holdings which are in need of preservation are routinely turned over to the UCLA Film and Television Archive. It has tried to address the preservation needs of West Coast avant-garde and independent filmmakers, preserving Gunvor Nelson's *Red Shift* and George Kuchar's *Corruption of the Damned.* Among early films which have been preserved by Pacific Film Archive are Georges Méliès' *The Palace of the Arabian Nights* in a tinted version, and the last reel of the 1918 Italian feature, *La Tosca,* starring Francesca Bertini. When funds become available, the Archive plans to preserve the Japanese silent feature *Arakuma Daihachi,* directed by Nishina Kumahiko.

Sheldon Renan tried initially to locate PFA at the San Francisco Museum of Art, but when his proposal was rejected by its board, Renan was successful in finding a home for his new organization at the University Art Museum, then located on the campus of the University of California at Berkeley but about to move to new quarters on Berkeley's Durant Avenue.

Tom Luddy was PFA's first curator from 1972 to 1980, succeeded for a brief period by Lynda Miles. As of 1992, Edith Kramer (who has been with PFA since 1975, and its director and curator since 1983) oversees an exhibition program which is, without question, the finest on the West Coast, and bettered in the United States only by that of the Museum of Modern Art. Since 1986, PFA has screened video on a regular basis, and it appointed its first video curator, Steve Seid, in 1988. Avant-garde film has been curated since 1987 by Kathy Geritz. The Archive also maintains a library facility open to the public.

With the establishment of an exhibition program, Sheldan Renan also sought to build up a film collection, and his first important acquisitions were the libraries of two major Japanese production companies, Daiei and Shochiku,†

---

*For more information, see Ehrenstein, David, "Queen of the Silver Screen," The Advocate, July 17, 1990, pp. 60–62.

†The Daiei Collection has been cataloged in Provinzano, Linda, Howard Besser, Stephanie Boris and Frank Motofuji, Films in the Collection of the Pacific Film Archive: Volume I: Daiei Motion Picture Co., Ltd., Japan (Berkeley: University of California Press, 1979).

an early acknowledgment of the partnership in the Pacific Rim of both Japan and America's West Coast. Pacific Film Archive continues to acquire films through donations and occasional purchases.

Anthropological films are just about as old as the cinema itself—shots of exotic people in exotic places have always been useful filler material in any film program—but the first attempt to archive such material came in 1981, when the Smithsonian Institution created the Human Studies Film Archives as part of its Department of Anthropology. The Archives has its origins in the Belmont Conference, sponsored by the National Science Foundation, at which anthropologists, filmmakers and social scientists acknowledged the need for a national center not only to preserve but also to produce, for research and documentation purposes, anthropological films. As a result, the National Anthropological Film Center was established in 1973, primarily to initiate filmmaking projects. In 1981, the Center's filmmaking and archival activities were separated, and the Human Studies Film Archives came into being.

In 1988, about 1.3 million feet of film created by the National Anthropological Film Center were transferred to the Human Studies Film Archives for processing and preservation. Shot under the direction of E. Richard Sorenson, the footage depicts ethnic life in Nepal, Tibet, Ladakh, India, Micronesia, Papua New Guinea, and Brazil. It represents less than one-third of the footage safeguarded by the Archives, one of the earliest items in which is *Beautiful Japan*, made in 1917 by Benjamin Brodsky. Unfortunately, the Archives has yet to find material on Brodsky's other important Asian travelog from 1917, *A Trip Thru China*.

Although somewhat akin to a stock footage library in that it is interested in trims and out-takes as much as cut picture, the Human Studies Film Archive has collected a considerable number of travelog-style "interest" shorts made by such well known pioneers in the genre as Burton Holmes. Among other material in its collection is documentary footage shot by E.C. Higbee, Laura Boulton, Paul Travis, and Ferdinand Rice. Nor is the collection limited to foreign peoples. Another of its early holdings is *Ye Old Time Coon Hunt*, shot in 1917 by E.F. Warner of *Field and Stream* magazine for Bray Studios, and showing a racoon hunt in the American South.

The preservation activities of the Human Studies Film Archives are explained by its director, Wendy Shay:

> Original film and video are not used for viewing, are subjected to a minimum of handling and printing, and are stored in temperature and humidity controlled vaults. Black and white films, audio tapes, and video tapes are stored in an existing vault at 50 degrees Fahrenheit and 50% Relative Humidity. In addition, the Film Archives is constructing a new color film vault which will operate at 35 degrees Fahrenheit and 25% Relative Humidity....
>
> The primary emphasis in film and video preservation, in addition to archival handling and storage of the original materials, is the production of preservation masters on which the best possible image is reproduced on as stable a format and

stock as possible. There are several factors to consider in this process. The first is identifying the original materials with the image quality to reproduce. The second is organization of the material prior to duplication. The HSFA's film archivists generally try to preserve camera rolls in the chronological order in which they were shot. The ideal is to work from uncut camera original material, but often this is not possible. Instead, out-takes, trims, and pre-print material such as A + B rolls may need to be assembled to provide the most complete record.

Once the original materials have been assembled and a preservation master has been produced, another master generation may be produced from which future copies may be made. The printing master is also maintained in archival storage. Only the reference copy, usually produced from the preservation or printing master, is used for viewing at the Archives.*

As indicated, in addition to preservation and cataloging materials, the Human Studies Film Archives makes its footage available for in-house viewing and for outside documentary use on a selective basis and taking into account the ethical use of the material. It has also sponsored occasional conferences, notably the 1989 two day event, "Changing Views: Filming the Peoples of the North Pacific Rim," which included a screening of Sakari Pälsi's *Travelling in the Arctic*, a restoration by the Finnish Film Archives of the 40-minute feature from 1917 (an important year in anthropological film production!).

With the use of "old film" becoming more and more attractive to producers of television commercials for the sale of everything from fast food to banking services, several archives, including the Human Studies Film Archives, have started to consider the ethical questions raised by the licensing of their holdings for outside use. In 1990, the New Zealand Film Archive (founded in 1981) became the first archives to adopt the protocol that indigenous people might retain "spiritual guardianship" of their images. As a result, the Maori tribes of New Zealand have the right to object to the use of archival film in such a way as to diminish the power and dignity of the original image.

Another type of film relevant to human behavior is pornography, the preservation of which first became a concern of archivists in the early 1970s. The initial reaction from both federal and local authorities is to rout it out and destroy it. As a result, an important aspect of American film culture may well be lost.

The obvious repository for pornographic films is the Kinsey Institute for Research in Sex, Gender and Reproduction at Indiana University. It houses a collection of pornographic films dating back to the early teens, together with a large number of clinical films, documentaries and even avant-garde films dealing with sexual matters, such as Kenneth Anger's *Fireworks*. A less likely repository for pornographic material is the National Archives, yet its holdings include a small collection of videotapes and 8mm films, collected by the

*Shay, Wendy, "Introduction to the Human Studies Film Archives," 1985, mimeographed report, p. 27.

Department of Justice as exhibits in Attorney General Edwin Meese's 1986 Commission on Pornography (and designated Collection No. RG60). It is more than a little ironic that the activities of a Commission seriously geared towards the abolition of pornography should have resulted in the safeguarding of a sampling of pornographic items.

The UCLA Film and Television Archive has two very different semipornographic collections. In September 1976, it acquired a major collection of 35mm positive and master elements, both nitrate and safety, from Sonny Amusement Enterprises. Dating from the 1930s through the 1960s, the collection includes such pornographic and exploitation subjects as *B-Girl Rhapsody*, *Buxom Beautease*, *Child Bride*, *Elysia*, *Valley of the Nudes*, *Sidestreets of Hollywood* (also known as *Virgin in Hollywood*), *Slaves in Bondage*, and *Love for Sale*.

In May 1983, UCLA received on deposit from Pat Rocco a collection of softcore gay pornographic films, which he had produced in the late 1960s and early 1970s. The collection includes *Pat Rocco Dares* (1969), *A Breath of Love* (1969), *Mondo Rocco* (1970), and *Sex and the Single Gay* (1970). The films are very important in the history of gay pornography, as Rocco explains:

> *A Breath of Love* is the first male nude ballet that received much notoriety because of a dance sequence shot nude on the Hollywood Freeway.... Impressionist Jim Bailey had a large part in *Mondo Rocco*, as did the Rev. Troy Perry.... *Sex and the Single Gay* featured, among its seven short stories, a serious look at transexualism and an original song, written and sung by me called "Changes."
>
> The very first program of all gay films to play anywhere was at the Park Theatre in Los Angeles, July 1968. It was a program of films called *The Original Pat Rocco Male Film Festival*, and ran 125 minutes, was a tremendous success, and launched me on a new career.*

At the American Film Institute, Lawrence F. Karr began an avid search for early pornography, and built up a considerable collection housed at the Library of Congress, and including the classic animated cartoon, *Buried Treasure*, featuring Eveready Harton. In the mid 1970s, the hardcore pornographic feature film *Deep Throat* was the subject of considerable furor, with its distributor, Sherpix, forced out of business and considerable effort being made by state and local prosecutors to prohibit the film's exhibition. Archivists at the American Film Institute including Karr and this writer, were concerned that *Deep Throat* and similar pornographic films might be lost forever unless immediate action was taken.

The staff at the Library of Congress felt it unwise to accept a collection of contemporary pornographic films in that, as a federal agency, the Library could not guarantee against subsequent government seizure, of the films or their use as evidence against the donor, or their possible destruction. In addition,

In an undated letter to the author, circa early 1970s.

producers of pornographic films were not happy with the notion that their works would be on file at the Library of Congress. One reason that most pornographic films have not been copyrighted is that their makers do not want deposited copyright prints easily accessible to federal prosecutors.

Eventually, the Museum of Modern Art agreed to accept *Deep Throat* and other titles from Sherpix for safeguarding. The next problem to be resolved was the transportation of the films to a Museum situated in the middle of a city which had just banned the movie. Happily, the Museum of Modern Art had storage facilities in New Jersey, and the films could be moved there without incident or violation of local laws. It was a minor event in the history of film preservation, but one that clearly demonstrates that preservationists must be just as diligent in their safeguarding of films of the present as well as films of the past.

There are two major archives devoted to the Jewish heritage in film and television. In 1980, the National Jewish Archive of Broadcasting was established at New York's Jewish Museum, with a grant of $500,000 from the Charles H. Revson Foundation. The grant came about as a result of a study published by the Foundation in cooperation with the Jewish Theological Seminary, and it led to the creation of a collection that preserves and makes available for study television programs and films of Jewish interest.

The National Center for Jewish Film was founded in 1976 as the Rutenberg and Everett Yiddish Film Library, a cooperative venture between the American Jewish Historical Society and Brandeis University. Housed on the Brandeis campus, it became an independent, nonprofit organization in 1981. The Center collects and preserves all manner of films relating to Jewish history and culture, including Yiddish-language features and short subjects, fund raising films for the state of Israel, and collections from the Organization for Rehabilitation through Training, the Jewish National Fund, the Joint Distribution Committee, the Jewish Defense Committee, and the United Jewish Appeal. It claims to be the largest archives of films of Jewish content outside of the state of Israel.

In 1989, the Center received considerable publicity for its restoration of the 1937 Polish feature, *The Dybbuck*, filmed in Yiddish. A nitrate dupe negative had been among the Center's first acquisition of 31 Yiddish-language features and 10 short subjects, and the restoration was made possible through additional materials provided by Britain's National Film Archive, the National Film and Sound Archive of Australia, and a private collector in Los Angeles. Supervised by Sharon Pucker Rivo and Miriam Krant, the restoration of *The Dybbuck* was hailed in an editorial by *The Boston Globe* (October 26, 1989) as "a triumph for the National Center for Jewish Film" and "an implicit rebuke for those who disfigured comparable classics of American cinema."

Other Yiddish-language features preserved by the Center include *East and West*, made in Austria in 1923, and *Uncle Moses,* shot in the United States in 1932, and featuring the great Yiddish actor, Maurice Schwartz. The National Center for Jewish Film also has an agreement with the German Bundesarchiv to acquire, for study purposes, copies of anti–Semitic Nazi films. Unlike many archives, the Center relies on the commercial useage of its footage for partial funding of its activities. Many of the early documentaries which it holds provide valuable stock footage material, and the Center works for the commercial re-release of films which it has preserved or restored for both theatrical and home video screenings.

Interestingly, the original collection of nitrate films from which the Center originated had been deposited at the Library of Congress in 1976, and preservation masters were subsequently made by the Library. However, the deposit of the films was accompanied by a restrictive instrument of gift, which protected the Center's right to exploit the films.

In the 1970s and 1980s, a considerable number of smaller archival film collections gained legitimacy. Many state and county historical societies had developed film collections in part because such holdings, devoted to local history, local news events and the like, held little interest for the national archives. With such lack of concern, these societies found it necessary to become a part of the film preservation movement. The Film Archives Advisory Committee of the National Center for Film and Video Preservation has been crucial in keeping these organizations familiar with what is happening in film preservation on the local, national, and international fronts.

Simply because of its size and the scope of its preservation efforts, the UCLA Film and Television Archive is the first university-sponsored film archives which comes to mind, but there are important film collections at other educational institutions, although they are generally more for study than for preservation. The Wisconsin Center for Film and Theater Research (sponsored by the University of Wisconsin at Madison) holds major 16mm study collections of Warner Bros., RKO, and Monogram features (donated by the United Artists Corporation). The American Archives of the Factual Film, located at Iowa State University, has already been discussed. The basis of the Yale Film Study Center is the 16mm film collection of John Griggs. The Center also has copies of television programs produced by Herbert Brodkin, notably *The Defenders* (CBS, 1961–1965), and a collection of 16mm prints of selected Columbia features.

The Harry Ransom Humanities Research Center at the University of Texas at Austin houses the voluminous David O. Selznick Collection, which includes not only all of the famous memoranda, but also prints of the producer's films, screen tests, home movies, and news items. The Research Center also has kinescopes of *The Mike Wallace Interviews* (ABC, 1957–1958), 16mm prints of *Perry Mason* (CBS, 1957–1966), and home movies from Norman Bel Geddes, Erle Stanley Gardner, Alfred A. Knopf, and others.

Master materials on 26 Selznick productions, excluding *Gone with the*

Wind, were turned over for preservation to the Museum of Modern Art in 1977 by ABC Entertainment, which had acquired all rights to the properties.* The American Film Institute had initated the negotiations for the preservation of the films as early as 1971, and the Museum of Modern Art agreed to accept responsibility for the work in the vain, as it happened, hope that by preserving the films, it could persuade the Selznick family to donate the producer's papers there.

The Kansas City Jazz Archives was created in 1985, when Kansas City, Missouri, used $200,000 of Community Development Block Grant Money to acquire the jazz film collection of Columbus, Ohio, resident John H. Baker. Reportedly, the collection includes 40 feature films, 200 short subjects, 100 kinescopes, and 2,000 soundies. The city acquired the collection as part of the Kansas City jazz renaissance, intended to bring visitors to a depressed neighborhood where once Count Basie had formed his band.

In the early seventies, the staff of the American Film Institute archives began an informal project to collect and preserve at the Library of Congress as many films as possible produced by or for black Americans. Because the majority of such films were not part of mainstream American filmmaking, they had been largely ignored. They have survived, to a large extent, only in 16mm prints owned by private collectors.

In 1974, New York collector Herb Graff permitted the AFI to copy his collection of unique 16mm prints of black features. In 1969, another private collector, Dennis Atkinson, had found the only surviving 35mm print of the 1927 feature *The Scar of Shame* (produced by the Colored Players Film Corporation of Philadelphia) in a trash can outside an abandoned Detroit theatre. A longtime supporter of the Institute's preservation program, Atkinson donated the film for preservation at the Library of Congress, along with prints of a number of other important black films: *The Blood of Jesus* (1941), *Broken Strings* (1941), *Bubbling Over* (1934), *The Girl from Chicago* (1932), *The Notorious Elinor Lee* (1940), *Tall, Tan and Terrific* (1946), and *Two Gun Man from Harlem* (1938).

By 1975, the Library of Congress was able to release a listing of more than 60 black films preserved there and available for study, including *By Right of Birth* (1921), *Dirty Gertie from Harlem* (1946), *Hi De Ho* (1947), *Killer Diller* (1948), *Moon over Harlem* (1939), *Sepia Cinderella* (1947), and *Spyin' the Spy* (1918).

In the early seventies, David Shepard of the AFI restored the 1933 Paul Robeson vehicle *The Emperor Jones*, utilizing 16mm prints from private collectors and additional 16mm material from the film's producers, John Krimsky and Gifford Cochran. The resultant restoration was blown up to 35mm, and received considerable attention. Unfortunately, as is quite often the case in

---

The physical preservation was handled by the Los Angeles–based Film Technology Company.

restoration work, after the project was completed, it was discovered that a
35mm print had survived in the Canadian Film Archive, from which Janus
Films prepared its video tape release.

In the meantime, John Krimsky began to claim, despite the film's being
in the public domain, that he controlled the AFI restoration, and actively
sought to prevent distribution of the film. Further research revealed that Krimsky had assigned his rights in the production to Gifford Cochran, who, in July
1955, had reassigned such rights to a gentleman named Joe Thall. The latter,
in turn, sold all the rights to Universal Pictures, which allowed the film to fall
into the public domain. Universal did, however, acquire original 35mm master
elements when it purchased the rights to the film, and such elements have
since been deposited with the Library of Congress.*

To a lesser extent, other U.S. archives have holdings of black films. One
important feature preserved at the International Museum of Photography at
George Eastman House is the 1925 Oscar Micheaux production *Body and Soul,*
starring Paul Robeson.

A prominent collection of feature films and short subjects made for all-
black audiences is preserved at the Southwest Film/Video Archives at Southern
Methodist University in Dallas. In August 1983, the Archives' director, G.
William Jones, received a telephone call from the manager of a warehouse
belonging to the Roosth and Genecov Corporation in Tyler, Texas. Housed in
the warehouse and awaiting disposal were more than 100 feature films and
short subjects, of which 30 were prints of films for all-black audiences. Roosth
and Genecov agreed to donate the films to the Archives, which had the
materials shipped back to Dallas.

With no funds available to preserve the films, the Southwest Film/Video
Archives issued a press release on the find, resulting in national publicity from
both television and the print media. As a result, funding for the preservation
came from an unlikely source, the Zale Jewelry Division of the Zale Corporation, whose senior vice president, William Harris, was an enthusiastic supporter of the project.

Thanks to Zale, the following all-black audience films were transferred
from nitrate to safety stock in 1985: *Boogie Woogie Blues* (1948, short), *Broken
Earth* (1939, short), *Girl in Room 20* (1946, feature), *Juke Joint* (1947, feature),
Midnight Shadow (1939, feature), *Miracle in Harlem* (1948, feature), *Murder
in Harlem* (1935, feature), *Souls of Sin* (1949, feature), *Vanities* (1946, short),
Where's My Man Tonight? (1943, feature), and four issues of *By-Line
Newsreels,* produced by William Alexander for All American News.

The Southwest Film/Video Archives was founded in 1965 by Dr. G.
William Jones; its first acquisition, in 1967, was 25 nitrate feature films from
Ginger Rogers. (They were subsequently desposited at the Library of Congress

Information provided by Scott MacQueen.

for preservation.) As of 1990, the Archives holds more than 8,500 film titles, including the Gene Autry film collection, a group of eight Ingmar Bergman features, and two million feet of 16mm news footage from WFAA–Dallas. In 1986, the Archives became an official entity of the Meadows Schools of the Arts at Southern Methodist University, and late in 1991 moved into a new archival, performance, and office facility, including a climate-controlled 3,700 square-foot vault, funded by actress Greer Garson.

Film preservation received national press attention in 1978 with the discovery of more than 500 reels of nitrate film at Dawson City, located in Canada's Yukon Territory. Dawson City was the end of the line for films in Canadian distribution, and rather than spend money in shipping the reels back to the distributors, an arrangement had been made long ago to store the films in the basement of the Carnegie Library, under the control of the Canadian Bank of Commerce. When space ran out, the films were buried in an old swimming pool, upon which an ice hockey rink was later constructed. Forty-nine years later, the films were uncovered when the Klondike National Historic Site began digging the foundations for a new recreation center. The films had survived because they had frozen. They were in reasonably good shape, and the National Archives of Canada, in cooperation with the Library of Congress, was able to thaw out, dry the reels, and hasten their transfer to acetate film stock.

Many of the films were unique, but, unfortunately, they were not important or famous enough to incite too much public enthusiasm, and plans for a 1980 national tour of selected items never materialized. A handful, including portions of the 1916 Pearl White serial, *Pearl of the Army*, and a 1915 Lionel Barrymore and Lillian Russell feature, *Wildfire*, were screened at the Museum of Modern Art on April 22 and April 25, 1980. Archivists trumpeted the finding of what was thought to be the "lost" Mae Marsh feature, *Polly of the Circus*, produced by Goldwyn in 1917, only to discover that a fairly complete print had survived in the vaults at M-G-M.

The following is a complete listing of all the feature films found at Dawson City. Virtually all are incomplete and consist only of one or two reels.

1915: *The Bludgeon, Her Shattered Idol, The Lure of Woman, Wildfire, The Price, The Patriot and the Spy.*

1916: *The Iron Hand, The Half-Breed, Gloriana, The Unattainable, The Rail Rider, The Mad Cap, The Folly of Desire, If My Country Should Call, The Closed Road, The Hidden Scar, Barriers of Society, The Female of the Species, The Social Buccaneer, End of the Rainbow, The Seekers, The Whirlpool of Destiny, The Place Beyond the Winds, The Unpardonable Sin, Rolling Stones.*

1917: *The Spotted Lily, The Awakening, The Little Orphan, The Recoil, The Hunting of the Hawk, An Even Break, Love Aflame, Princess Virtue, Polly of the Circus, Threads of Fate, Her Soul's Inspiration, The Mysterious Mrs. M., The Stolen Paradise, A Girl's Folly.*

1918: *The Voice of Destiny, The Sea Waif, The Stolen Hours, A Soul for Sale, Bread, Scandal Mongers, The Marriage Lie.*
1919: *A Sagebrush Hamlet, The Exquisite Thief, The Silver Girl.*
1921: *The Little Clown.*
The following is a complete listing of all the short subjects found:
1910: *His Sick Friend* (IMP), *The Joke They Played on Bumptuous* (Edison), *Unexpected Help* (American Biograph), *The Girl of the Northern Woods* (Thanhouser).
1911: *Vindicated* (Thanhouser).
1912: *For Professional Services* (Edison), *Guiseppe's Good Fortune* (Essanay), *The Lake of Dreams* (Selig), *A Christmas Accident* (Edison), *The Judgement of the Sea* (Méliès), *His Madonna* (Powers), *The $2,500 Bride* (Pathé), *Out of the Deep* (Edison), *Pansy...The Story of a Bear* (Selig), *A Winter Visit to Central Park* (Edison), *The New Woman and the Lion* (Selig), *The Office Boy's Birthday* (Edison), *The Junior Officer* (Selig), *For the Papoose* (Pathé), *Circumstantial Evidence* (Selig), *A Windy Day* (Lubin), *Brutality* (American Biograph).
1913: *Balaoo* (Eclair), *The Dancer's Ruse* (American Biograph), *The Wedding Gown* (American Biograph), *The Star* (Essanay), *Draga the Gypsy* (Rex), *The Fifth String* (Selig), *A Mixup in Pedigrees* (Majestic), *Up and Down the Ladder* (Vitagraph), *The Angel of the Desert* (Vitagraph), *The Pajama Parade* (Majestic), *The Rose of San Juan* (American), *Hello Central, Give Me Heaven* (IMP), *Rastus and the Game-Cock* (Keystone).
1914: *Slippery Slim, the Mortgage and Sophie* (Essanay), *His Responsibility* (Reliance), *The Mysterious Mr. Davey* (Vitagraph), *The Pit and the Pendulum* (Solax), *The Servant Girl's Legacy* (Lubin), *Sweeney's Christmas Bird* (Vitagraph), *The Tie That Binds* (Majestic), *White Dove's Sacrifice* (Sawyer), *Casey's Vendetta* (Mutual Komic), *The Demon of the Rails* (Kalem), *For Her Father's Sins* (Majestic), *Daybreak* (Reliance), *A Double Error* (Vitagraph), *The Hand of Destiny* (Eclectic), *Environment* (Majestic).
1915: *Fun Among the Pharaohs as Seen by Homer Croy* (Universal), *The Child Needed a Mother* (L-KO), *Hushing the Scandal* (Keystone), *Ambrose's Lofty Perch* (Keystone), *The Burglar's Baby* (Domino), *The Heart of Jabez Flint* (Kay-Bee).
1916: *The Inspector's Double* (Joker-Universal), *Love and Brass Buttons* (Nestor).
1917: *Bliss* (Rolin-Pathé), *Little Bo-Peep* (Universal).
1918: *It's a Wild Life* (Rolin-Pathé), *Do Husbands Deceive?* (Rolin-Pathé).
1919: *All Jazzed Up* (L-KO).
Unidentified titles: *The Gypsy's Trust, The Quest, The Mystery of the Glass Coffin, The Sphinx, or Mrs. Carter's Necklace, It Happened to Adele, The Salamander, The Girls of Grassville, A Mixup in Court, Birth of Flowers,*

The Frog, Frivolity, Saved in the Nick of Times, Bread upon the Waters, Kate O'Day, Avenged by the Sea, Justice, The Vicar of Wakefield, An Excursion to the Gorge du Loup, Tails of Providence, The Taking of the Saragossa, Leo the Indian, Little Old New York, The Baited Hook, Dread of Doom, Virginia's Triumph, plus miscellaneous newsreels and cans with no title identification.

A number of incomplete serials were also part of the Dawson City find: *Lucille Love...The Girl of Mystery* (1914), *The Hazards of Helen* (1915), *The Girl and the Game* (1915-1916), *Lady Baffles and the Duck* (1915), *The Strange Case of Mary Page* (1916), *The Crimson Stain Mystery* (1916), *Pearl of the Army* (1916-1917), *The Neglected Wife* (1916-1917), *The Purple Mask* (1917), *Mystery of the Double Cross* (1917), *The Red Ace* (1917), *The Seven Pearls* (1917-1918), and *The Lightning Raider* (1918-1919).

Another example of a "treasure trove" of nitrate films, admittedly a much smaller collection, which received some press attention is the April 1987 find of 300 reels in a Temperance, Michigan, barn. The films were discovered by a University of Toledo student, Robert Uhl, whose grandfather, Clement Uhl, had apparently been a film collector in the 1920s. Fifty reels of film were too deteriorated to save, but the remainder were transported to the Library of Congress, and in the collection were found to be three reels of the 1914 Sessue Hayakawa vehicle, *The Typhoon*, produced by Thomas H. Ince, and a complete print of the 1915 George Beban starring vehicle, also produced by Ince, *The Italian*, which had survived up to that point only in inferior copies.

The discovery of new material on *The Italian* following preservation/restoration from poorer quality elements illustrates an aphorism usually attributed to David Shepard. Archivists should find a completely shabby copy of a film and lavish great amounts of time and effort over its restoration in order to ensure that another, complete, pristine copy will turn up.

8 NEW AREAS
OF PRESERVATION

Until the advent of safety film in the 1950s, film preservation, as such, did not exist. Archives retained and "safeguarded" nitrate prints or master elements on films. Such nitrate elements would be stored under what was then considered the best possible conditions, but if the nitrate decomposed, it was an uncontrollable reality accepted by an archives. Until the late 1960s, only limited funds were available for preservation. In fact, in 1967, the total monies spent on film preservation by the Library of Congress, the Museum of Modern Art, the National Archives, and George Eastman House amounted to only $150,000. Thanks in large part to the creation of the American Film Institute, the National Endowment for the Arts and various private sources began to fund film preservation in earnest.

Between 1967 and 1979, the American Film Institute made available $4.6 million in preservation funding from the National Endowment for the Arts. The total amount of money available for film preservation, from both private and public sources, was $11.2 million. As of 1979, annual expenditure on film preservation by America's film archives was more than $2.5 million.*

Motion picture film exists in a variety of gauges, the most common of which are 16mm, 35mm, and 70mm. It can consist of black-and-white silver images or color dye images. It can be on unstable nitrate base or the longer-lasting safety base. The most common types of the latter are diacetate, the earliest form of safety film which dates from 1909; triacetate, the most widely-used type of safety film base, dating from 1950; and polyester, an extremely tough and long lasting film base, invented in 1941, which is resistant to shrinkage and has a greater chemical stability than other forms of safety film. In addition to the film itself, the motion picture may consist of audio elements, such as magnetic sound recordings on sprocketed 16mm, 17.5mm or 35mm celluloid, ½-inch or ¼-inch magnetic tape recordings, or the Vitaphone discs used for early sound films in the late 1920s.

*Statement by George Stevens, Jr., to the House Government Information and Individual Rights Subcommittee, June 19, 1979, pp. 2–3.

Sound elements can provide their own problems for the preservationist. Magnetic recordings may exhibit oxide shedding and are, of course, subject to accidental erasure. Vitaphone discs are fragile, and can easily be broken. A soundtrack can be photographically duplicated, but often there is an increase in background noise and audio distortion. Older soundtracks, particularly variable density tracks, must be printed with special attention to exposure and contrast in order to obtain acceptable results. Tracks which are shrunken or cannot be satisfactorily copied photographically may have to be re-recorded to make a new optical soundtrack negative. Equalization and noise reduction techniques will have to be utilized to restore the sound to its original quality. At the same time, an effort must be made to ensure that modern sound processing does not alter the soundtrack so that it bears little resemblance to the original.

The procedure for preservation of a film is fairly standard from archives to archives. The following description is based on the mode adopted by Robert Gitt, film preservation officer at the UCLA Film and Television Archive. First, the film is carefully inspected for damage. Torn perforations are repaired, bad splices are fixed, new head and tail leaders are attached, and dirt and oil deposits are carefully removed through cleaning. Quite often, it may be necessary to combine, restore, and reconstruct a complete version of the film from a variety of sources. Selection and assembly of such footage is undertaken using a Steenbeck or other similar flatbed editing table.

When the film is ready for sending to the laboratory, a number of printing techniques are available. The least expensive method, but one whose speed may result in a fuzzy or unsteady image if the original material is shrunken, is continuous contact printing. Here, the original film is held in contact with the undeveloped raw stock, and both are passed continuously past a slit of light.

In step contact printing, the original film and the raw stock are advanced one frame at a time, and held stationary in front of an aperture while the exposure is made. The result is a sharp and steady image at a relatively low cost.

Step optical printing involves the use of an optical printer, which, in its basic form, consists of a camera and projector aimed at each other, thus enabling the film to be rephotographed one frame at a time through a lens system. The optical printer can handle a higher degree of shrinkage than any other type of laboratory printing, but it is a slow and expensive process, which can also result in exaggeration of scratches and a build-up of contrast in the copy.

If the original film is severely shrunken, redimensioning can be used. This is a method in which the film is soaked in chemicals, causing it to expand for copying, temporarily, to its original size. If the film to be copied is badly scratched, a chemical treatment may be employed to dissolve the scatches out of the base, or diffused light can be used in printing, to minimize the appearance of scratches in the copy. Another technique is to immerse the film to be copied in a liquid bath, consisting of a volatile liquid with the same refractive index as the film itself. Wet gate printing can make all but the most severe scratches completely invisible in the new copy.

The number of laboratories available to handle archival film printing has substantially diminished since the 1960s. In the late 1960s and 1970s, archives utilized commercial laboratories, such as Movie Lab, Guffanti, Triangle, and WRS. The results were often far from satisfactory by contemporary standards. The American Film Institute relied heavily on Pittsburgh-based WRS in 1969 and 1970, but within a few years was forced to have much of the work redone elsewhere. Archivists seldom veer from a policy of preserving 35mm films in 35mm, but for many years the American Film Institute made 16mm preservation negatives on films which it considered of only minor importance, usually silent "B" pictures and minor silent short subjects. In copying such films on 16mm, the Institute was also able to make 16mm prints, cheaply, for collectors in exchange for the loan or donation of nitrate originals. Both the 16mm negative and the original nitrate went to the Library of Congress, which could determine whether or when to copy the latter.

Most of the Institute's 16mm laboratory work was handled by the New Jersey–based Rozelle Motion Pictures. Archivist Lawrence F. Karr recalls that Rozelle's prices for 16mm prints in 1971 were extremely low at $10 a reel.* The Institute maintained a listing of minor, public domain features, 16mm prints of which were available to collectors in exchange for nitrate. One of the "hottest" items on the list was the 1925 Fay Wray feature *The Coast Patrol*.

The American Film Institute also accepted 16mm preservation in the mid–1970s, when a private collector named Andy Sordoni offered to pay for the making of 16mm picture and track negatives on a number of Charles Starrett "B" Westerns. An arrangement was worked out with the copyright owner, Columbia Pictures, that in return for paying for the 16mm preservation of the films, Sordoni was to receive a 16mm print on each title. Of course, the original nitrate on the Starrett Westerns was retained by the Library of Congress, which had the theoretical option of one day copying the films in 35mm.

Aside from the cost in terms of archival staff time, it is expensive to preserve any feature film in 35mm. The average laboratory cost to make preservation elements on an average 90-minute, black-and-white feature in 1992 is $15,000. The cost of preserving a color feature can range from $20,000 to $70,000. Yet the average grant from the National Endowment for the Arts to an American film archives is little more than $100,000 a year. Such figures indicate only too well the impossibility of preserving more than a small percentage of America's film heritage.

Unfortunately, while new preservation concerns develop, the amount of money available for preservation remains the same.

In a letter to the author, May 31, 1990.

Two preservation areas which began to garner attention in the 1970s were color and television. They make an interesting juxtaposition in that color preservation was a matter to which film archivists had given scant attention for many years, and television preservation was only discussed in the mistaken belief that preservationists already had the archival film preservation field well under control, and now there was a need to move on to something new. To many it might well appear, with reason, that some in the archival film community were trying to hide their relative lack of success in coping with nitrate film preservation by deflecting attention to a new area of concern. It was very much a matter of covert admission of failure to raise funds for one form of preservation, and the need to try to find money for another area.

One of the first color restoration efforts was in England rather than the United States—but the film concerned was an American one. In 1959, the Museum of Modern Art had determined that it was unable to adequately safeguard various of its nitrate negatives. The negatives were deposited with several foreign archives, and those for Douglas Fairbanks' 1926 two-color Technicolor feature, *The Black Pirate,* came to Britain's National Film Archive.

In 1970, at the request of Douglas Fairbanks, Jr., the Archive's preservation officer, Harold Brown, began the arduous task of restoring the film, working in concert with Technicolor Ltd. in England. Because *The Black Pirate* was filmed using the two-color, rather than the later full-color Technicolor process, Technicolor Ltd. had to adapt one of its printers to copy alternate rather than consecutive frames of film. Because the original negatives had shrunk, special pins had to be installed to engage with the shrunken perforations. Missing footage was another problem. All that had survived on the film were one print and two incomplete negatives. (The negatives had, apparently, been used to provide stock footage for later productions.)

It took two years to produce a new safety negative and print, and even then Brown was forced to admit that the resultant work was not a perfect reproduction of the original. According to Brown, original prints of *The Black Pirate* had "an overall appearance of orange and green," whereas the new prints were more pink and blue.*

The need for color preservation arises from the fact that the dyes used for both negatives and prints produced in Eastmancolor (and other similar color systems, such as Fuji) fade relatively quickly. Modern color film is basically unstable. Without the fire risk, it provides almost as many problems as nitrate film. The same is not true of Technicolor, a two-color (red and green) process introduced in 1921, with a full-color (utilizing the primary colors of blue, red and green) process first utilized in 1932. Unfortunately, the Technicolor process was in use primarily during the nitrate film era. The Technicolor

---

*For more information, see Andrews, Nigel, "Resurrecting The Pirate," BFI News, *January* 1973, p. 3.

Company phased out the use of the Technicolor camera in the mid-1950s, and Technicolor printing, as such, ceased in 1975. When a current film bears the phrase "Print by Technicolor," it means simply that the process was handled by the Technicolor Company, but the color stock used was Eastmancolor.

Eastmancolor was introduced by the Eastman Kodak Company in 1950; it received an Academy Award for its efforts in 1952. Far cheaper and easier to handle than Technicolor (which required a special camera and specialized developing), Eastmancolor was quickly adopted by the film industry. Some studios even gave it different names—Metrocolor, Warnercolor, Color by DeLuxe, etc.—but the film was still Eastmancolor. (Interestingly, Eastman Kodak had introduced another color film, Kodachrome, in 1935. Unlike Eastmancolor, it was stable and seldom faded. It was primarily used in 16mm filmmaking.)

Unfortunately, Eastmancolor is not a preservation medium. Both prints and negatives can and do fade, with prints eventually becoming one color—pink. Eastmancolor can fade in as little as five years, although with proper processing and storage (at low temperature and humidity), it can survive intact for ten years or more. Library of Congress archivist Paul Spehr has written:

> The first color elements to fade are usually the yellows and greens. Since these are frequently the softer, less intense colors, their absence is less obvious. A change in flesh tones occurs, and the outdoor scenes are less vital. This can become especially destructive. I recently saw a print of *Tom Jones* which had lost so much yellow and green that the romantic revels of Sophie and Tom had completely lost the intended effect of youthful, springtime joy. The roses in the garden were now tinged with a reddish brown that totally destroyed the playful spirit of the original production.
>
> In the extreme stages of color fading, the picture images are gradually reduced to ugly pinkish purple shadows of the original. The color now looks something like overaged veal—a macabre abstraction never imagined by the film's creator.*

Most archivists agree that the worst examples of color fading are with prints and negatives developed in the 1950s by the Hollywood-based DeLuxe Laboratories. The problem was based on unreliable and speedy film processing, but because DeLuxe was, and is, a subsidiary of 20th Century–Fox, it is a problem which affected all of that studio's features during the decade.

The only manner in which to preserve a color film is to revert to the style in which the Technicolor negatives were made: with three different pieces of film for each of the primary colors. By copying the original one-strip Eastmancolor negative through red, blue, and green filters, three black-and-white separations of the red, blue, and green color records can be made. Separating out the color on black-and-white films means that there are no color dyes to fade, and the color is permanently preserved. Of course, the black-and-white

*Spehr, Paul C., "Fading: The Color Film Crisis," American Film, vol. 5, no. 2, November 1979, p. 57.

separations must be stored under perfect conditions, with no danger of one of the records shrinking and thus affecting the color registration.

Archivists do use Eastmancolor stock to manufacture prints of color films which they have preserved in black-and-white separations. Eastmancolor is also useful as a quick, and relatively cheap, means of retaining the color tints in a silent film. Although not relevant from an archival viewpoint, the advent of videotape, with its ability for color correction, does mean that a faded Eastmancolor print can be restored to full color—but only in video.

While the problem of color fading was long known to archivists around the world, it became an issue to the public and the film industry through the efforts of director Martin Scorsese. He told *Daily Variety* in 1980:

> I started to be concerned about this in 1972 after *Mean Streets*. I finally just couldn't stand anymore. Forget about me as a filmmaker; I'm just sick and tired of it as a moviegoer. I've had it. I'm getting older and I'm getting sick and tired of seeing these pictures year after year get worse and worse. It took me seven years to find a 35mm print of Luchino Visconti's *The Leopard*—and it's pink. It's a pink leopard.*

Scorsese's initial criticism was of Eastman Kodak for failing to provide nonfade or low-fade color stock. However, the company responded that long lasting color film had been available, but was rejected by the film industry as too expensive. "When I first got into this, I was naive," Scorsese commented to *The New York Times*. "I thought it was only the film and Kodak; now I realize it's more complex."† From Eastman Kodak, the director turned his attention to the industry, urging that black-and-white separations automatically be made on all color films (something which at least one studio, Walt Disney, had been doing for a number of years).

With considerable publicity, Scorsese presented a petition to Eastman Kodak, signed by, among others, Federico Fellini, Jean-Luc Godard, Joseph Losey, Paul Newman, Jack Nicholson, Leni Riefenstahl, Steven Spielberg, Jacques Tati, François Truffaut, and William Wyler. At the New York Film Festival, on October 5, 1980, Scorsese screened a compilation of films illustrating color fading and concluding with Sergio Leone's *Once Upon a Time in the West* (1968) in its entirety. The program was titled "The Moving Image: Cultural Suicide." A similar presentation, with Paul Schrader substituting for Scorsese, was given at the Directors Guild in Hollywood on March 17, 1981.

As a result of Scorsese's efforts, Eastman Kodak did introduce a low-fade film stock, adopted by the industry. Of course, it was still subject to fading in time, but if a print on the new stock was stored under ideal conditions and not projected, it would have a life span considerably longer than Eastmancolor prints

---

*Jacobson, Harlan, "Old Films Don't Die, But They Are Slowly Fading," Daily Variety, July 10, 1980, p. 1.

†Lindsey, Robert, "Martin Scorsese's Campaign to Save a Film Heritage," The New York Times, October 5, 1980, p. 19.

of earlier decades. A few directors tried to press for clauses in their contracts requiring producers to make black-and-white separation masters on their films. Ironically, the only directors who could enforce such clauses were those, such as Steven Spielberg and George Lucas, whose films were so popular that it was in the best interests of the producers to make such masters.

Before Scorsese's impassioned pleas, archivists had not been idle in trying to resolve a problem whose solution was basically financial. On October 17, 1977, George Stevens, Jr., spoke at a luncheon of the Society of Motion Picture and Television Engineers and urged the scientific community to find a means to preserve color films. One such method discussed was holography. And in August 1979, the American Film Institute/National Endowment for the Arts program included grants of $35,530 to the University of Delaware "for research in the archival preservation of color films by the Fourier color holographic process," and $24,200 to Wayne State University "for research into the archival preservation of color films by the one-step rainbow holographic process." In Hollywood, veteran special effects technician Linwood Dunn (inventor of the Acme optical printer) was experimenting with a modified 70mm optical printer which would make possible the recording of three black-and-white separation images on one single strip of film. (Because of the cost, Dunn's idea was eventually rejected by American archivists.)

Archivists generally agreed that cold storage was the only acceptable means of vaulting color film. Yet as of 1978, the Library of Congress was the only American archives with vaults capable of reaching a low temperature of 34 degrees Fahrenheit and 35 percent relative humidity (at its Landover, Maryland, Center Annex). The lower the temperature, the longer the life of the color film. Henning Schou, president of the FIAF Preservation Commission noted that the reduction of temperature by approximately 6 degrees Centigrade (11 degrees Fahrenheit) would double the useful life of almost any material.*

At the same time, cold storage presented its own problem in that there must be a gradual withdrawal of the film from the refrigerated vault. Rapid removal from cold storage can result in moisture seeping into the emulsion and lifting the image off the base of the film. So many initial concerns were expressed with regard to cold storage that from April 21 to 23, 1980, the American Film Institute and the Library of Congress jointly sponsored a conference to discuss the pros and cons of adopting cold storage as a standard procedure for keeping color film.

The revival of interest in color film preservation was given a boost in 1984 by Robert Gitt's restoration of *Becky Sharp* (1935) for the UCLA Film and Television Archive. Directed by Rouben Mamoulian, *Becky Sharp* was the first three-, or full-color, Technicolor feature. Through the years its length of 84

Schou, Henning. Preservation of Moving Images and Sound *(Brussels, FIAF, September 1989),* p. 26.

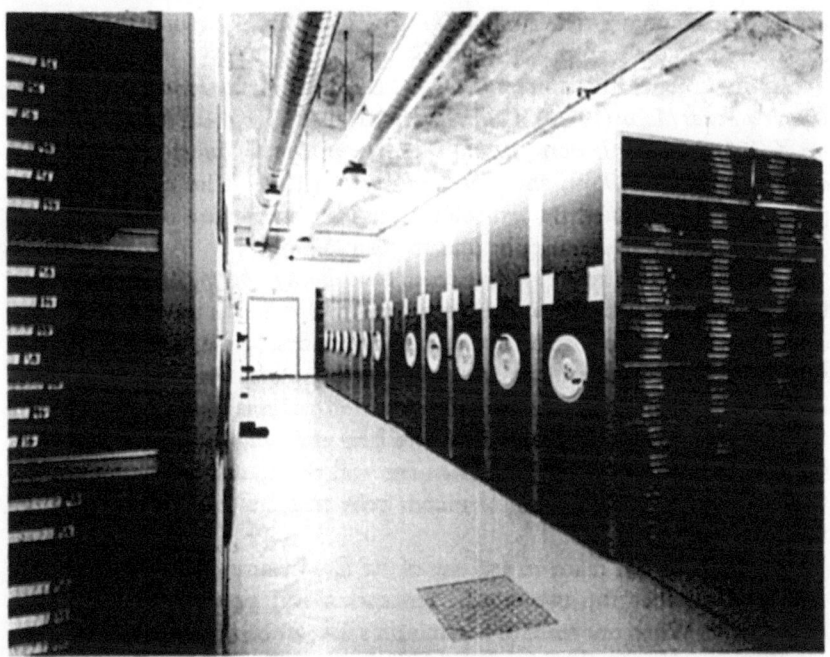

The cold storage vaults of the Finnish Film Archive.

minutes had been cut to 66 minutes and reissue prints had been made either in black-and-white or in the two-color Cinecolor process. Of the 448 prints originally made in Technicolor, all that had survived was one print of reel one only, retained by the Technicolor Company. Using that print as a color guide, Gitt, working in collaboration with Richard Dayton of YCM Laboratory, restored the film from a patchwork quilt of incomplete negatives, protection masters, 16mm negatives, and prints. The result of Gitt and Dayton's work was first seen at the 1984 New York Film Festival, and was widely praised and admired.

Under Gitt's supervision, the UCLA Film and Television Archive soon gained an international reputation for its color preservation and restoration. *Becky Sharp* was followed in 1986 by the restoration of the first two-color Technicolor feature, *The Toll of the Sea* (1922). The restoration here was less complex in that most of the original negative had survived at the Technicolor Company. The end of the film was missing, but Gitt and Dayton were able to restore the final titles from a continuity on file in the copyright records at the Library of Congress. With considerable ingenuity, they took an original two-color Technicolor camera to a Southern California beach and filmed an ending showing the waves breaking on the shore, as the sun went down, much as the film's original closing must have looked. As Gitt tells it, their novel approach to restoration means that *The Toll of the Sea* is not only the first two-color Technicolor feature—it is also the last.

Other color features preserved by UCLA are *The Vagabond King* (1929), *Under a Texas Moon* (1930), *Viennese Nights* (1930), *Follow Thru* (1930), *Doctor X* (1932), *A Star Is Born* (1937), *I've Always Loved You* (1946), *She Wore a Yellow Ribbon* (1949), and *The Quiet Man* (1952). The Archive has also preserved and restored the two-color Technicolor sequence to *Hell's Angels* (1930), the only appearance in color by Jean Harlow.

Thanks in part to the public response to *Becky Sharp*, "restoration" has become as fashionable a word as preservation. Often it is unwisely and inaccurately used in place of preservation. In its broadest sense, preservation consists of little more than the ordering of a new safety negative or fine grain master from the laboratory. A minimal amount of technical work is involved. In comparison, restoration of a film can be a long and complex task, often involving the matching of incomplete negatives and prints, and a reworking of the film's soundtrack. Restoration demands both technical and artistic decisions from the restorer.

Unfortunately, many in and out of the film industry appear to be under the delusion that the two words, restoration and preservation, are interchangeable. When one reads of Paramount's restoration of, say, *The Ten Commandments* or *Funny Face*, it may mean little more than a company executive's ordering new prints from the laboratory. So out-glamorized has preservation been by restoration that whenever one of the silent features presented by Thames Television receive an airing, they are always described as restorations by Kevin Brownlow and David Gill. While there have been "genuine" restorations in the Thames Television series, such as the 1990 presentation of Raymond Bernard's *Le Joueur d'échecs/The Chess Player* (1927), it is doubtful that some of these so-described restorations involved anything more than a satisfactory transfer of a negative or print to videotape.

It is, of course, Kevin Brownlow who began the restoration movement in film preservation with his astonishing and dedicated work on Abel Gance's 1927 feature, *Napoléon*. That restoration developed from Brownlow's 1968 documentary, *Abel Gance—The Charm of Dynamite*. As Brownlow puts it, "serious work on the restoration of *Napoléon*"* got underway the following year, and Brownlow's efforts were first seen at the American Film Institute Theater in Washington, D.C., in April 1973. The restoration continued and culminated in a 1980 screening in London and a series of screenings at New York's Radio City Music Hall the following year.

Napoléon was a French film restored by a British film historian. The American restoration movement can be dated back to 1975, when Robert Gitt

---

*Brownlow, Kevin, Napoléon: Abel Gance's Classic Film *(New York: Alfred A. Knopf, 1983)*, p. 205.

and Lawrence F. Karr first began work at the American Film Institute on *Lost Horizon*. Restoration work in the United States gained its first major recognition in 1981, when Ronald Haver, director of the film department at the Los Angeles County Museum of Art, began to explore the possibility of restoring George Cukor's original edit of the 1954 version of *A Star Is Born*. The film had been cut by Warner Bros. prior to its general release, and it had long been the hope of many fans of the star, Judy Garland, that the edited musical numbers and other footage might be restored.

With the backing of the Academy of Motion Picture Arts and Sciences, Haver began a thorough search of the Warner Bros. vaults, pulling in all extant footage on the film (and, coincidentally, finding other "lost" footage, such as *The Animal Kingdom*, subsequently preserved by UCLA). Haver hired Craig Holt to handle the technical aspects of the editing, and was lucky enough to have the film's original art director, Gene Allen, and (at least until his death) the film's director, George Cukor, to serve as advisors on the project. Haver's restoration received its premiere at Radio City Music Hall on July 7, 1983, followed by special screenings in Washington, D.C., Chicago, Dallas, Oakland, and Los Angeles.

One of the most controversial aspects of Haver's restoration was the use of still photographs to bridge sequences where sound existed, but the picture image did not. George Cukor approved what was then a revolutionary idea in film restoration, but did not live to see the realization of the work. Under the supervision of Lize Bechtold, $25,000 was spent in the careful photographing and editing of still photographs to match the soundtrack.

In his restoration of *Lost Horizon*, Robert Gitt was faced with much the same problem. There were several minutes of soundtrack for which no picture existed anymore. Initially, Gitt had inserted cards reading "Scene Missing," while the soundtrack played. This approach seemed rather lackluster, and, mainly for commercial reasons, it was decided to use still photographs. In the case of *A Star Is Born*, the film's director had a complete set of stills and there was considerable choice available for the restorer. The same was not true with *Lost Horizon*, for which almost no still photographs existed for the sequences where the picture image was missing. As a result, Gitt was forced to hold the same photograph on screen for an exceptionally long period of time or resort to very slow camera movements across the photographs. Interestingly, while $25,000 was available for the photographic sequences in *A Star Is Born*, Gitt had only a budget of $500 for similar sequences in *Lost Horizon*.

The use of photographs, along with the recreation of the ending of *The Toll of the Sea*, resulted in major questions as to the ethics of restoration. How far might a restorer go in attempting to make a film restoration palatable for a general audience? Obviously, there are two variant types of restoration. One is limited to what film material survives and can result in a restoration of only scholarly interest. The other is concerned with enhancing a restoration as much as possible, without interfering with the original concept of the film, and thus making its viewing an enjoyable experience.

Eileen Bowser is outspoken in her definition of film restoration:

> As far as the Museum of Modern Art is concerned, our chief goal in doing film restoration is to try and get as close as we can to what the audience saw on opening night. I don't think we have any interest in what might be popular. I think that belongs more to the commercial world than the world of archives. In other words, we have the interest of a film historian to try the best we can to recreate that original experience, although, of course, we're not the same audience at all, and we know that.*

Unfortunately, there does not seem to be a happy middle course. The Library of Congress policy seems to be to leave the film basically as it is when it arrives in the collection. The result can be that scenes are copied out of order, or that an end title obviously belongs to another film. Preserving the integrity of the film as it survives seems almost more important that the integrity of the original work.

The use of still images to bridge gaps in a sound film is, arguably, acceptable. Far more controversial is the use of still photographs in a silent film restoration. The two major restorations from the Museum of Modern Art, both coordinated by Peter Williamson, have been of D.W. Griffith's *Way Down East* (1920) and *Intolerance* (1916), and both have made heavy use of still photographs and frame enlargements. The *Way Down East* restoration, completed in 1984, was based on a complete list of shots and intertitles in the copyright records of the Library of Congress. It included considerable still photographs and reproductions of illustrative materials from contemporary periodicals. The use of such images was not particularly intrusive, although it did generate some criticism from the film's star, Lillian Gish. As an academic exercise, if nothing else, it proved worthwhile and praiseworthy. It is arguable that the same can be said of the restoration of *Intolerance*, which took four years, cost $75,000, and involved the reshooting of the intertitles and provision for full silent aperture.

In 1972, Arthur Lennig, a New York State University professor, had restored Erich von Stroheim's *Foolish Wives* (1922). Working with Robert Gitt and the American Film Institute, he had integrated two prints of the film — the American and foreign versions — and created the most complete version available. It was Lennig's boast that he was the only editor to add footage to an Erich von Stroheim film! Aside from being a von Stroheim scholar, Lennig was also a D.W. Griffith historian. It was his devout wish to restore *Intolerance* to the form in which it was presented at its premiere, and working on his own, in 16mm, he put together the most nearly complete version available of the film. On October 14, 1975, he screened his restoration for Eileen Bowser and this

Interview with the author, February 4, 1991.

writer at the Museum of Modern Art. Lennig's plan was to continue the restoration in 35mm, utilizing the Museum's materials. Largely because of the intransigence of both parties, his plans came to naught. Eileen Bowser was unable to allow the use of the Museum's materials without permission of Paul Killiam, whom she insisted had commercial control of the footage. Lennig, perhaps with good reason, refused to permit Paul Killiam to have commercial control, and to make money, from his restoration, which was a labor of love of a film unquestionably in the public domain.

The Lennig restoration was forgotten, as apparently was Paul Killiam's control of the Museum's material on *Intolerance*, and in 1981, Peter Williamson began the official Museum of Modern Art restoration of the film. The basis was a 1917 print of *Intolerance*, owned by the Danish Film Museum. (As luck would have it, after the restoration's first screening, it was discovered that the original from which the Danish print was copied was extant at the International Museum of Photography at George Eastman House.) The restoration itself was based on two major elements at the Library of Congress; the original music score and the copyright frames (one for each shot in the film and deposited for copyright purposes). The resultant restoration includes hundreds of these frame enlargements, many damaged by staples used to attach the frames to pages of a scrapbook. Such restoration is far from being a disaster, but it does hamper the flow of the film, and an audience's ability to enjoy the director's work. This is particularly true of the last portion of the film, as each of the separate stories moves to a conclusion. The French story at this point seems to contain more blown-up copyright frames than it does actual footage.

Purists might argue, So what? The film has now been restored, albeit in an incomplete fashion, to the way it looked at its premiere. But is this true? Griffith certainly never intended for frame enlargements to slow down the emotional mood created by his editing. Further, the copyright frames were deposited at the Library of Congress three months prior to *Intolerance*'s first public performance. There is no evidence that the copyright frames match Griffith's final cut of the film. In fact, knowing the director's love for "tinkering" with his productions up to and past their first screenings, it seems very unlikely that the copyright frames do match the version of the film shown at its premiere.

There is a need for academic discussion of this supposed academic restoration of *Intolerance*. Certainly the one-page article by Peter Williamson, published in *Sightlines*, fails to meet any scholarly argument against the restoration.*

What is apparent is how unlikely it is that there will ever be a restoration

---

*Williamson, Peter, "The Reconstruction of Intolerance," Sightlines, vol. 23, no. 2, spring 1990, p. 4.

project that will satisfy all audiences, general and academic. Certainly, the restoration of *Intolerance* indicates the need to look at established classics of the cinema and discuss what work, if any, needs to be done to make them look as they were first seen by an opening night audience. In Germany, Enno Patalas, curator of the Munich Film Museum, has been doing just that, reconstructing versions as complete as possible of such German classics as *Die Niebelungen* and *M.**

If nothing else, the restoration projects of American and foreign archives illustrate just how far the archival movement has progressed. It is astonishing to read of the technical work involved in the restoration, say, of *Becky Sharp* or *A Star Is Born*, and compare it to Harold Brown's early activities at the National Film Archive. Brown, who retired in August 1984, joined the Archive in April 1935, one month after the British Film Institute was founded, and became its film preservation officer in 1951. A year later, he invented a printing machine:

> The mechanism was my childhood Meccano set plus such pieces of timber and electrical plugs and sockets I could find. I borrowed sprockets from a 1905 Gaumont showman's outfit, a roller from an editola, other bits of things I could solder out of tin-plate, camera tape, rubber bands, paper clips, what the others insisted on referring to as knicker elastic. When I first put the things together I had no separate motor. To have asked for the price of an electric motor would have been not on in the financial state of the Archive.†

Despite the politics, restoration and preservation have progressed far beyond the possibilities first envisioned by the pioneers of the film archives movement.

No other area of preservation is quite as complex and yet seems as relatively simple as television. The medium has been around far fewer years than the motion picture. Yet its output is far greater than that of the American film industry, and just as the latter experienced a major technological change from silent to sound production, the television industry has undergone a similar change from live television, supplemented by film, to videotape.

Much live television programming from the late 1940s and early 1950s is lost, simply because it was never recorded on any medium. Largely because of the time difference between the East and West Coasts, it was necessary to record live programming in some manner, for later broadcast. That led to the making of a kinescope, usually a 16mm, but occasionally a 35mm, film copy directly from a cathode ray tube with the use of a motion picture camera. These kinescopes, as well as prints and negatives of filmed television series such as *The*

---

*For more information, see Gillett, John, "Munich's Cleaned Pictures," Sight and Sound, vol. 47, no. 1, winter 1977–78, pp. 37–39.

†Quoted in Sussex, Elizabeth, "Preserving," Sight and Sound, vol. 53, no. 4, autumn 1984, p. 238.

George Burns and Gracie Allen Show (CBS, 1950–1958), are on safety film. The very act of archiving, storing them, is preservation.*

Television production began to change in 1956, when Ampex introduced two-inch black-and-white videotape. Two-inch color videotape came into use two years later. In the late 1970s, two-inch videotape became obsolete, and was replaced by a one-inch tape. In addition, most news gathering, which first involved 16mm film, is handled on ¾-inch or ½-inch Beta videotape.

The first problem which television archivists face is the constantly changing technology. Every time a new tape standard comes in to replace an older one, the video transfer and postproduction houses dispose of the old equipment. Similarly, the operators are only familiar with the newest equipment, and cannot handle what might appear on the surface to be a simple transfer operation.

The only means of preserving videotape is to transfer it to another videotape. Tape to film transfers are too expensive for consideration by any archives. The problem is that videotape decomposes far faster than nitrate film, and can have a shelf life of possibly less than ten years. An oxide-binder problem has the effect of separating the emulsion from the base, and there are also inherent problems with print-through and magnetic debris. Tape life is also dependent upon the stock itself. Dan Einstein, who has been Television Archivist at the UCLA Film and Television Archive since 1979, points out that a batch of Sony and Scotch brand tapes from the early 1970s were particularly inferior, apparently because the 1973 oil crisis had an impact on the petroleum products used in tape manufacture.

Archival storage requirements for videotape are similar to those for film, in terms of low temperature and humidity. Videotape should always be housed upright on shelving (similar to books) and never placed one on top of the other. There are advocates of rewinding nitrate film every year to prolong its life, many others argue that videotapes should be rewound at least once every three years.

The introduction of digital tape and high definition television augurs well for future videotape preservation. While there is a virtually imperceptible loss of quality in dubbing one tape to another, it will be possible to make a digital transfer without any resultant loss in picture or sound quality. At the same time, television archivists must be vigilant not to embrace new electronic technologies which may "enhance" or change the original material, through colorization, time compression, false "stereo" sound, panning and scanning, or more subtle means.

The selection process for television archivists is a difficult one. Between 1948 and 1974, ABC, CBS and NBC broadcast 360,000 hours of programming.

There have been examples of nitrate kinescopes, which must be treated in just the same manner as any piece of nitrate film.

Only 60 percent of that is believed to survive, but even that amount is too much for any television archives to preserve. In 1975, officials at the Corporation for Public Broadcasting estimated it would cost at least $1 million a year to tape all original television programming in the United States. Of necessity, most television archives must be selective. Regional archives concentrate on regional programming, usually news broadcasts, while the three major archives—the Library of Congress, the Museum of Broadcasting and UCLA Film and Television—try to be eclectic even as they concentrate on entertainment programming. Dan Einstein at UCLA explains:

> Right now we don't have a set collection development policy. We're interested in collecting as many original materials as we can. If kinescopes are offered to us, we generally take them, because they're generally one of a kind, and two-inch tapes the same way. If somebody offered us every single episode of *Happy Days*, we wouldn't take that. It depends on the show and its historical value. If it's a show like *The Brady Bunch*, let's say, which is formulaic, one show is much like another in terms of plot and character, and we won't take the whole series. We'll try and take the first ten episodes, the first and last episodes from a season, episodes that reflect cast changes, or ones that are of particular interest in terms of plot. If somebody offered us a complete run of *The Adventures of Ozzie and Harriet*, for preservation reasons we might not want it, but in terms of interest by students and researchers, we might.*

Both the quantity of television programming and the vulnerability of videotape has resulted in the loss of a considerable amount of television. Videotape can be reused, and so it is a far more attractive financial situation for a television network to erase tapes than pay their storage costs. The lack of residual commercial value in many of the programs, particularly news, information and talk shows, makes it unlikely that a network or an independent television station would keep them. Ronald Simon, television curator at the Museum of Broadcasting, once commented on the ironic situation that there is a better chance of preserving kinescopes from the 1950s than videotapes from later decades because "you can erase tape, but of course you can't erase film."† Unfortunately, however, you can destroy it, and in the late 1960s ABC junked its entire library of pre–1968 kinescopes for no other reason than it needed more storage space.

On March 31, 1957, CBS broadcast *Cinderella*, a new musical specially written for television by Richard Rodgers and Oscar Hammerstein II. The cast, including Julie Andrews in the title role, recorded the musical numbers for a Columbia recording. The recording survives, but the record of the show was destroyed by the network. Such a loss might be understandable if no effort had been made to create a television archiving program, but, even in the 1950s,

---

*Interview with the author, January 24, 1991.
†Quoted in Stilson, Janet, "'B'Cast Museum on Quest for Early TV Artifacts,'" Daily Variety, February 13, 1985.

the need to preserve television was apparent. As early as 1956, *TV Guide* had editorialized:

> There certainly is a need for a permanent television library, and for a way to repeat top programs from time to time for the viewing public. . . . Using kinescope recordings, or the new tape recording process, the best of these programs should be kept in a library similar to the Museum of Modern Art motion picture film library and used for study and enjoyment.*

The first major attempt to create a television archives came in 1965 when what was then the National Academy of Television Arts and Sciences (and is now simply the Academy of Television Arts and Sciences) created the NATAS-UCLA Collection on the campus of the University of California at Los Angeles. Similar collections were also to be developed at New York University and American University in Washington, D.C., but did not materialize. The driving force behind the NATAS-UCLA Collection was Robert Lewine, who described the development of the collection as "a seek and grab operation."† Nevertheless, despite its lack of formality, the collection had grown to 3,000 titles by 1974.

Sometime after the establishment of the UCLA Film and Television Archive, the NATAS-UCLA Collection became part of its holdings. While it has not received the publicity generated by the Museum of Broadcasting, the television collection at UCLA has grown in statute, numbering more than 25,000 titles as of 1991. A catalog of its holdings was published in 1981.§ The university is responsible for what is probably the first major restoration of television programs, three Fred Astaire specials, which was coordinated by Dan Einstein and technical consultant, Ed Reitan. The former explains:

> Fred Astaire did three specials in 1958, 1959 and 1960, which were produced on color videotape. The 1958 show, *An Evening with Fred Astaire* was, as far as we can determine, the first time that color videotape was used as a pre-recorded medium and then played back. The show was basically live, except for the three main dance numbers and the commercials, which had been pretaped, and were rolled in.
>
> We found the original tapes at Universal, and Astaire himself had some. We decided to use the new digital technology to transfer the two-inch originals, then edit digital to digital, restoring these shows to exactly as they were aired, commercials and all. All three shows presented their own set of problems. When we tried to play the original tapes of the first show, we couldn't, because as we learned later, the machine on which they were recorded at NBC in Burbank was an Ampex black-and-white machine, which had been modified by RCA engineers to play

*"As We See It," TV Guide, May 12, 1956, p. 2.
†Robert Lewine at AFI meeting, March 8, 1974.
§ATAS/UCLA Television Archives Catalog: Holdings in the Study Collection of the Academy of Television Arts & Sciences/University of California, Los Angeles, Television Archives. Pleasantville, N.Y.: Redgrave Publishing, 1981.

color—it was an experimental machine. The calibrations to which that machine was set were totally different to the low band color standards that came in a few months later. We had to figure out how to modify an existing two-inch machine to play that stuff, which we were only able to do after locating a vice president of RCA labs who had the specifications in his file.

Other problems included the fact that the shows were rebroadcast in the 1960s, and in the rebroadcast all the original commercials were taken out and thrown away. In one show, Astaire makes a reference to *On the Beach*, which had come out in 1960, but when they showed it in 1964, it wasn't topical anymore, so they threw it out. We didn't have any of the color masters. We went to kinescopes, we went to record albums, we found the original audio engineer and he had his own audio tape of the first show, so we were able to fill in missing audio.*

All in all, the restoration required the cooperation of MCA/Universal, Fred Astaire and KTLA–Los Angeles, which permitted the use of its tape equipment. The restoration cost approximately $150,000, and garnered an Emmy for Einstein and his colleagues.

Aside from the work of the Archive, since the early 1970s, UCLA's Communications Studies Department had been taping the national news, local news, government hearings, press conferences, and even popular talk shows such as *Donahue* and *Oprah*. The tapes are considered for research and study, rather than preservation, and the program continues, in a more limited form, as part of the UCLA Film and Television Archive's activities.

The first taping of network news programs began on August 5, 1968, when a Nashville businessman, Paul C. Simpson discovered that ABC, CBS and NBC were routinely erasing the tapes of their nightly news broadcasts two weeks after transmission. The program became part of the Jane and Alexander Heard Library at Vanderbilt University, was named the Vanderbilt Television News Archive, and has been headed since 1971 by James Pilkington. The Vanderbilt Television News Archive is concerned with news programs as a resource rather than preservation. It details each news item in its monthly *Television News Index and Abstracts*, and is able to compile tapes on specific subjects for loan to researchers.

The networks were far from happy to learn of Vanderbilt's activities, particularly as later study of the tapes might indicate bias or questionable interpretation of the news. On December 21, 1973, CBS filed suit in federal court, requesting an end to the taping and the transfer of all existing tapes to CBS, whose attorney Val Sanford indicated they would be erased. Such an attitude evoked anger from a variety of sources, including Tennessee's Senator Howard Baker. In *TV Guide*, Patrick Buchanan commented,

> That act would be an atrocity against the people's right to know. And while CBS president Arthur Taylor quickly denied the existence of any such book-burning mentality in the upper reaches of his communications empire, the fact that the

---

Interview with the author, January 24, 1991.

network has systematically destroyed tapes of the Cronkite show — two weeks after their airing — is hardly grounds for confidence in CBS as the custodian of the Vanderbilt tapes.*

A compromise suggestion by CBS that Vanderbilt be allowed to continue to own and tape its news broadcast, but without indexing, categorizing or loaning of tapes, was rejected. Vanderbilt continues to tape the CBS and other network news broadcasts, and in almost a protest mood, CBS entered into a 1974 agreement with the National Archives and Records Service, creating an archives of television news broadcasts, including the CBS nightly news. Just prior to its lawsuit against Vanderbilt, CBS had considered establishing an in-house television archives, to be named after Dr. Frank Stanton, but the proposal fell through because of lack of financial support from the network.

As early as 1969, Senator Howard Baker had introduced a bill to empower the Library of Congress to tape television network news and other public affairs programming. Eventually, as part of the 1976 Copyright Act, he was able to make provision for the creation of the American Television and Radio Archive, as part of the Library of Congress. Funding for the new Archive began on October 1, 1978, and permitted the Library of Congress to preserve "television and radio programs which are the heritage of the people of the United States and provide access to such programs to historians and scholars without encouraging or causing copyright infringement." The planning meeting for the Archive, hosted by Erik Barnouw, took place at the Library on February 13 and 14, 1978.† A few months later, on July 31, 1978, Barnouw was appointed chief of the Motion Picture, Broadcasting and Recorded Sound Division.

A year earlier, NBC had donated its entire collection of 20,000 television programs, 1948–1977, to the Library of Congress, in celebration of the network's sixtieth anniversary. In 1978, NBC donated 80,000 hours of radio programming from 1926 to 1970.

In 1989, the Library published *3 Decades of Television: A Catalog of Television Programs Acquired by the Library of Congress 1949–1979*, compiled by Sarah Rouse and Katharine Loughney. This publication made the valid point that prior to the mid-1960s the Library had acquired only a small number of television programs registered for copyright purposes. The Library's attitude towards television acquisition changed in 1966 when the selection process became the responsibility of the then Motion Picture Section.

The American Film Institute became interested in television preservation in 1972. In December 1974, the Ford Foundation convened an Ad Hoc Committee on Television Preservation, with three subcommittees concerned with Selection Criteria, Acquisition Techniques, and Technical Preservation.

*Buchanan, Patrick, "Study the Record? If CBS Wins Suit It May Be Hard to Do," TV Guide, April 6, 1974, pp. A3–A4.
†Reported in LC Information Bulletin, March 17, 1978, pp. 172–174.

On November 9, 1976, the Museum of Broadcasting, sponsored by the William S. Paley Foundation, opened its doors to the public in New York. The Museum's chief function appears to be exhibition of television programming either for groups in its theatres or on highly publicized tours or at individual consoles in the Museum's building. Physical aspects of television preservation are seldom discussed. For example, when the Museum announced plans for its new building at 23 West 52nd Street, William S. Paley commented that "this wonderful new building . . . is a landmark in the preservation of our cultural and social and political heritage as a nation." Yet, the article, from *The New York Times* (July 8, 1988), in which he is quoted makes reference to the theatres, individual screening facilities, and the architectural design, but nowhere indicates how the programming is to be preserved or vaulted.

The claim of the Museum's president, Robert M. Batscha, is that "We are not a museum of technology but of the creative art of television."* The Museum has little interest in acquiring kinescopes and is basically happy to make copies from original tapes held by the networks, rather than acquire such tapes for archiving. One positive aspect of the Museum's work was a $3.5 million grant from the Sony Corporation in 1988, consisting of digital equipment, to make possible the transfer of the Museum's entire collection to digital masters. One can only hope that such work will enable the Museum to make better quality tapes available for its public programming. At present, much of the videotape offered by the Museum of Broadcasting (which changed its name in 1991 to the Museum of Radio & Television) gives the impression that early television had a soot and whitewash look, rather like the way the uninformed believe silent films looked.

Another television museum is the Museum of Broadcast Communications in Chicago. Opened in the spring of 1987, it specializes in the preservation of the history of broadcasting in the Chicago area. It is just one of a growing number of television oriented institutions, such as the Purdue University Public Affairs Video Archives (which tapes and catalogs all the C-SPAN broadcasts). (Since 1988, selected master tapes of C-SPAN broadcasts have also been deposited with the National Archives and Records Service.) Television material is also archived at many institutions, known primarily for their film holdings. For example, the Wisconsin Center for Film and Theater Research has 35mm negatives and prints, as well as original scripts, for 2,000 television programs produced by Ziv Television Programs, Inc.

Between 1952 and 1965, the television presentations of the Academy Awards shows were recorded only on 16mm kinescopes. It was not until 1980 that the Academy transferred the films to ¾-inch videotape, and not until 1990 that it realized the urgent need for one-inch video masters. In the mean-

---

*Quoted in Boxer, Sarah, "*Giving New and Longer Life to Vintage Shows,*" The New York Times, *July 31, 1988, p. 29.*

time, the 16mm kinescopes, unique records of the best known activity of the Academy of Motion Picture Arts and Sciences, were being used for viewings and other nonarchival purposes.

Even as late as 1990, it seems there is more discussion about television preservation than action. On March 16, 1990, the Canadian Broadcasting Corporation hosted a roundtable discussion on the current state of broadcast preservation in Canada. (Ernest J. Dick had recently been seconded to CBC from the National Archives of Canada to evaluate archival procedures and practice at the network.) Television archival practices among the Canadian television companies was mixed, but the meeting did agree to support the Association for the Study of Canadian Radio and Television in its promotion and preservation of Canadian television.

On May 19, 1989, the Annenberg Washington Program (part of the Communications Policy Studies at Northwestern University) held a roundtable discussion on television preservation. The main point to come out of that meeting appears to be that television is no longer merely "popular culture," but is now an art form, recognized as important source material for the professional historian. Perhaps such a change in status will mark a new beginning for television preservation — not a call for more academic discussions, but for action.

9 COLORIZATION

"Colorization" has become the generic name for the electronic coloring of black-and-white films. It has also become one of the most controversial topics within the film industry, and one that is linked, without a great deal of reason, to film preservation. Utilizing a computerized system, which breaks down each frame of film into thousands of separate dots, the process converts black-and-white motion picture film into color videotape. In its final form, the colorized subject exists only on videotape — it cannot be projected as colorized motion picture film.

Colorization is the registered trademark of one of the two major companies in the field, Colorization, Inc. The other company, American Film Technologies, Inc., uses the trade name Colorimaged for its process. The latter is the more successful of the two systems, invented in 1977 for exploitation by the predecessor company to American Film Technologies, Color Systems Technology. The colorization process was developed by Wilson Markle, utilizing the Dubner Graphics Computer, for Vidcolor Image, Inc., of Toronto, Canada.

The concept of colorizing black-and-white films, via computerization, is not new. In the 1960s, Universal experimented with a Japanese process, and added color to reels of Alfred Hitchcock's *Psycho* (1960) and Lewis Milestone's *All Quiet on the Western Front* (1930). Both the studio and Alfred Hitchcock were dissatisfied with the end result, but the experiment did lead to a rumor among film buffs that Hitchcock had filmed *Psycho* in color. Pete Comandini describes the test footage as "reasonably poor."

In 1983, Universal also considered another color conversion proces, Chromaloid, developed in the late 1960s by sound and video engineer Deloy J. White. Following a protracted legal suit with 3M, which had a financial interest in the process and had also applied for patents in its name, White, along with two partners, William C. Miller and Jay Levin, established a color conversion laboratory, Telechrome Internacional, in Mexico in 1971. Universal's initial idea was to convert some of its black-and-white stock footage to color. The studio also considered the possibility of converting some of its black-and-white feature films to color, but Pete Comandini, the head of Universal's optical department, commented with remarkable prescience, "Purists may object to putting classic black-and-white films in color."*

Wilson Markle's colorization process was first developed, in association with Image Transform, in the early 1970s. An agreement between Markle and that company, a prominent Los Angeles–based film and video laboratory, prevented the former's further development of the process until 1981. In that year, Markle formed his own Canadian company, Vidcolor Image, in association with art director Brian Holmes. Initially, the colorization process was used in the production of television commercials, adding color to black-and-white scenes and changing the color of a prop or makeup.

The expansion of the colorization process began when Hal Roach Studios, Inc. (by then unassociated with the producer whose name it carries), acquired a 35 percent interest in Vidcolor Image in 1983, and changed its name the following year to Colorization, Inc. On August 29, 1984 (a day which will live in infamy, as some might say within and without the industry), Earl Glick, chairman and chief executive officer of Hal Roach Studios, Inc., presented the company's first examples of the colorization process to its shareholders. Included in the demonstration tape were extracts from *Topper* (1937) and *Rebecca* (1940).

Topper was the first feature film to be released to the home video market in the colorization process, in the spring of 1985. It was followed by Laurel and Hardy's *Way Out West* (1937), Howard Hughes' *The Outlaw* (1947), and Frank Capra's *It's a Wonderful Life* (1947). Initial reaction from some former members of the film industry was surprisingly enthusiastic. Cary Grant, the star of *Topper*, wrote to Earl Glick, "I found the process extremely interesting and trust your company will continue to colour other memorable films in the same manner."† First Lady Nancy Reagan commented, "I didn't think *Topper* could ever be improved, but we were most impressed with the colorization of that fun movie. The soft colors were not intrusive but added just the right touch. A clever idea."§ Stan Laurel's daughter Lois Hawes, wrote to Glick, "I know that my father would surely have raised his Derby to you and all the wonderful technicians at the Hal Roach Studios."**

Frank Capra, director of *It's a Wonderful Life*, was somewhat confused in his reaction to the colorization process. Initially, the director wanted to become a partner in the colorization of *It's a Wonderful Life*. However, by March 1985, Capra was denouncing the decision to colorize his film, commenting, "My films were beautifully made in black-and-white, and meant to be in black-and-white. I don't think it's fair to the public to take *It's a Wonderful Life*, which

---

Quoted in The Hollywood Reporter, *April 4, 1983, p. 4.*
†*Letter to Earl Glick, August 19, 1985.*
§*Letter to Raymond Caldiero, August 6, 1985.*
**Letter to Earl Glick, August 13, 1985.*

they like, and have it colorized. The consequences are monetary, and I think the audiences will smell out the truth."*

Capra's comment was, in part, a reference to *It's a Wonderful Life*'s being in the public domain, unprotected by copyright, and available for anyone to use as they might see fit. One of the major advantages of the colorization process and its competitors was that by adding color to black-and-white films, it was possible to copyright them as new titles, thus adding additional years of copyright life to a copyright protected black-and-white feature and starting a whole new copyright life for a film already in the public domain. Of course, the colorization process does not affect the copyright status of the black-and-white original.

In September 1986, the Copyright Office at the Library of Congress began consideration of copyright questions raised by the colorization of films. In June 1987, it announced that colorized versions of films could be registered for separate copyright protection. In the unlikely event that any producers might have missed the implications of the Copyright Office's announcement, American Film Technologies placed a full page advertisement, headed "Add 75 Years to Your Life," in the June 29, 1989, edition of *Daily Variety*, which stated in part, "Colorimaged films for television can expand the life span of your feature films soon to be in public domain. Insure your company's valuable assets."

Color Systems Technology, Inc., the predecessor company to American Film Technologies, was founded by inventor Ralph Weinger in association with two well known Hollywood publicists, Charles Powell and Buddy Young. With remarkable acumen, in January 1985, the company retained Gene Allen as a creative consultant. Not only was Allen then president of the Academy of Motion Picture Arts and Sciences, he was also a noted art director (winning an Oscar for his work on *My Fair Lady* and Academy Award nominations for *A Star Is Born* and *Les Girls*). "Color conversion is an idea whose time has come," Allen told *The Hollywood Reporter* (January 8, 1985). "When CST first approached me for advice on coloring George Cukor's *Camille*, I began to realize that I had a unique opportunity to protect Mr. Cukor's artistic intent. Having worked with him for 18 years, I felt it was more than an opportunity—it was almost an obligation."

Allen's appointment gave a certain amount of legitimacy to the work of Color Systems Technology. It also marked a dramatic change in the attitude of the art director, who had earlier denounced the colorization industry. "Many great films could be harmed," he told *Time* in 1985. "I shudder to think what they might do to *Casablanca*."† In fact, *Casablanca* was already awaiting

---

*Quoted in Rothman, Cliff, "Colorized Classics Raise Capra's Ire," The Hollywood Reporter, March 15, 1985, p. 1.

†Quoted in Elmer-DeWitt, Philip, "Play It Again, This Time in Color," Time, October 8, 1984, p. 83.

colorization when Gene Allen became part of the Color Systems Technology team the following year.

An art director is very important to the colorization process in that he must decide, much as with a new film in production, what the colors of clothes and props should be. Obviously, there are some predetermined colors—actress Maureen O'Hara must have red hair—but other colorings must be based on research, with art directors and their associates often checking through production records and consulting with original art directors on the films to be colorized.

Colorizers have reason to be unhappy when critics compare their recreations to the lifeless colors of lobby cards. Certainly the colorization process has drastically improved through the years since 1986, when George Romero, director of *Night of the Living Dead*, commented, "I think the actors in all of these movies look like the living dead."*

Unlike its competitor, Color Systems Technology was able to boast contracts with major studios. In January 1985, it announced that work was about to commence on the color conversion of *Yankee Doodle Dandy* (1942), the first of 20 features under a contract with MGM/UA. On September 28, 1985, the "Glowworm Cleaning Powder" episode from *The Honeymooners* series was seen on television for the first time in a color version from Color Systems Technology. On November 24, 1985, KCOP–Los Angeles presented the world television premiere of the Colorimaged version of *Miracle on 34th Street* (1947). (At that time, the Color Systems Techology process was known by the somewhat unwieldy title of Color Spectography.) Based on its initial success with *Miracle on 34th Street*, 20th Century–Fox decided to colorimage its package of Shirley Temple features. It was an announcement greeted with some glee by cynics, who noted that two of the features which the studio proposed to colorimage had been filmed in Technicolor.

The average cost for colorizing a feature film is $200,000. The cost is high, but so are the potential returns in that the colorized film can be licensed to independent television stations not as part of a package of black-and-white features for late night viewing but as potential prime-time material, with a potential prime-time material fee. The same increased value applied to black-and-white television series. Viacom, one of the major television distributors, experimented with the colorization of the "Miniature" episode from *The Twilight Zone* (first seen in its new version in October 1984), and was pleased with the public response. Of the colorization process, a Viacom spokesperson said, "It gives old black-and-white a new life."†

Following the first steps into the new technology by MGM/UA and 20th

---

*Quoted in Corliss, Richard, "Raiders of the Lost Art," Time, October 20, 1986, p. 98.
†Quoted in Elmer-DeWitt, Philip, "Play It Again, This Time in Color," Time, October 8, 1984, p. 83.

Century–Fox, other studios began to consider the possibility of colorization. The Samuel Goldwyn Company, which had an in-house restoration and preservation program in the 1980s headed by Tom Bodley, announced that none of its films would be colorized. Over at Columbia, its chairman, David Puttnam, announced that he would never permit the colorization of any of Frank Capra's features without the director's consent. He did, however, confirm that the studio was not opposed to colorization, and was interested in colorizing certain of its features on a film-by-film basis.*

In the final analysis, it was not a Hollywood studio which made a major issue of the colorization concept, but an Atlanta businessman named Robert E. "Ted" Turner. In March 1986, Turner acquired the M-G-M Film Library, and within two months announced plans to colorize a first group of 24 features. In September of the same year, through his Turner Broadcasting System, Ted Turner released a list of additional 100 titles to be colorized. In 1987, Turner acquired the RKO Film Library, and announced plans for the colorization of its films, including Orson Welles' *Citizen Kane* (1941). Turner was thwarted in his plans by the director's contract which prohibited any tampering with the film. There was a charming arrogance to Ted Turner. He owned the films, and he was going to do what he liked with them. He did not buckle under to attacks on his decisions—he relished the controversy.

Public reaction to colorization was mixed. A 1985 poll in the *New York Post* found readers opposed to colorization three-to-one.† On November 24, 1986, KTLA–Los Angeles presented the local premiere of the colorized version of *It's a Wonderful Life*. Following the airing, viewers voted 53.3 to 46.5 percent against colorization. Colorized versions of classic films were finding a marketplace on home video. As of September 1985, Hal Roach Studios reported sales of 10,000 copies of its colorized version of *Topper*.

The fight against colorization was, and is, led by the Directors Guild of America. In the summer of 1986, the Guild created a presidental committee, headed by Elliot Silverstein, to review the situation. Members were united in their opposition to colorization. "Determining the colors that people wear, or what colors the walls are and so on are major creative decisions," stated Woody Allen. "To have a group of people from the outside making those decisions is criminal and ludicrous." Billy Wilder was equally outspoken: "Those fools! Do they really think that colorization will make *The Informer* any better? Or *Citizen Kane* or *Casablanca*? Or do they hope to palm off some of the old stinkers by dipping them in 31 flavors? Is there no end to their greed?"§

Following the television presentation of the colorized version of his feature

See "Puttnam: Col Will Weigh Colorizing Case-by-Case," Daily Variety, November 18, 1986, pp. 6, 14.
†Reported in the New York Post, April 18, 1985, p. 25.
§Quoted in Matthews, Jack, "Film Directors See Red Over Ted Turner's Movie Tinting," Los Angeles Times, Part VI, September 12, 1986, p. 1.

The Maltese Falcon (1941), John Huston called a press conference at the Directors Guild on November 13, 1986. Supported by a group of directors, including Peter Bogdanovich, Richard Brooks, Arthur Hiller, Ronald Neame, and George Schaefer, Huston urged a boycott of companies which sponsored the television presentations of colorized films. He began his prepared comments with a joke:

> A couple of generations back, screenwriters used to tell a story about two producers lost in the desert and dying of thirst. About to give up the ghost, they crawl into view of a miraculous spring of pure effervescent water and they go joyously to drink, when one says, "No, wait. Don't drink. Wait 'til I piss in it." To bring the story up to date, one has only to add that, in my opinion, both producers are members of the Turner organization.*

Not an organization to ignore the publicity potential of the dispute, the American Film Institute decided to become involved in the colorization argument, calling a press conference on October 1, 1986. The Institute issued a position statement from its board of trustees, which read in part: "The Trustees are opposed to the computer coloring of films which were originally conceived and presented in black and white. We maintain that it is the ethical responsibility of the copyright holders to protect and preserve the artistic integrity of black and white films."

Heading the anticolorization forces at the press conference was James Stewart, who commented on *It's a Wonderful Life*, of which he is the star, "I feel the things that are lacking in the color version are detrimental to the story and to the whole atmosphere." In response, Earl Glick of Hal Roach Studios, claimed, "We have increased and improved on Joe Walker's original photography in *It's a Wonderful Life*."

In response to the press conference, Roger Mayer, president and chief operating officer of Turner Entertainment, wrote a letter to the Institute, which read, in part,

> I feel that it is totally inappropriate for the AFI to take sides in an issue that in my opinion is political in nature and that might have an adverse economic effect on the very companies within the industry which have been most supportive of the AFI and its activities over the years.... I do not believe it is consistent with the AFI's purposes to interfere with the entrepreneurial or creative aspects of the business, particularly without giving us the opportunity to present our position.†

Mayer had a valid point in that the American Film Institute's board has always included the heads of a number of Hollywood studios. Not surprisingly, a 1987 national conference on the question of colorization, to be organized by the American Film Institute, never materialized.

---

*Quoted in Robb, David, "Huston's Cup Overfloweth with Harsh Words for B & W Colorizing and Ted Turner," Daily Variety, November 14, 1986, pp. 1, 35.

†Quoted in McCarthy, Todd, "Color Institute B & W When It Comes to Vintage Films," Daily Variety, October 2, 1986, p. 28.

The Institute tried to make colorization an issue in film preservation, linking it to the destruction of "our national film history and the rich heritage which it represents."* Such an attitude was rejected shortly after the Institute press conference at a meeting of leading American film archivists, who felt it inappropriate for them to take a stand on the issue.

In reality, colorization has nothing directly to do with film preservation or the physical destruction or alteration of a film. The colorization process does not affect the original negative of a film or any other master elements. In order to colorize a film, the best possible black-and-white print of the subject must be made. It is then transferred to a one-inch videotape, which is utilized in the colorization process. In that a producer is required to provide the best possible film elements to start the colorization process, it might be argued that colorization can help in the preservation of a film.

Certainly there can be no argument that the Turner Entertainment Company has always been a staunch supporter of film preservation. It has a high reputation within the archival community, and has also been generous in permitting access to the films which it controls for both study and preservation. Curiously, the Directors Guild of America and its members, while paying lip service to the concept of film preservation, have been noticeably quiet when it comes to providing much-needed funds to preserve this country's and their film heritage.

The Academy of Motion Picture Arts and Sciences found itself in an awkward situation with regard to the colorization dispute. Two of its board members, Charles Powell and Gene Allen, were highly visible figures in Color Systems Technology, while two other board members, Gilbert Cates and Franklin Schaffner, were leading opponents of colorization within the Directors Guild. When Cates and Schaffner introduced a motion at the December 16, 1986, meeting of the Academy's board, calling for it to make a stand against colorization, the organization was able to table it on the basis of the Academy's by-laws denying it involvement in political or economic matters.

Colorization had a surprising supporter in Thomas M. Pryor, former editor of *Daily Variety*, who published an editorial in the September 3, 1986, edition of that trade paper stating categorically that "Colorization Has a Place." Also questioning the dispute was Ron Haver, head of the film department at the Los Angeles County Museum of Art. He called it "a tempest in a teapot," and instead urged filmmakers to turn their attention to the evil of "panning and scanning," the method of presenting widescreen films on television through rephotography and recomposition.†

Restrained commentary on colorization was rare in Hollywood, and most

---

*Position Statement of the Board of Trustees of the American Film Institute, October 1, 1986.
†Reported in Osborne, Robert, "Rambling Reporter," The Hollywood Reporter, October 7, 1986, p. 2.

guilds and unions joined the Directors Guild of America in its fight. On September 29, 1986, the board of directors of Writers Guild of America West passed a motion which "deplores and opposes computerized coloring of black and white motion pictures as an act of cultural vandalism and a distortion of history." Similar views were expressed by Camera Local 659 and the Costume Designers Local 892. The American Society of Cinematographers issued a statement claiming that colorization "represents an unwarranted intrusion into the artistry of the cinematographer who photographed the work."* In November 1986, the Screen Actors Guild also came out against colorization.

In the United Kingdom, the fight against colorization was led by director Fred Zinnemann. The Directors Guild of Great Britain released a curious statement on the subject, signed by Zinnemann, along with Lindsay Anderson, Sir Richard Attenborough, John Boorman, Roy Boulting, Stephen Frears, Hugh Hudson, Roland Joffe, Neil Jordan, Stanley Kubrick, David Lean, Alan Parker, Michael Radford, Karel Reisz, Ridley Scott, John Schlesinger, Michael Winner, and Peter Yates. In part the statement read:

> We are not asking for a colourisation ban on all British black-and-white films. What we do earnestly seek, however, is the protection of a limited number of classics—such masterpieces as *Brief Encounter*, *Rebecca*, *The Third Man* and Olivier's *Hamlet*. The concept is effective with "listed buildings," so why not with films?

Aside from the fact that *Rebecca* is not a British film, the statement did not explain how this list of "untouchables" was to be compiled. None of the directors were able to explain by what right they could decide which films were worthy of protection and which not. A call for action by the British government brought a sensible response from the Department of Trade and Industry: "Where copyright still subsists then it is a matter for the copyright owner, and not the Government, to decide whether or not to allow coloured reproductions to be made."†

It was increasingly obvious that the directors both in the United States and the United Kingdom were getting nowhere with their protests. As a whole, the public was little interested in the dispute, and Ted Turner was not about to change his mind on the matter. In fact, the publicity generated by the protests were increasing television viewer interest in the colorized versions of black-and-white films. What might have been nothing more than a passing fad gained in prominence because of the protests from the Directors Guild and others. Turner announced plans to utilize a new coloring process, developed by Entercolor Technologies Corporation in 1968, by which black-and-white cartoons

---

*Quoted in Robb, David, "ASC Joins Opposition to B & W Coloring," Daily Variety, October 8, 1986, p. 1.

†Letter, July 17, 1986, from Geoffrey Pattie, Department of Trade and Industry, to Anthony Smith and Fred Zinnemann.

could be converted to color on film. The process would not work with live action subjects, but by 1990, Turner had converted 120 black-and-white Popeye
cartoons to color utilizing the Entercolor process.

In 1987, the Directors Guild decided to take its fight to Washington,
D.C., and on May 12, Elliot Silverstein, Woody Allen, Milos Forman, and
Sydney Pollock testified before the Senate Judiciary Committee's subcommittee on Technology and the Law. The directors hoped to persuade Congress to
institute new legislation protecting films from new technologies which might
tamper with the original intentions of their makers.

This action by members of the Directors Guild of America came to the
attention of Representative Robert J. Mrazek. He was a man who understood
art; "I would rather watch the scene where Fredric March returns to his family
[in *The Best Years of Our Lives*] than a roomful of Renoirs," he told *The New
York Times*.* Mrazek sponsored a bill creating a national film commission,
which he described as "a significant first step towards the ultimate recognition
of artists' moral rights."† Filmmakers were not ungrateful for Mrazek's support, and in May 1990, Steven Spielberg and Barry Levinson announced they
had raised $100,000 for the Congressman's re-election campaign.§

The legislation, sponsored by Mrazek, is a compromise which serves no
valid purpose; simply it increases the legislative bureaucracy and adds an additional quarter-of-a-million dollars to the taxpayers' burdens. As approved by
a House-Senate conference committee on August 9, 1988, the bill permitted
a 13-member panel to classify 25 films a year as worthy of "protection" through
listing in a national film registry. If one of the films selected by the panel were
"materially altered," a disclaimer label was required to be placed on the film
indicating such alteration was made without the participation of the film's
creators. The same disclaimer had to appear at the beginning and end of the
film when it was aired on television. Initially, it had been suggested that the
Secretary of the Interior should serve as secretary to the proposed panel, but
the ultimate choice was the Librarian of Congress.

The bill was the subject of considerable lobbying efforts by Turner Broadcasting. The National Association of Broadcasters urged defeat in the legislation. It was also opposed by Jack Valenti, on behalf of the Motion Picture
Association of America, who urged, "We ought never to abandon the principle
that government intrusion in the creative screen, for whatever reason, is wrong,
and should never be tolerated."** There was much talk that President Ronald

*Quoted in "Hope Is Slim for Legislation to Ban Film Coloring," The New York Times, June
19, 1988, p. 44.
†Quoted in Harris, Paul, "Nat'l Film Panel Up to Reagan," Daily Variety, August 10, 1988, p.
19.
§King, Andrea, "Mrazek Gets Directors' Funding," The Hollywood Reporter, May 21, 1990, p. 1.
**Valenti, Jack, "Nat'l Film Preservation Board Is a Dangerous Chink in Showbiz' Armor," Daily
Variety, July 20, 1988, p. 10.

Reagan would veto the legislation, but to the surprise of many, on September 25, 1988, he signed what was now called the National Film Preservation Act of 1988 (2 U.S.C. 178) into law.

The name of the bill is, of course, a misnomer. It has nothing whatsoever to do with film preservation. All the bill does is have the Librarian of Congress, in collaboration with his appointed panel, select 25 films a year which can still be altered in any way by their copyright owners, but if they are altered must bear a label forewarning the viewer. It is all rather ridiculous, an exercise in bureaucratic futility, designed primarily to confuse the American public into believing that Congress has, in some mysterious way, arranged for certain important American films to be preserved.

As further evidence of the Act's noninvolvement in film preservation, none of the members of the National Film Preservation Board have anything to do with film preservation. The Board is comprised of representatives of the following organizations or institutions: the Academy of Motion Picture Arts and Sciences, the Alliance of Motion Picture and Television Producers, the American Film Institute, the Directors Guild of America, the Motion Picture Association of America, the National Association of Broadcasters, the National Society of Film Critics, the Department of Cinema Studies at New York University, the Screen Actors Guild, the Society of Cinema Studies, the University Film and Video Association, the Department of Theater, Film and Television at the University of California at Los Angeles, and the Writers Guild of America.

The Board quickly became embroiled in controversy as it tried to develop selection criteria, first in public meetings and then in private, for fear of embarrassing itself. Politics, of course, played a major part in the Board's decision. One noted Hollywood feminist on the Board refused to consider Alfred Hitchcock's *Psycho* because it showed violence against women. Liberal advocates of freedom of speech in public became censors in private, and refused to consider D.W. Griffith's *The Birth of a Nation* for inclusion on the list, for fear of offending black Americans. What is arguably the most important film in the history of American cinema is thus denied a place in the National Film Registry.

After compiling its lists of "culturally, historically or aesthetically significant" American films," the board was required to turn the choice of the first 25 films over to James H. Billington, Librarian of Congress. On September 19, 1989, he revealed his choices, noting they were made to "suggest to the American public the breadth of great American filmmaking":*

The Best Years of Our Lives (1946), *Casablanca* (1942), *Citizen Kane* (1941), *The Crowd* (1928), *Dr. Strangelove* (1964), *The General* (1927), *Gone*

---

*Quoted in Harris, Paul, and Joseph McBride, "U.S. Cites 25 Pix in First Cut," Daily Variety, September 20, 1989, p. 1.

with the Wind (1939), *The Grapes of Wrath* (1940), *High Noon* (1952), *Intolerance* (1916), *The Learning Tree* (1969), *The Maltese Falcon* (1941), *Mr. Smith Goes to Washington* (1939), *Modern Times* (1936), *Nanook of the North* (1922), *On the Waterfront* (1954), *The Searchers* (1956), *Singin' in the Rain* (1952), *Snow White and the Seven Dwarfs* (1937), *Some Like It Hot* (1959), *Star Wars* (1977), *Sunrise* (1927), *Sunset Boulevard* (1950), *Vertigo* (1958), and *The Wizard of Oz* (1939).

To calm charges of racism, a minor film directed by a black, *The Learning Tree*, was included. *Nanook of the North* was obviously on the list to indicate the board's concern for documentaries. *Dr. Strangelove* was included presumably because the Board and the Librarian of Congress thought it was an American film—it is, of course, British-made.

For its next selection of titles, the Board promised greater public contribution, but at its February 19, 1990, meeting in Los Angeles opted for privacy and decided to share its recommendations by mail rather than discuss them in front of a reporter from *Daily Variety*.*

The second group of 25 titles for the National Film Registry were announced by the Librarian of Congress on October 18, 1990. He revealed that 472 titles were suggested by the Board and 1,500 by members of the general public. The final choice was made by the Librarian in consultation with staff members from the Library's Motion Picture, Broadcasting and Recorded Sound Division. The selection was again strange and obviously influenced by compromise, including one experimental film, *Meshes of the Afternoon* (1943), directed by Maya Deren, three documentaries—*Harlan County, U.S.A.* (1976), *Primary* (1960), and *The River* (1937)—and one black-directed film, *Killer of Sheep* (1977). The others were:

All About Eve (1950), *All Quiet on the Western Front* (1930), *Bringing Up Baby* (1938), *Dodsworth* (1936), *Duck Soup* (1933), *Fantasia* (1940), *The Freshman* (1925), *The Godfather* (1972), *The Great Train Robbery* (1903), *How Green Was My Valley* (1941), *It's a Wonderful Life* (1946), *Love Me Tonight* (1932), *Ninotchka* (1939), *Primary* (1960), *Raging Bull* (1980), *Rebel Without a Cause* (1955), *Red River* (1948), *Sullivan's Travels* (1941), *Top Hat* (1935), *The Treasure of Sierra Madre* (1948), and *A Woman Under the Influence* (1974).

The inclusion of *It's a Wonderful Life* was ironic in that the colorization of that film more than any other was at the heart of the controversy leading up to the creation of the National Film Preservation Act. Capra had sent a passionate letter to the House Appropriations Committee in the early stages of the writing of the legislation; it read in part:

See McBride, Joseph, "Pic Preservers Mum on Next Titles," Daily Variety, February 20, 1990, pp. 1, 24.

I appeal to you for the chance for redress and justice, not only for myself but for colleagues who are no longer here to defend their reputations for themselves: For if they have not already been under attack by insults of shortening and lengthening, electronic speeding up and slowing down, by editing, colorization, rescoring and possible computerized recasting and other electronic revisions, they will be shortly.*

How little did Capra and his fellow directors accomplish was revealed at that October 18, 1990, announcement, for not only did the Librarian of Congress reveal the next 25 titles, but also he defended guidelines which permitted films on the National Film Registry to be panned and scanned, edited and time compressed, without a required warning label.†

At the same time, the Library of Congress attacked the film industry, as a whole, for its failure to preserve America's film heritage. It accused the industry of claiming to spend large sums of money on film preservation when, in reality, that money was used for the so-called restoration of films by their transfer to videotape. "There's a big difference between restoration and preservation," commented one Library spokesman.§

Meanwhile, the Hollywood directors continue to lobby for new laws to protect the artistic rights of filmmakers. Steven Spielberg told *Daily Variety* (May 21, 1990),

> We are terrified of technology. It wakes me up at night. I used to trade on technology to make my movies more effective. Now I fear technology because it's going to make my movies more defective. . . . The technology is such today, and will be even more quantum in 10 years, that they will truly be able to replace actors in existing movies, continue the backgrounds, and all the action and all the shots, and put other actors in their places.**

The fears of colorization have given birth to a new impetus for filmmakers' rights. Sadly, what it has not done is raise consciousness within the Hollywood community for financial support for film preservation.

---

*Capra'a letter was published in its entirety in Daily Variety, June 16, 1988, pp. 2, 15.
†The federal guidelines for labeling of films in the National Film Registry took effect August 9, 1990. A warning label was not required if fewer than six minutes were removed from a film in the National Film Registry through a combination of methods. For more information, see Wharton, Dennis, "Altered Pic Label Rules Lenient," Daily Variety, August 21, 1990, pp. 1, 30.
§Quoted in Wharton, Dennis, and Joseph McBride, "Second Wave of Classic Pix Cited," Daily Variety, October 19, 1990, p. 23.
**Spielberg's worst fears became reality at the end of 1991, when Diet Coke unveiled a television commercial featuring colorized images of Humphrey Bogart and James Cagney, "lifted" from old films.

10 STOCK FOOTAGE LIBRARIES

The primary function of a film archives is to preserve films. It has no responsiblity to make such films available for commercial use, although some archives have begun to understand that by permitting outside use of their holdings they can also levy fees which can be used for film preservation. For example, the UCLA Film and Television Archive has operated a commercial services division for a number of years. The Library of Congress and the National Archives have no choice but to make their holdings of public domain films available for outside use, charging nothing more than a handling fee plus the laboratory cost of making whatever elements the user may need.

Vast as are the holdings of these two archives, they are far from adequate in satisfying the needs of those using film for purposes as varied as documentary production and television commercials. As a result, a number of commercial film libraries have been established — and the quantity if not the quality of their holdings is continually growing — to accommodate the new market. Most call themselves stock footage libraries, but, in reality, they license film clips and newsreel subjects, neither of which fit the definition of stock footage.

The copyright laws of the United States are so written as to permit, usually by accident, many films to fall into the public domain. Prior to the Copyright Act of 1976 (which went into effect on January 1, 1978), films could only be copyrighted for an initial period of 28 years, and these then had to be renewed for a further 28-year copyright period. (The new act gave motion pictures copyright for 75 years from the first publication of the work. However, it was not retrospective, and all films in their first 28 years of copyright needed to be renewed to gain the additional 28 plus 19 years to take advantage of the new 75-year copyright period.) Many famous and even more less famous films were never copyrighted or did not have their copyrights renewed. As a result, such classics as Frank Capra's *It's a Wonderful Life* (1947) and D.W. Griffith's *Intolerance* (1916) are in the public domain. Newsreels were seldom copyrighted, and fewer still had their copyrights renewed.

With so many films in the public domain, a number of commercial libraries have been established to "license" clips from these productions for use in documentaries, corporate presentations, television commercials, and the like. Several entrepreneurs have purchased vast quantities of public domain footage from the Library of Congress and the National Archives, and now "license" such footage to clients unaware of the existence of the two governmental archives or unwilling to wait the lengthy periods of time it can take either institution to fulfill requests for film or video.

There are, of course, underlying problems in the use of public domain footage, as many users have found to their cost. Just because a film is in the public domain, it does not mean that the music from such film is free of copyright. Members of the Screen Actors Guild must be paid residuals for their work in television from 1952 onwards and in motion pictures from 1960 onwards regardless of the copyright status of the production in which they appeared. Celebrity rights laws in many states require the celebrities be paid if their images are used to promote a product, and most such laws also apply to the heirs up to 50 years after the death of the personality.*

These commercial libraries may call themselves stock footage libraries, but they do not meet the industry definition of a stock footage library. Stock footage should be used to refer only to trims and out-takes from productions or to specially shot color footage. It should never be used to describe clips from features or short subjects, either black-and-white or color. Footage which cannot be cut into another production without its use being apparent to the average viewer is not stock footage. It says much for stock footage that although it is often overlooked and seldom discussed, it continues to play an important role in the production of television programs and commercials, as well as a lesser part in independent feature film production.

The value of using stock footage can be seen in the opening credit sequence of *Newhart*, utilizing out-takes from *On Golden Pond*,† or the opening of *Highway to Heaven*, which uses an out-take from the 1968 M-G-M feature *Ice Station Zebra* that had earlier been used in *Superman*.§ When the Joan Collins character drove her car off the bridge in a season finale of *Dynasty*, the footage used was, in reality, an out-take from a minor 1984 feature called *Impulse*.**

The two most prominent agencies representing personalities and their estates in the field of celebrity rights are Curtis Management Group (1000 Waterway Boulevard, Indianapolis, Indiana 46202; 317-633-2050) and the Roger Richman Agency (9777 Wilshire Boulevard, Suite 815, Beverly Hills, California 90212; 310-276-7000). Among the latter's clients are the estates of Charlie Chaplin, Marilyn Monroe, and Mae West. Curtis Management Group represents the estates of Fred Astaire, Abbott and Costello, John Belushi, Humphrey Bogart, James Dean, and Judy Garland, among others.
†*Licensed from Cameo Film Library.*
§*Licensed from Sherman Grinberg Film Libraries.*
**Licensed from Producers Library Service.*

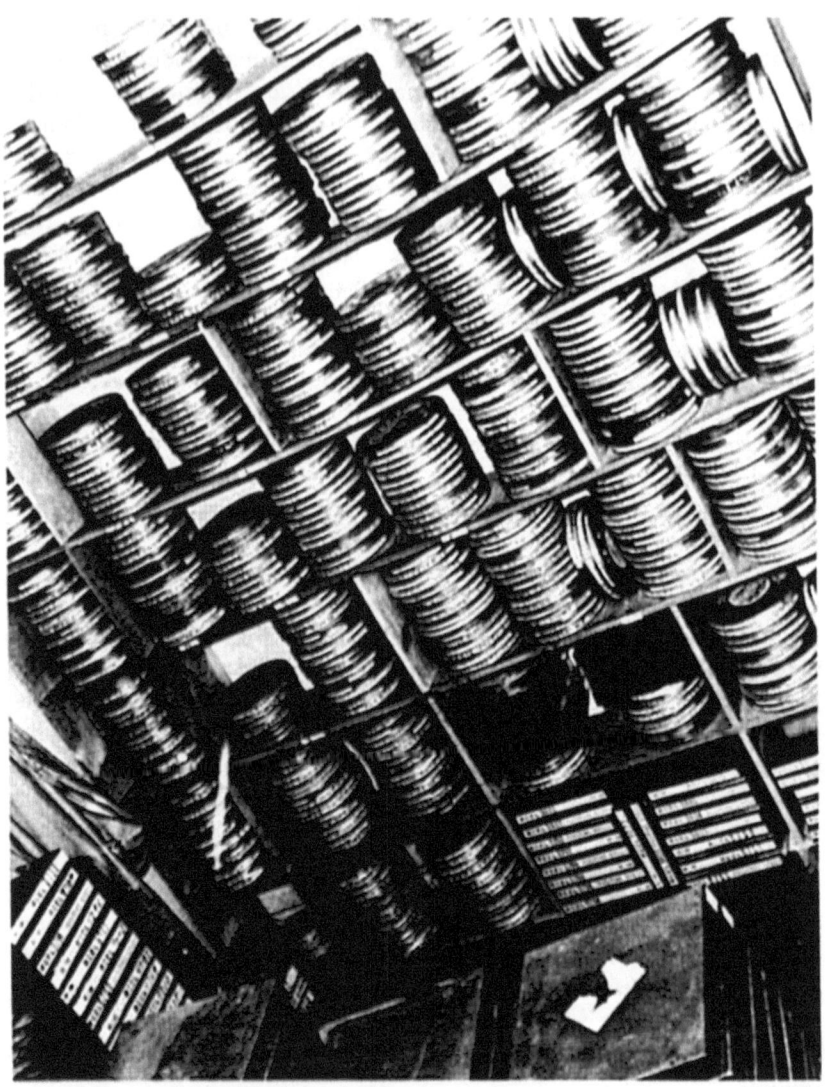

A typical studio film library in the 1930s or 1940s (courtesy of the Academy of Motion Picture Arts and Sciences).

The creation and use of stock footage illustrates how the efforts of one producer can benefit another. Studio libraries retain footage which they generate, not only for their own use, but also to service outside producers. Independent stock footage libraries generally acquire their holdings from consignees, producers who place with the library film shot for but not utilized in a specific production. In return for so doing, the consignees receive a portion of the license fees charged by the libraries for the use of such footage (usually 40 percent), have the film cataloged at no charge, and enjoy free access to it for future projects. Thanks to the foresight of the original producers, other filmmakers can utilize this footage at prices which are minimal in comparison to the cost of reshooting the same scenes.

It was a fairly common occurence for freelance cinematographers to work in tandem with independent stock footage libraries, shooting film wherever they happened to be, but such practice has declined in recent years with the increased cost of film stock and film processing. Video shooting makes more financial sense, but, as of 1991, the demand from major producers remained for film rather than video footage. Certainly any library will welcome footage of exotic locations, but it will appreciate just as much film which might, at first seem almost mundane, such as a shot of an Eastern home in the rain or a small American town with snow on the ground. Stock footage is far more than establishing shots of foreign locales. Producers are much more likely to ask for matching shots of a home at day and night, or of an Eastern expensive restaurant. At the height of summer, they will need snow scenes or Christmas decorations. Certainly, there will be calls for cars or helicopters exploding, but there will be a greater demand for a 747 jet flying by day or night, or a taxicab run-by on a suburban street.

The earliest known stock footage library was created by Abram Stone in 1908, and it remained in existence until the Second World War. (Its card index has survived and is housed in the Motion Picture, Broadcasting and Recorded Sound Division of the Library of Congress.) Situated on the East Coast, the Film Library (as it was called) suffered as a result of the Western migration of the film industry, and by the thirties was more concerned with the production of series utilizing its own stock footage, notably *Flicker Frolics*, than in acquiring new film or promoting the old.

Because the Film Library was some 3,000 miles removed from the Los Angeles producers, a method had to be devised to provide viewing prints which could not be pirated. The answer was the "scratched print," still in use today. As Stone's daughter, Dorothy, recalled in a 1951 magazine article:

> This was a print made from the negative, usually a selection of scenes, and much more footage than that required by a scenario. This print was scratched from end to end through its middle, so it could not be used. The director or editor who needed footage had the privilege of using it as a rough work print in combination with his rushes and other material. When the final editing was finished, this scratched print was returned to the library with paper markers indicating the actual footage the director or editor wanted to buy. These lengths were then matched to the negative and a duplicating positive [known as an I.P. or interpositive] was delivered to the purchaser, who had a duplicate negative made and inserted it in the complete production negative.*

---

*Stone, Dorothy E., "The First Film Library," Films in Review, August-September 1951, p. 31.

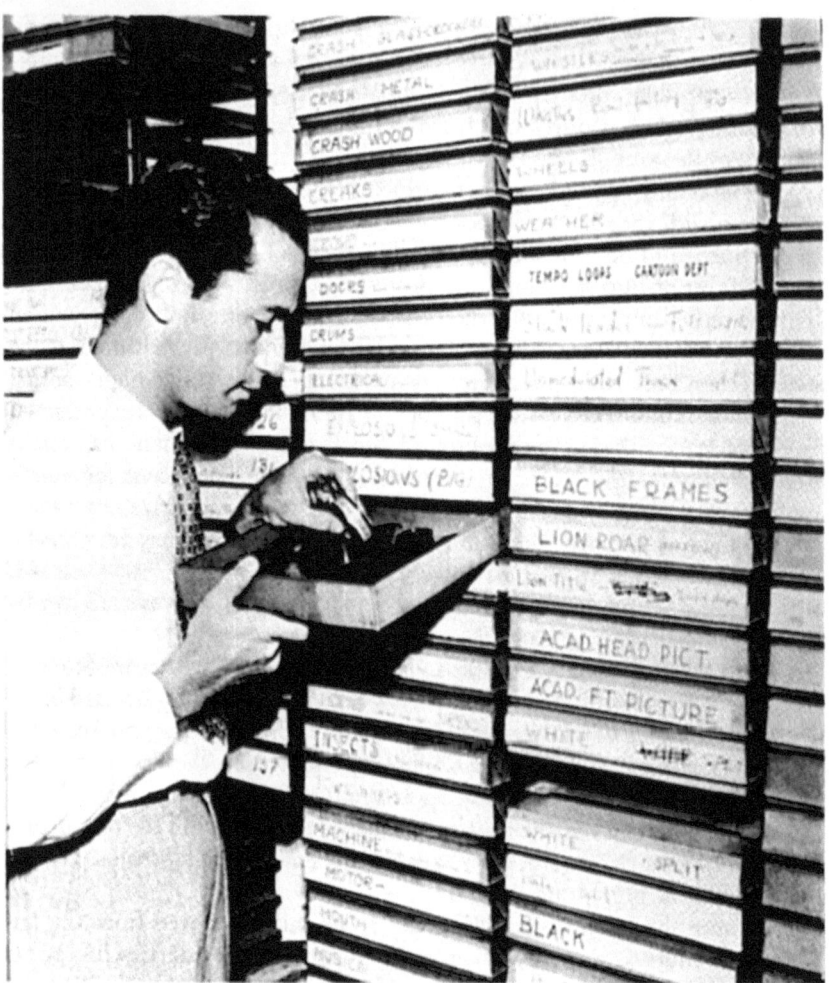

A studio librarian examines a can in a studio stock sound library typical of the 1930s and 1940s (courtesy Marc Wanaker Bison Archives).

Then, as now, prints and negatives are matched through the key numbers on the edge of the film. "Scratched prints" are generally utilized today if a producer needs a workprint to determine if a stock shot will work when cut into his production. However, most producers can decide if they need a specific shot by looking at a library's viewing print, and based on that, they will order negative. Because it is industry practice for a library to charge a license fee once a negative is pulled and released to a client, "scratched prints" tend to be used less and less, and many laboratories today are unfamiliar with the term.

Film historian William K. Everson has written extensively—notably in

*Films in Review** — on films of the twenties, thirties and forties which have utilized scenes from other, earlier productions. However, it should be stressed here that stock footage is not film used in earlier productions but rather film shot for but *not* used in an earlier feature. Strictly speaking, films such as *Isle of Love* from 1922, which re-edits footage from a feature of two years earlier, *An Adventuress*, to emphasize the presence of Rudolph Valentino, is not an example of the use of stock footage. The most important criteria for film to be culled and used as stock footage is that it must not include actors or actresses in the scene. Any footage with recognizable individuals in the shot is deemed "production," requiring residual payments to the performers, and would not be acceptable to a stock shot library. The only exception is footage of a stunt, such as a car crash. Even with residual payments to the stunt people involved, it is cheaper for a producer to utilize this footage than to reshoot it.

Film in a stock shot library is not generally released until at least two years after the feature has gone into distribution. It is also restricted until a television version of the film has been cut and aired.

During the first half of this century, independent producers had to rely for stock footage on two major sources, Progress Film Library and the General Film Library. The latter was operated by Sidney Kandel and Morris Landres, and because he had so much footage — some 20 million feet — available to the independent producer, Landres was dubbed "the Mayor of Poverty Row" by *Motion Picture Herald*. Founded in 1920, with offices in both Los Angeles and New York, the General Film Library included two earlier libraries, Horsley and Dawes, as well as a complete run of the *Kinograms* newsreel.

In an interview with *The New York Times*, Sidney Kandel revealed that the most profitable film in his library was of the sinking of the Austrian battleship *St. Stephen* by an Italian torpedo boat during the First World War. That one scene, showing hundreds of seamen swarming over the overturned hull of the boat, was licensed to First National for use in its 1927 release, *Convoy*, for $10,000.†

(Such a license fee is excessive even by modern standards. The average license fee in 1991 for use of a seven second cut in a television production is $400; the use of the same cut in a nationwide television commercial would cost a minimum of $1,000.)

Morris Landres produced a number of low budget feature films which made extensive use of his library's holdings. He died on July 18, 1987, at the age of 96. The General Film Library was acquired by Ziv Television in the late forties; its news footage was used in the compilation of various early fifties televison series.

---

*"Stock Shots," Films in Review, *January 1953, pp. 15–20; and "Movies Out of Thin Air,"* Films in Review, *April 1955, pp. 171–180.*
†*Strauss, Theodore, "History's Happy Hunting Ground,"* The New York Times, *June 22, 1941.*

The New York–based Progress Film Library was apparently founded in 1914 as the Joe Miles Library, with the slogan "Miles of Stock Shots." It was operated in partnership with Lloyds Film Storage Corporation.

Aside from General and Progress, the only other major, independent stock footage library operating prior to the fifties was the Elmer Dyer Film Library, founded by the highly regarded aerial cinematographer in 1920. Inactive for a number of years, it was acquired in 1988 by the New York–based Petrified Film & Photos.

In 1989, Petrified acquired the Warner Bros. nitrate stock footage library, consisting of approximately 20,000 cans of 35mm out-takes, process plates, and special effects footage from the period 1930–1951. Stock footage from more than 400 Warner Bros. features and short subjects was included in the purchase, including out-takes from such classic films as *The Adventures of Robin Hood, Casablanca, Mildred Pierce,* and *Yankee Doodle Dandy*. Petrified moved the footage from the Warner Bros. lot in Burbank to vaults in Kearney, New Jersey.

For many years, the major studios did not want it known that stock footage libraries existed on their lots. There was a strong feeling that if the public became aware that a feature had utilized stock footage it would diminish the film's production values. Nevertheless, several of the major studios did operate stock footage libraries, with one of the oldest and most important being on the Paramount lot, under the guidance of Hazel Marshall.

Marshall became Paramount's librarian in 1924, when she left the laboratory in which she was working, and went in to help the woman who was supposedly in charge. When Hazel Marshall joined the library the most recent can of cataloged film was numbered 173. When she retired on June 15, 1975, there were more then ten thousand cans in the vault. (Hazel Marshall was succeeded by Connie Bulmer, who remained the Paramount librarian until her death in the spring of 1990.)

Marshall recalls that there was little restriction placed on the use of footage in a studio library. Any independent producer who had the money to pay the bills could have access to the footage (although there were certain Paramount producers, notably Cecil B. DeMille, who did not permit the use of their out-takes for stock footage purposes). Process plates were also restricted for internal Paramount use only. Wherever a production crew was filming, it was expected to shoot many thousands of feet of process footage for use in later Paramount features.

It was Hazel Marshall who introduced the ten-foot minimum charge per cut, which remains a standard in stock footage library practice to the present. Any client utilizing stock footage must pay a minimum fee for the use of ten feet of 35mm film (the equivalent of seven seconds) per editorial cut, no matter how little film he may actually use in that cut. As Marshall recalls, "Around 1940, I was feeling guilty about sending out such small bills for the use of two or three feet of film at $2.50 per foot. And the accounts department was raising Cain about paperwork involved costing more than the film was bringing in." Prior to the forties, there had been no standardized minimum cut within the industry, although Abram Stone's library did, apparently, charge for a 25-foot minimum.

As an example of the "treasures" which may occasionally turn up in a stock footage library, out-takes from Orson Welles' abortive 1941-1942 film project, *It's All True*, survived in the Paramount library. The footage, both color and black-and-white, had been acquired by Paramount from RKO in the fifties. Welles' contract had forbidden the use of his trims and out-takes as stock footage — Woody Allen has a similar clause in his contract with Orion — but the director's wishes had been overlooked, and preservation and restoration of the material, in cooperation with the American Film Institute, began in 1988.

Studio stock footage libraries were also maintained at Republic, Walt Disney, M-G-M, Universal, Warner Bros., and Columbia. The last three remain active, although the Columbia library houses only stock footage from the company's television productions. Stock footage culled from the features is handled by the independent Cameo Film Library, under a 1989 contract.

Cameo, which is operated by Janet and Norman Meyer, also handles stock footage from Tri-Star, NBC Productions, and Viacom. Janet Meyer was formally the librarian at the CBS/MTM Film Library, which handles the stock footage created by Republic and also has the out-takes from two David O. Selznick features, *A Star Is Born* and *Nothing Sacred*. With the demise of Republic in the mid-fifties, its stock footage was initially handled by the independent EVCO Film Library, which was founded in 1962 and ceased operations in 1989.

Each of the studios and the two major independent libraries dating back to the fifties utilized a different color with which to identify their film cans. Paramount's cans were (and still are) yellow; Warner Bros.' were orange; CBS/MTM's were blue; Sherman Grinberg's were green; and Producers Library Service cans were pink.

Doris Dashiell (1910–1989) began her career with Gene Autry's Flying A Company. Subsequently, she became a librarian with Columbia and then with Desilu, when it took over RKO. When the RKO library was acquired by Paramount, Dashiell founded her own library in 1964. "I had the benefit of working at a studio," she recalled, "and I knew what the studios had, and, more importantly, I knew what they did not have." She also realized that 16mm was now viable for use as stock footage, and made it a point to acquire 16mm color footage from cinematographers around the world. When Doris Dashiell retired, the Dashiell Film Library was absorbed by Producers Library Service.

Hazel Marshall points out that stock footage libraries came into their own with the Second World War, and the shortage of raw stock. "Anywhere you could save ten feet of negative stock by using somebody else's establishing shot of City Hall, you would go with it."

A further resurgence in the importance of stock footage libraries came in the fifties with the ready availability of 16mm footage. Prior to that decade, few went out and shot film just for its possible use as stock footage, but with 16mm that became a viable, and reasonably inexpensive, proposition. The Lem Bayley Library, consisting entirely of 16mm film, was founded in 1953. (The library is now operated by the Chicago-based White Production Archives, Inc., which also has the Guy Haselton Library.) Actor Jon Hall founded his company, the Torrejon Film Library, three years later. It was noted for its underwater footage. Currently, three major stock footage libraries continue to offer a substantial collection of footage which their owners have shot, but in 35mm: Larry Dorn, Carl Barth's The Stock House, and Telecine International Productions.

The last is owned by Nick Archer, who has a policy of not promoting his library for outside use by independent filmmakers. Yet his proud boast is that he has serviced and billed over 4,000 Hollywood and New York productions, from *Studio One* and *Playhouse 90* in 1957 through *I'll Take Manhattan* and *The Two Mrs. Grenvilles* in 1987.

Many stock footage libraries operating in the 1950s and 1960s are forgotten today. Among these once-prominent companies are Cinerama, Inc., Film Library (established in 1962), Seth Larson's Continental Film Library (founded in 1964), Dynamic Films, Inc. (founded in 1948 and specializing in auto race footage), Guy Haselton (with 16mm color footage of national parks), Arthur Lodge Productions (founded in 1953), Marathon International Productions (established in 1947), and Stock Shots To Order, Inc. (founded in 1956).

Changes in the film industry in the fifties led to the creation of other libraries. Reggie Lyons (son of the noted ASC cinematographer of the same name) and Jack Reilly, the respective librarians at RKO and M-G-M, decided to form their own company, Producers Library Service, in 1957. The Library was intended to represent stock footage from independent producers, acting as a service to both the consignee and the buyer. Currently, Producers Library Service also represents stock footage from the BBC Location Library, ABC Entertainment, and Orion Pictures Corporation.

Also in 1957, the best known name in stock footage libraries, Sherman Grinberg (1928–1982), founded his library, after almost a decade working as an editor at 20th Century–Fox and elsewhere. Grinberg realized that the demise of the theatrical newsreel was close at hand, and that the newsreel archives could form a valuable resource for both television interest series and documentaries. He was able to acquire the libraries of both Pathé News (1912–1957) and Paramount News (1927–1957), and eventually, in 1963, also added ABC Television News to his holdings (CBS and NBC news footage is controlled and licensed by their respective networks).

As well as licensing stock footage, Grinberg also embarked on an ambitious production program. In 1962, in collaboration with David Wolper, he produced for television 39 episodes in the *Biography* series, narrated by Mike Wallace, with a further 26 episodes released the following year. Earlier, in 1960, he had produced 130 episodes in the *Funny Worlds* series, and 260 *Greatest Headlines of the Century* programs. In 1961 Grinberg produced 260 one-minute *Sportfolios* and, in 1964, made 30 *Survival* shows and 39 *Battleline* episodes. By 1965, Grinberg boasted a staff of 55, and his production activities were budgeted at $5 million.*

That same year, Grinberg moved his operation from the Columbia Studios lot to a building he had purchased, and from which the library still operates, at 1040 North McCadden Place in Hollywood. A New York office had opened earlier, and in 1965 it was placed under the control of Bernie Chertock, who had been with Grinberg since 1959, and continues as its East Coast head of operations.

Along with its black-and-white news footage, Grinberg also represents color and black-and-white stock footage from the productions of 20th Century–Fox, M-G-M, Allied Artists, ITC, and many others. Television productions from which the company represents stock include *Nova, Odyssey, Wide World of Animals*, and those from Home Box Office.

Aside from the Sherman Grinberg Film Libraries, the other major sources for black-and-white news and actuality footage are the UCLA Film and Television Archive, with its 27 million feet of newsreel footage from Hearst Metrotone and elsewhere,† and the New Jersey–based library and laboratory operation of John E. Allen, Inc. Founded in 1950, John E. Allen has some 28 million feet of film on file, including the *Kinograms* newsreel (1915–1931) and *Telenews* (1947–1953). As late as the 1960s, John E. Allen was also known to movie buffs for its fabulous collection of paper memorabilia from the teens, which it sold outright to collectors. Today, John E. Allen, Inc., is widely respected in the archival community for its laboratory, specializing in preservation and restoration of nitrate films.

Smaller sources of black-and-white archival footage are Archive Film Productions, Inc., and Killiam Shows, Inc. The former is operated by Patrick Montgomery, who received his training with Paul Killiam, and who has been actively involved in film production since 1979. Archive's major acquisition, in 1989, was the complete run of *The March of Time* from 1935 to 1951. Paul Killiam controls the estate of D.W. Griffith, and has built up an enviable reputation for his superior quality releases of silent features and short subjects in

---

*For more information, see Ornstein, Bill, "Grinberg Spending Near $5 Mil During This Year," The Hollywood Reporter, January 6, 1965, pp. 1, 4.

†Not all the Hearst Metrotone material is at UCLA. Hearst Metrotone News (235 East 45th Street, New York, New York 10017) still controls and licenses footage from its series Hearst Almanac, Hearst Reports (1958–1983), Telenews Weekly (1954–1963), Time Capsules, Time Out for Sports, Big Moments in Sports, Farm Newsreel, Perspectives on Greatness, History Makers, and American Insight.

television series such as *Movie Museum* (1954-1955) and *Silents Please/The History of the Motion Picture* (1960-1961).*

Recent years have seen some changes in the stock footage industry. New companies, such as Energy Productions and Dreamlight Images, have been created to shoot 35mm film specifically for stock footage, with a specialization in time-lapse and slow motion photography. The advent of video has resulted in the formation of a number of houses specializing exclusively in video as opposed to film, most notably the Los Angeles–based Video Tape Library, Ltd. Smaller production companies, including Stephen J. Cannell and Lorimar, have found it profitable to create their own stock libraries to compete with and supplement the holdings of the major studios. In New York, Film Search and Second Line Search specialize in finding stock footage for their various corporate clients, and the former, in association with the Image Bank photographic library, also maintains a stock footage library.

In April 1985, Jill Hawkins, the head of BBC Library Sales, hosted a meeting of representatives from various commercial audiovisual libraries at the MIP Television Market in Cannes. A second meeting was held in London in October of the same year, and the Federation of Commercial Audio Visual Libraries (FOCAL) became a reality. International in scope, but with its membership and activities primarily located in Europe, FOCAL's aim is to represent both the interests of commercial film and television libraries, and those of professional film researchers.†

*For more information on Paul Killiam, see the entry in Films on Film History *by Anthony Slide, Metuchen, N.J.: Scarecrow Press, 1979, pp. 110–112.*
†All correspondence for FOCAL should be addressed to P.O. Box 422, Harrow Middlesex, HA1 3YN, United Kingdom; telephone: 081-423-5853.

11 INTO THE NINETIES

The archival movement had a sad year in 1988 in that three of its leaders died. On May 22, George C. Pratt, curator emeritus of the International Museum of Photography at George Eastman House, and a prominent figure in its development from 1953 to 1984, died at the age of 73. On June 6, Jacques Ledoux died at the age of 66; he had been curator at Belgium's Cinémathèque Royale since 1948. Vernon S. Harbin, who died on July 31, 1988, at the age of 79, was one of the few individuals in the film industry to have held a long-time concern for preservation. He joined RKO in 1931, and was still with the company in 1958 when Howard Hughes decided to dispose of its assets. It was Harbin who selected which of the company's records were to be saved, and spent the next 20 years cataloging and organizing them. (They were subsequently donated to UCLA.) Actress Ginger Rogers echoed the thoughts of many when she commented, "Vernon Harbin deserves his own Academy Award for keeping movie history alive."*

The passing of these prominent figures in film preservation symbolized the end of an era. Not only were new archivists coming along, but also training programs in the field were beginning to appear.

Aside from the occasional summer school for new archivists, organized by FIAF and held at the Staatliches Filmarchiv der DDR, and the equally infrequent single-session university classroom surveys of film preservation, there had been no attempt to offer courses of study in film preservation and film archives administration. The obvious reasons were that there are insufficient positions available for would-be film archivists, and most of the work involved in the running of a film archives is far removed from the world of academia. The major figures in the American film archival field trained themselves. Eileen Bowser, at the Museum of Modern Art, was Richard's Griffith's secretary before she became an archivist. Robert Gitt of UCLA ran the Dartmouth College Film Society before embarking on a career in film preservation. Archivists such as the National Film Archive's Ernest Lindgren or Paul Spehr at the Library of Congress started at the bottom and slowly graduated to administration.

*Quoted in Daily Variety, *August 2, 1988, p. 22.*

Harold Brown joined the British Film Institute in April 1935, one month before the National Film Archive (then the National Film Library) was established. He became its preservation officer in 1951 and retired in August 1984. (Since then, he has been active as an advisor to the New Zealand Film Archive.) He had no training in film preservation and, as he once commented, "You just did what was called for, and the things you weren't very good at people stopped asking you to do."*

Despite the obvious job limitations in the field, the British University of East Anglia, located at Norwich, began offering a master of arts degree for film archivists in October 1990. (The university is also the home of the East Anglian Film Archive.) In some ways, the course indicates the progress which has been made in the field, but progress, as is so often the case, is not always productive. Preservation may now be acceptable, but it has also become an academic exercise.†

One of the crucial problems facing archivists in the future is public access to their collections. Researchers are constantly frustrated by the lack of a central database of information on the holdings of American archives and libraries. Some archives have attempted to publish catalogs of their holdings, usually out of date long before publication is achieved. The UCLA Film and Television Archive published a *Catalog Listing of Holdings* in March 1975, and in 1981 issued the *ATAS/UCLA Television Archives Catalog* (Pleasantville, N.Y.: Redgrave Publishing). Jon Gartenberg compiled *The Film Catalog: A List of Holdings in the Museum of Modern Art* (Boston: G.K. Hall, 1985). In 1978, the American Film Institute published *Catalog of Holdings: The American Film Institute Collection and the United Artists Collection at the Library of Congress.*

An important advance in the area of cataloging was the creation of the National Moving Image Database (NAMID) by the National Center for Film and Video Preservation. Some archives already have computerized listings of their holdings, but the systems are generally incompatible. Commercial operations have also agreed to make their lists of holdings available to NAMID; in June 1990, the Turner Entertainment Company provided a data storage tape describing the printing and projection elements for its holdings of pre–1948 Warner Bros. features and short subjects.

The National Center has also been providing grants to individual archives for the development of computerized catalogs of their physical holdings, for inclusion in NAMID. The International Museum of Photography at George Eastman House and the Wisconsin Center for Film and Theater Research have

---

*Quoted in Sussex, Elizabeth, "Preserving," Sight & Sound, vol. 53, no. 4, autumn 1984, p. 237.

†For more information, see Barr, Charles, "East Anglia Teaches a Neglected Art," Sight & Sound, vol. 60, no. 2, spring 1990, pp. 75–76; and Cleveland, D., "East Anglian Film Archive," Framework, autumn 1980, pp. 44–45.

been receiving such grants since 1988; the Museum of Modern Art since 1989. The Library of Congress became involved in making its records available to NAMID in the summer of 1990.*

The American Film Institute's interest in establishment of a Film Information System is not new. The Institute's 1969 annual report contains the following statement:

> Is there a print of *Intolerance* in the Chicago area? What films deal with problems of migrant workers during the Depression? Which museums or archives hold films directed by Erich von Stroheim?
>
> Such questions as these will be answered by the Film Information System, to be established in New York early in 1969. Utilizing the National Film Catalog and computerized cataloging techniques the System, with access to specialized film agencies, will collect and disseminate all types of data on all types of films. The basis of the System will be a comprehensive film reference service linked by Telex to regional centers around the country. To complement this national service the System will act as a clearinghouse for all film information and publish an interlocked series of resource directories.

Of course, nothing came of this grandiose scheme. The first major conference on cataloging and documentation was held November 1–3, 1978, at the American Film Institute in Washington, D.C. Attended by representatives from 34 institutions, it was organized by the Wisconsin Center for Film and Theater Research, the Museum of Modern Art, the Charles K. Feldman Library of the American Film Institute, the National Archives and Records Service, and the Library of Congress.

A national database is important in ensuring access for archivists to information on the holdings of other institutions, and thus eliminating duplication of preservation efforts. As Frank Hodsoll, then chairman of the National Endowment for the Arts, wrote in 1983, "Informed decisions about preservation priorities will continue to be difficult to make until the contents and physical condition of films in major collections across the country are listed in one database."†

Similarly, students and scholars have a need, not to say a right, to know what films are held or preserved where. The FIAF has a database at its Brussels headquarters, listing all American films held by foreign archives, but it is accessible only to member archives. This type of secrecy is wrong, antischolarly, and, ultimately, harmful to the public relations image of archivists.

In 1971, Eileen Bowser of the Museum of Modern Art prepared a 20-page

---

*Major publications relating to archival film cataloging are: Gartenberg, Jon, Film Cataloging Manual: A Computer System *(New York: Museum of Modern Art, 1979); White-Hensen, Wendy,* Archival Moving Image Materials: A Cataloging Manual *(Washington, D.C.: Library of Congress, Motion Picture, Broadcasting and Recorded Sound Division, 1984); and Yee, Martha,* Moving Image Materials: Genre Terms *(Washington, D.C.: Library of Congress, Cataloging Distribution Service, 1988).*

†Hodsoll, Frank, "Our Heritage Must Be Saved," Variety, January 19, 1983, p. 132.

listing of American feature films since the 1920s known to exist in world archives. An invaluable piece of documentation, the listing was distributed only to the Museum's colleague archives, and accompanied by a memorandum (dated November 17, 1971), which read, in part, "I am not prepared to advise you of the location of films just so you can borrow them for a show. . . . The list is not for publication nor for showing to anyone except the members of this committee." In the intervening 20 years, archives have opened up their holdings to a limited extent, but there is still a strong need to overcome the negative, "need-to-know" thinking of the older generation of archivists, who had experienced a certain amount of paranoia from dealing with Raymond Rohauer as well as an early distrust of film archives by film company executives.

Inextricably linked to the public cataloging of archival collections is the need for access to films both for individual viewings and group presentations at events such as retrospectives and film festivals. Individual access to films varies considerably from archives to archives. The Library of Congress and the National Archives are the most cooperative, making their holdings available for in-house study without charge on an appointment basis. Most other U.S. archives offer lesser availability, often at a nominal charge per film. Certainly, the situation has improved dramatically for the American film scholar, and the days in which it was a matter of whom one knew at an archives rather than the validity of the research project are gone forever.

In September 1989, the UCLA Film and Television Archive opened its Archive Research and Study Center on the Westwood campus. According to its glossy brochure, the goals of ARSC are to

> encourage the use of film and broadcast media as primary sources for education and research; enhance the curricular resources available to the University, facilitate multi-disciplinary approaches to film and broadcast media; promote creative and critical advancement of media literacy; expand use of archival materials to the widest range of disciplines within the arts, sciences, and humanities; develop curricular and research applications for new media technologies; provoke critical dialogue on issues related to film and television.

Located in the university's Powell Library, ARSC is an impressive-looking facility, with its individual carousels and video monitors resembling the viewing rooms at the Museum of Broadcasting.

Unfortunately, the films available for study at ARSC are primarily limited to the more popular preserved titles and films which the Archive held in 16mm and which it was able cheaply to transfer to video. As a result, there is not a great deal of difference between the films available on video at ARSC and the films available on video at a local video store. What are not easily accessible are the thousands and thousands of unique 35mm nitrate titles in the UCLA collection, the very titles which need to be made available for scholarly study.

Along with all the other major U.S. archives, UCLA offers daily public screenings as part of its activities, but, as is so often the case, the majority of

screenings are devoted not to the holdings of the archives but to outside programming, often from Third World countries. In public, archives generally express a willingness to loan out their holdings for public screenings, but, in
private, such "loans" are often subject to not only the matter of rental charges
but the highly political issue of the publicity such a loan will garner for the
archives in question.

When Bob Epstein founded the UCLA Film and Television Archive, his
attitude was to make films available at no charge:

> Working in an archives, it's like working in a restaurant, the customers are the
> biggest nuisance in the world. But what the hell are you there for? My feeling was
> open access. Any print in the collection, unless we knew it was unique or hadn't
> been copied, was viewable. When we got our first Steenbeck, the viewing room
> was open four days a week, nine to five. Anybody could call and make an appoint-
> ment. We limited them to four hours a week. We didn't ask for their credentials.
> Occasionally, if somebody was coming from out of town, one of us would stay in
> the evening, or come in on Saturday to accommodate them.
> The Paramount prints in the collection are the best prints because in most cases
> they are the original answer prints. Let people see them, because they are not go-
> ing to be around forever, and the ideal place to see them is in a theatre. If any
> place wanted to use a print, I was happy to let them have it at no charge. The
> fact that it's a commercial enterprise doesn't mean it's corrupt. I cared about those
> people going to the Vagabond Theatre in Los Angeles to see, say, *The Love
> Parade*, and not seeing one of MCA's crummy 16mm prints, but seeing what the
> film really looked like. One of the patrons of the Vagabond Theatre turned out
> to be David Packard, who was amazed at how good these movies looked. It was
> what sparked his interest in the archive, and he became a major benefactor of the
> archive [funding preservation through the David and Lucile Packard Foundation].
> Now if I hadn't been doing that, he probably never would have.
> [Archive Director Robert] Rosen is always saying, "We aren't getting anything
> out of it" — one of his favorite sayings — but here it came back to benefit the Ar-
> chives many times over. On the subject of access, I always told folks at the Archive,
> we want to be more like the Cinémathèque Française than the Museum of Modern
> Art — a place that is founded on a love of film, not on a love of procedure and
> bureaucracy.*

The future holds the need not only for better access to archival prints, but
also an urgent need for archives to make their holdings available on videotape
for sale or rental. While archives quite obviously cannot transfer their copyrighted holdings to video, there are literally thousands of films in American
archives which are in the public domain, and which could be made available.
Videotape can make films accessible to a wider public, which may for the first
time become aware of the work of film archives, and it can also be an obvious
source of income. Yet archivists remain stubbornly opposed to the obvious.
Many criticize the poor quality of videotape of films which they hold in superior quality, but they make no effort to enter the video marketplace. *Becky*

Interview with the author, December 21, 1990.

Sharp is in the public domain, and it would be relatively easy to release UCLA's restoration of it on video. But all that is available to the public are videotapes of the shortened, unrestored version, often in black-and-white. The National Endowment for the Arts should insist that grants for the preservation of public domain films be contingent upon archives' working for the videotape release of such titles.

Preservation can and should be a source of income for archives, not merely a constantly losing proposition. There is a serious need for the National Endowment for the Arts and lawmakers to consider the profits made from the public funding of film preservation not by the public but by commercial concerns. At present, public money is daily used to restore or preserve copyrighted films without any financial participation by the copyright owners. Once the film has been preserved at the public expense, the preservation elements are made available to the copyright owner, without charge, for his or its financial benefit. It is not unusual for television programming to present stories of preservation, utilizing clips from restored films. Although such programs offer no financial rewards for the archives involved, they do for the copyright owners of the preserved films being excerpted. Such copyright owners charge as much as $2,000 or $3,000 for use of the clips. Such commercialization of publicly-funded "art" is morally and legally wrong. Commercial owners of publicly-preserved films must be required to return a percentage of their profits from the use of the preservation elements to the public's preservation efforts.

The interrelationship between commercial interests and film preservation has often been an uneasy one, marred by mutual suspicion and self-interests. Happily, the situation has been steadily improving through the years, reaching a new high in 1990. The subject of commercial film and television preservation touches on a number of areas, but all, ultimately, are financial in nature.

Aside from the benefits of an averted risk of a nitrate fire and the positive financial side to having a public archives spend public money to preserve a film over which a company or an individual has commercial control, many have been persuaded to deposit their films with archives to avoid the high cost of storage. Such a consideration was influential in Mary Pickford's decision to donate her films to the Library of Congress, and it also played a part in the actions of many who donated films to the Museum of Modern Art at the formation of its film library. Film storage is not, and never has been, cheap. In 1930, the Thomas H. Ince Corporation signed an agreement to store its films with Lloyds Film Storage Corporation in New York. The monthly storage charge back then was as high as 40¢ a reel for the first five reels and 20¢ per reel for all additional films.

Another major advantage to commercial producers in donating the physical rights in their films to archives was a tax advantage. Despite the donors' retaining all other rights, including copyright, in their films, tax laws permitted substantial write-offs, often based on replacement cost of the footage involved. Most archives required donors to find and pay for appraisers to evaluate the gifts. The exception was the Library of Congress which provided in-house evaluations of the donated materials.

Initially deposited in 1971, a collection of 91 films dating from 1914 to 1943 was eventually deeded to the Library of Congress by Paramount Pictures in 1979. Paramount retained the copyright in the material, and also the right of access to the preserved films. Aside from ensuring that the films were preserved for posterity, the Library of Congress and the people of the United States got little from the arrangement. The same is not true for Paramount. The Library divided the gift into three categories: those films which were unique (and valued at $1 per foot), those films which might exist elsewhere (valued at 50¢ a foot), and those which were definitely duplicates of films already in U.S. archives (valued at 20¢ a foot). The Library's total recommended evaluation of the Paramount gift amounted to $412,830.*

A major blow to the concept of producers and distributors' donating physical property to archives in return for substantial tax deductions came on May 8, 1990, when the United States Court of Appeals for the Federal Circuit ruled against Transamerica Corporation and affirmed the disallowance of its claim for a charitable contribution deduction in the amount of $10,045,480.

Transamerica had claimed the deduction in 1969, following its donation of original nitrate elements on more than 700 pre–1948 Warner Bros. feature films (owned by Transamerica subsidiary United Artists) to the Library of Congress. (The company had made a similar gift of 16mm viewing prints of the same titles to the Wisconsin Center for Film and Theater Research, but the Center had rejected the nitrate.) The gift to the Library of Congress consisted only of the "physical property," which the Library was permitted to convert to safety film, at its expense.

The Court of Appeals upheld a 1988 verdict by the U.S. Claims Court, noting:

> The cost of the conversion to safety film which the Library undertook to make was well over $1 million. . . . Taxpayer contributed nothing towards this cost, although it received the right, to the exclusion of other members of the public, to obtain access to the Library's safety film for commercial purposes in perpetuity. Even after the relinquishment of copyright, the Library agreed to make such materials available only to educational institutions for scholarly research and then only with taxpayer's consent.
>
> The Claims Court found that there was no market at the time of the transfer in which taxpayer could have sold its nitrate negatives, stripped of all intangible rights in the motion picture, for scholarly or archival uses or as historical artifacts.

---

*Information taken from Draft Evaluation Memo prepared by Robert C. Sullivan, Paul Spehr and John Finzi. At the end of this chapter is a list of the films in the Paramount gift.

Per the Claims Court, the nitrate films as physical property had no fair market value in November 1969.*

While the decision of the Courts of Appeals may be harmful to archives in that it discourages commercial companies from donating films for preservation, there can be no question that it is in the best interests of the American taxpayers. Such taxpayers would, and did, pay for the protection and preservation of Transamerica's corporate assets, and further, through a flawed instrument of gift, were a party to the circumvention of American copyright laws (which do not give copyright protection in perpetuity to any individual or company).

In an effort to encourage more studio participation in film preservation, director Martin Scorsese organized the Film Foundation. Joining Scorsese in the organization's formation, announced on May 1, 1990, were Steven Spielberg, Woody Allen, Francis Ford Coppola, Stanley Kubrick, George Lucas, Sydney Pollack, and Robert Redford. The Film Foundation's initial goal was to raise a minimum of $30 million for joint restoration projects by American studios in cooperation with American film archives.†

Valid and sincere as its goals might be, it was obvious that the Film Foundation was unlikely to address the most critical issue facing American film archives in the 1990s, and that is the preservation of the minor films, the nonglamorous film titles which mean little to the public or to the self-interested in the preservation field. Unfortunately, directors such as Scorsese or Spielberg are primarily interested in the preservation of their favorite films, the majority of which have been adequately safeguarded. Somewhat typical of the danger of permitting professional filmmakers, too close a contact with film preservation was a telegram from Woody Allen, read at the announcement of the Film Foundation's creation, which ended with the comment, "P.S.: Just don't bother to preserve *Porky's.*" Here is an ill-considered, fatuous comment, suggesting that simply because a film appeals to a lower mentality than that of Woody Allen, it should not be preserved.

Another problem with the concept encouraged by the Film Foundation is that studios have a strong vested interest in seeing that their libraries of films are preserved. It is no major financial hardship for a studio to commit a million dollars or more for the in-house preservation of its film library. What is needed, and what the Film Foundation does not seem able to accomplish, is the extra-studio preservation of a studio's library under the ideal archival and restoration conditions that a studio might consider unnecessary. Just because a film is "preserved" by Paramount or Universal on their studio lots, in their studio

---

*United States Court of Appeals for the Federal Circuit, decision No. 89-1428, Transamerica Corporation, plaintiff-appellant, v. the United States, defendant-appellee, May 8, 1990, p. 5.
†For more information, see McBride, Joseph, "Eight Form Preservation Band," Daily Variety, May 2, 1990, pp. 1, 18.

vaults, does not necessarily mean that the film is adequately preserved for posterity.

The announcement of the Film Foundation came at a time when studios were taking a serious look at the value of some of their older films. The sale of the M-G-M Film Library to Ted Turner and his successful marketing of its holdings was clear proof that a studio's major asset was often its film library. As UCLA's Robert Rosen commented, "People around the world have discovered that their holdings are not dead storage but are in fact capital assets."* Turner spent $350,000 to restore *Gone with the Wind*, and netted $7 million in profit from its reissue on film and videotape. *The Wizard of Oz*, which required no restoration, resulted in a $10 million profit for Turner from its release on videotape. In 1989, Columbia released the restored version of *Lawrence of Arabia*, and netted a $2 million profit.

By the late 1980s, studios were willing to spend considerable sums of money in the restoration and reissue of their older films. The situation had changed drastically in only a few years. For example, in 1982, 20th Century–Fox was agreeable to paying $1,000 per title to make new prints on some 80 films to be distributed to revival houses. However, the studio balked at spending $2,000 to restore the magnetic stereophonic soundtrack to a new print of *The King and I*.†

Paramount was one studio which expressed initial surprise at the audiences for its 1990 reissues of *The Ten Commandments* and *Funny Face*. Those reissues coincided with the studio's in-house film and television preservation activities, designated as "Asset Protection Program." In the summer of 1990, the studio opened its own 40,000 square foot archive building on the Hollywood lot, under the directorship of Milt Shefter. In addition, beginning in January 1989, Paramount began storing duplicate preprint safety elements in a former limestone mine outside of Pittsburgh.§

Paramount's recent concern for archival storage mirrors an earlier corporate decision from 1914, described in *The Moving Picture World*:

> In connection with the new studios the Jesse L. Lasky Feature Play Company contemplate building in the East shortly, there will be a fireproof, explosion-proof, negative vault.
>
> The vault will be composed of small separate vaults with each negative being in a separate and distinct enclosure, which will have an outlet to the open air. A cooling plant will keep the air at fifty degrees Fahrenheit permanently.

*Quoted in Citron, Alan, "Value in the Vault," Los Angeles Times, Section D, May 29, 1990, p. 1.

†See Cohn, Lawrence, "Fox Archival Restoration Project Rejuvenates 80 Vintage Titles," Variety, April 21, 1982, pp. 7, 28.

§For more information, see McBride, Joseph, "Studio Mounts Re-Release Campaign Following Program to Restore TV, Pic Classics," Daily Variety, April 27, 1990, pp. 1, 34, 43. An editorial, "Pic Preservation Must Be of Paramount Importance," by Thomas M. Pryor, also appeared in the May 3, 1990, edition of Daily Variety.

The separate vaults will be so constructed that if one were to be affected by combustion or fire the damage will be confined to the one vault only, in that the individual outlets will carry off the gases and combustible air, so that even in the event of a fire, which is almost impossible, but one negative vault will be affected.*

Commercial interest in film preservation diminished as "old" negatives and prints appeared to have little value with each passing decade. If they were worth anything at all, it was for the silver which might be recovered from them. The advent of television sparked the first renewal of interest in films of the past as viable money-making entitites, and a second surge of interest occurred with the coming of the video revolution. Even so, the attitude of many companies was summed up by Sid Samuels, director of worldwide print operations at 20th Century–Fox: "Economics is always a factor to be contended with. We're not a museum. We're not an archives supported by public funds. We're a commercial company that has to account to its chairman, its board of directors and, beyond them, its stockholders."†

As a result of such an attitude, the transfer of nitrate to safety was often conducted in a hurried manner, with little or no regard for archival standards. Columbia Pictures made poor quality safety masters on its classic films, failed to inspect such masters, and then, worst of all, destroyed the nitrate originals. The company displayed minor concern for its lesser features. These it did not bother to copy at all, but it did retain the nitrate originals. As an ironic result, the company and archives with which it works have been able to obtain far better quality safety materials from these films compared to such classic features from the studio as It Happened One Night (1934). Similarly, MCA/Universal was lax in its initial copying to safety of the Paramount features, from 1928 to 1948, owned by the studio. It has since transpired that far superior quality preservation elements can often be made from the original Paramount nitrate prints donated to the UCLA Film and Television Archive.

Two studios whose track records are blameless as far as film preservation is concerned are Walt Disney and Metro-Goldwyn-Mayer. Disney has made black-and-white separation masters on all of its color animated and live action productions. All its nitrate elements have been carefully transferred to safety stock, and the company has worked with archives, notably the American Film Institute, to locate and acquire any missing early cartoon titles. One minor problem which the studio was forced to face in the 1970s was the shipment of nitrate film to the lot for copying. Previously, such film had been carried by air, but studio executives suddenly had a vision of a nitrate fire on board, the plane crashing and there among the ashes would be discovered a shipping label with Mickey Mouse's image. The public relations fear of any diaster linked to

---

*The Moving Picture World, June 20, 1914, p. 1843.

†Quoted in Wiener, R.M.M., "Vanishing Art: Fading Color Threatens Film Archives," Box Office, April 28, 1980, p. 14.

Mickey Mouse was such that Walt Disney decided to ban all air shipments of nitrate film. Instead, it opted to go with UPS, presumably on the assumption that the loss of one or two UPS drivers would not have the same impact on the American public.

Fear of the potential danger of nitrate film in recent years has created a number of problems for commercial companies and their relationship to the archival community. Culver City, in which the M-G-M Laboratory is located, has strict rules on the number of reels of nitrate film which can be housed inside the city limits at any one time, and, as a result, the laboratory could only handle half a dozen reels of nitrate film in any one job. In the late seventies, 20th Century–Fox decided to ban the screening of nitrate prints of any of its films, a major blow for museums and film institutions wanting to provide their audiences with the best possible prints of scheduled films.

In 1965, despite the Culver City regulations, M-G-M began a preservation program to transfer all of its nitrate films, features, shorts and trailers, to safety. When the library was taken over by the Ted Turner organization in 1986, all the program had been completed. "It was one of the most thorough conversions of nitrate to safety," notes Turner Entertainment's Richard May.*

The preservation program at M-G-M included not only all of its own films, but also the extant titles from the earlier Goldwyn Pictures Corporation (founded in 1916). There were, and are, of course, some missing titles, notably Lon Chaney's *London After Midnight* (1927) and Greta Garbo's *The Divine Woman* (1928). The latter is the only missing Garbo American feature — and the Swedish Film Institute has done a remarkable job in preserving the actress' European films — but there are other missing Chaney films, from before the M-G-M era, as well as missing scenes from a number of the actor's features from the 1920s.

Aside from the nitrate transfer program, the studio also embarked in the mid–1970s on a project to restore the music and sound effects to a number of late silent features. Many M-G-M silent films from 1927 onwards were originally released with music and sound effects not on a combined soundtrack but on a separate disc (similar to the Vitaphone process introduced by Warner Bros.). Among the features now restored are *Trail of '98, Tide of Empire, Show People, Woman of Affairs, The Viking, White Shadows in the South Seas, Wild Orchids, West of Zanzibar, Spite Marriage, Our Modern Maidens, Our Dancing Daughters, The Wind, While the City Sleeps, The Pagan, Desert Nights, The Kiss,* and *Where East Is East.*

In the mid–1970s, M-G-M worked out an arrangement with the International Museum of Photography at George Eastman for the staff there to supervise the remaining conversion to safety film and for the Rochester institution to store the original nitrate negatives. The storage agreement continues to the

Telephone conversation, January 9, 1991.

present, but M-G-M helped in the financial cost involved in preserving the films, ultimately spending $30 million on the project.

When MGM/UA was created in 1983, the company acquired the entire pre–1950 output of Warner Bros. United Artists had already converted about half of the feature films to safety, and had made 16mm reduction negatives on the entire library as part of its television exhibition program; MGM/UA converted the remainder of the feature films to safety.

Turner acquired the M-G-M and pre–1950 Warner Bros. libraries in 1986, and continued with the preservation work. Two years later, Turner acquired the RKO library of 800 features, and embarked on the preservation of 270 titles which had not been converted to safety film. Improvements in color preservation techniques inspired Turner to "represerve" some of the films in its library, beginning with the 1989 restoration of *Gone with the Wind* at a cost of $350,000. Other films similarly "restored" by Turner are *Lassie Come Home, Meet Me in St. Louis, Show Boat,* and *Lovely to Look At.* Several of the color films in the RKO library have not been converted to safety stock, and Turner began work on those in 1991. When the M-G-M Laboratory closed in 1989, the preservation work was taken over by Guffanti Film Laboratories in New York, YCM Laboratory in Burbank, California, Film Technology Company in Hollywood, California, and Cinetech in Riverside, California.

Richard P. (Dick) May, Turner's vice president for film services, confirms the company's commitment to film preservation:

> We have every intention of keeping our entire library in the best possible condition for the longest period of time that technical advances will allow. Without preservation of the film the library is useless and it is a happy combination that the commercial use of all of these films also brings about historic preservation.

In lesser ways, some smaller companies have been concerned with various aspects of film preservation. Modern Talking Pictures, owned by Keith Smith, and headquartered in Omaha, Nebraska, owns all rights to the 1927 Cecil B. DeMille feature, *King of Kings.* In the early 1970s, the company made 35mm acetate negatives and fine grains on the feature, with Technicolor manufacturing safety negatives and fine grains on the color sequences. Modern Talking Pictures then made a hundred 35mm prints from the original negatives, again with Technicolor printing the color inserts. In addition, the company acquired all extant films produced by Cinema Corporation of America and Sack Amusements (excluding its black-oriented films), made 35mm acetate negatives and prints on everything, and then destroyed the nitrate originals. In 1975, it purchased 12 minor features and one serial in the so-called TelePrompter package from Blackhawk Films and again, promptly, manufactured new safety elements on all the films.*

Information taken from a conversation with David Shepard, April 25, 1975.

In New York, Paul Killiam founded his own company, Killiam Shows, in 1950, and a few years later acquired the "rights" to the films of D.W. Griffith (most were in the public domain) and the "rights" to the early American Biograph productions (all were in the public domain). He worked closely with the Museum of Modern Art, ensuring that these films and others which he acquired were properly preserved. Additionally, Killiam "restored" the films for television release, adding artificial tints and new music scores.* Aside from his work with the Museum of Modern Art, Paul Killiam also worked closely with the American Film Institute, making his first donation of films in December 1972. In 1977, he donated 30 feature films and 75 short subjects to the American Film Institute Collection at the Library of Congress.

The archival involvement of some companies arose from their dissolution rather than from their active lives. When Studio Films, Inc., went bankrupt, Neptune World Wide Moving acquired its films stored at a Neptune warehouse. More than a million feet of 35mm film from the 1950s was handed over to the American Film Institute in the spring of 1973, including many, many copies of *Rhythm and Blues Review* and *Rock 'n' Roll Review*. It is doubtful that there is a film archives, however small, in America which does not have a print of these titles!

As an example of how the past can catch up with the present, in October 1989, Edwin Thanhouser donated $40,000 to the Library of Congress. The money was to be spent on the acquisition and preservation of films produced by the New Rochelle–based Thanhouser Film Corporation, which Edwin Thanhouser's grandfather had founded in 1909, and which remained in existence through 1918.†

There can be no question that the film industry has awakened to the need for film preservation. As a result of the Film Foundation's propaganda efforts, Columbia Pictures embarked in 1990 on a preservation and restoration program in cooperation with the UCLA Film and Television Archive. In June 1990, Columbia announced the creation of a film and tape preservation committee, which included, along with senior company officials, Mary Lea Bandy from the Museum of Modern Art, Robert Rosen of UCLA, Pat Loughney from the Library of Congress, and George Stevens, Jr. Similar committees were formed by Paramount and Warner Bros., with the latter announcing a program to restore 26 of its classic features, including *Rebel Without a Cause* and *East of Eden*.

In an act emblematic of the resolve by various studios not only to preserve the quality of later productions, Columbia has asked UCLA's Robert Gitt to restore its 1961 feature, *The Guns of Navarone*. Ron Haver of the Los Angeles

---

*For more information, see Montgomery, Patrick, "Killiam Film Restorations," Blackhawk Film Digest, May 1979, p. 74.
†Library of Congress Information Bulletin, October 30, 1989, pp. 381–383.

County Museum of Art has long been working, in association with United Artists, to restore director Billy Wilder's original cut of *The Private Life of Sherlock Holmes* (1970).

The relationship between archives and film companies has become far more a cooperative arrangement and less a matter of the former's being used by studios to preserve films for which they were unwilling to allocate funds. In 1977, 20th Century–Fox offered to let the Museum of Modern Art make, at its expense, color negatives from the studio's nitrate YCM masters. In return, the Museum of Modern Art was to be allowed to keep and store the nitrate, while 20th Century–Fox would take over the newly-made safety negatives. In 1977, such an offer was rejected by the Museum as inappropriate. Today, neither 20th Century–Fox nor any other studio would have the audacity to suggest such a one-sided arrangement.

In 1991, the Academy of Motion Picture Arts and Sciences at last decided to improve its image in the area of film preservation and acquisition by appointing Michael Friend as the first director of the Academy Film Archive. Friend previously spent four years as deputy director of the AFI's National Center for Film and Video Preservation.

Film companies have also shown more concern for the professional storage of their films. Turner Entertainment, 20th Century–Fox, Walt Disney, Columbia Pictures, United Artists, and Lorimar are some of the major companies which safeguard their assets by storing films with Underground Vaults & Storage, Inc., of Hutchinson, Kansas. The vaults here are 650 feet underground in a former salt mine, a natural constant environment where the temperature remains stable at 68 degrees Fahrenheit and the humidity at 50 percent. With its slogan, "Protection in Depth," the storage facility first gained attention when it was utilized by M-G-M for the vaulting of its safety preservation elements in the early 1960s.*

Underground Vaults & Storage, Inc., was formed by a group of Wichita, Kansas, businessmen, on June 11, 1959, at the height of the Cold War when underground storage of records for security purposes was a priority. The businessmen rented space in the mines of the Carey Salt Company. As of 1991, 60,000 reels of film are stored in Hutchinson, including master copies of 7,000 first-run features.

Within the archival community, it seems that no sooner is one major problem solved than another develops. While it might be argued that preservation by a commercial entity is not the equivalent of archival preservation, it is better than nothing. And certainly there is no way that America's publicly-funded archives can possibly preserve the entire output of the major studios. In addition, many producers simply do not want their films preserved by anyone other than themselves.

Underground Vaults & Storage, Inc., Box 1723, Hutchinson, Kansas 67504-1723.

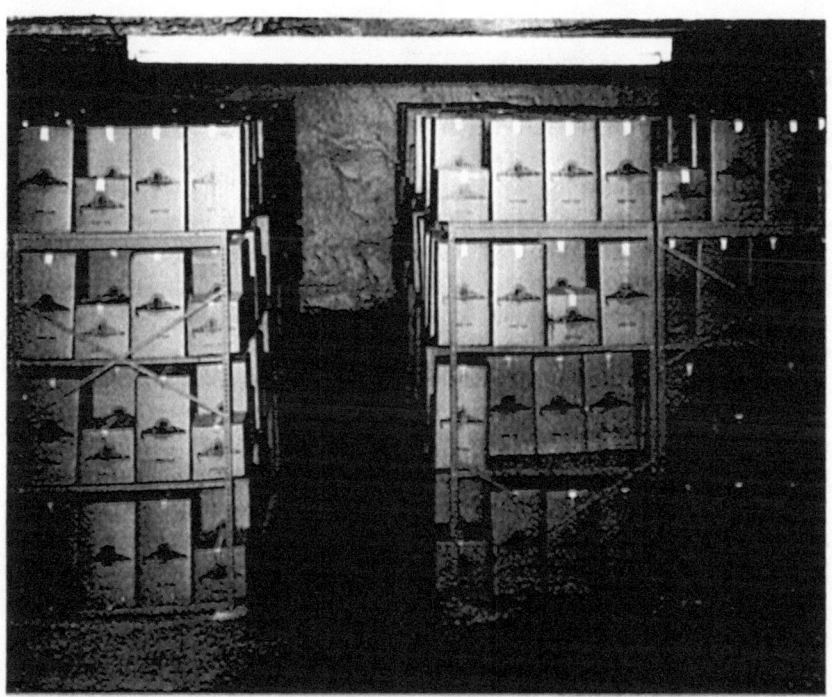

M-G-M's safety elements in storage at Underground Vaults & Storage, Inc., located in a Kansas salt mine.

The creation of the Association of Moving Image Archivists is significant in that it proves there are a whole host of new faces, new archivists, who have or wish to have responsibility for at least a part of the moving image archival action. They face the problems of their predecessors. Public funding is inadequate, and private funding from sources such as the David and Lucile Packard Foundation is minuscule in comparison to the need. What the United States needs is private funding on the same level as that provided in the United Kingdom to the (British) National Film Archive by J. Paul Getty. The manifold problems of selection, retention, conservation, and preservation are insoluble. Never will enough money, staff time or technological facilities be available, and future archivists must accept the inevitability that the sheer quantity of films in need of perservation will override the requirement that moving images must be preserved in their original format to the highest standard of quality.

The biggest problem new archivists must face is only now becoming evident, and that is the discovery that safety film, just like nitrate, is subject to deterioration. For a number of years, archivists have been noticing the pungent odor of acetic acid emanating from some safety films, evidence of the film stock's deterioration. Because of the smell, the phenomenon has come to be known as the vinegar syndrome.

The deterioration of cellulose triacetate (the technical term for safety film) was first noted by Eastman Kodak in the 1950s with regard to Indian governmental film which had been stored in a hot, humid climate. Eastman Kodak began laboratory studies on the problem in the 1960s, and in 1991 revealed that safety film deterioration "derives from the same chemical mechanism (hydrolysis) and the same triggering factors in the environment (heat and humidity) that nitrate decomposition does." Without the hoopla and publicity surrounding nitrate film decomposition, it transpires that safety film has also been decomposing with the same finality.

In addition to the Eastman Kodak testing, the Belgium-based Afga Company conducted a scientific study in 1987. Two years later, scientists at England's Manchester Polytechnic undertook a second study, financed by the National Film Archive and the Eastman Kodak Company. This confirmed the earlier findings on the potential deterioration of cellulose triacetate film, linking it to improper storage and to the metal cans in which the film is housed, and which, they noted, act as a powerful catalyst.

As a result of these studies, it seems likely that safety film may have a life of 50 years or less. Further, archivists must now consider the need to store their films not in cheap and easily obtainable metal cans but in glass (which is chemically inert), plastic or acid-free paperboard containers. The regular checking of safety film is now as important as the continual watch over nitrate film holdings, because, just like nitrate film, once a piece of safety film shows evidence of deterioration, such deterioration can spread to other films in the same storage area. As this book is written, archivists are working with Eastman Kodak to determine if polyester film, used for projection prints but not preprint materials, can be manufactured by the company as a successor (at least for archival use) to cellulose triacetate.

Perhaps the most extraordinary result of these studies is that nitrate film may have a longer life than safety. Archivists have slowly come to realize that it is as important to store nitrate under ideal conditions (low temperature and low humidity) as it is to copy it to safety. Of course the tragedy is that many archives, as a matter of routine, junked their nitrate holdings once they had been transferred to safety.*

While it is unlikely that any major "lost" film will be discovered at this

*Much of the information on the vinegar syndrome is taken from a draft report by William T. Murphy, "The Vinegar Syndrome: An Archival Response to the Deterioration of Cellulose Triacetate Motion Picture Film," presented at the Film and Television Archives Advisory Committee Annual Conference, Oregon Historical Society, Portland, Oregon, November 1, 1990, and from "Brief Summary Report of Research, Storage Conditions and Deterioration in Acetate and Nitrate Film, to the Film Foundation Archival Council," the Image Permanence Institute, Rochester, N.Y., February 1, 1991.

late date, important features are still being recovered and preserved. For example, in England, Jessie Matthews' 1938 starring vehicle, *Climbing High*, which also features Michael Redgrave and Alastair Sim, and was directed by Carol Reed, was considered a "lost" film until 1990, when material on the feature was discovered in the vaults of Pinewood Studios. The "find" resulted in a half-page feature article in the September 23, 1990, edition of *The Observer*, proof that any film rediscovery is still considered newsworthy.

The Ptolemaic kings of Egypt—in the second and third centuries before Christ—had an ambition to build a library which would house all the books ever written. That Library of Alexandria is considered one of the wonders of the ancient world, but its disappearance and the fate of its books have led some scholars to question its very existence.

Certainly future scholars will have no doubt as to the reality of American film archives and American film preservation in the 20th century, but they may well question the paucity of work, the failings of the archivists, for whatever reasons, to preserve the bulk of this country's film heritage. Sadly, archivists cannot emulate the Ptolemaic kings and try to preserve everything. They must of necessity be highly selective. Like Iris Barry in the 1930s, they will need to be influenced by what is considered art and what has social significance as much as by what is commercially important. They cannot preserve everything—they must have strong, valid opinions about film. As the dean of American film historians, Lewis Jacobs, points out, "You can't do what [Henri] Langlois did in Paris. He took everything—anything at all, rubbish, cigarette stubs. I would only take what I think are the top films. Other people may not like those films, but I would be very selective. And I may be very wrong, because, after all, it's an entertainment industry, not an industry for art."*

The fate of the holdings of America's archives rests as much in future technologies and future fund-raising efforts as it does in the activities of past and present archivists. Like the Library of Alexandria, the American film archives may well be curating collections of films whose ultimate survival still remains in doubt.

A list of the films in the Paramount gift listed by category.

Category I		
Affairs of Anatol *(1921)*	Bluff *(1924)*	Conrad in Quest of His
American Consul *(1917)*	The Breaking Point *(1924)*	Youth *(1920)*
Bedroom Window *(1924)*	Broadway Bill *(1934)*	Crooked Streets *(1920)*
Behind Masks *(1921, in-*	The Captive *(1915)*	The Cumberland Romance
complete)	The Carnation Kid *(1929)*	*(1927)*
Black Birds *(1915, incom-*	The Case of Becky *(1917)*	Divorce Made Easy *(1929)*
plete)	Castle for Two *(1917)*	Dr. Jekyll and Mr. Hyde
The Blue Angel *(1929,*	Changing Husbands *(1924)*	*(1933)*
English version)	Circus Man *(1914)*	Each Pearl a Tear *(1916)*
	Code of the Sea *(1924)*	The Enemy Sex *(1924)*

Interview with the author, January 27, 1991.

Eve's Secret *(1925)*
Excuse My Dust *(1920)*
A Farewell to Arms *(1932)*
Forbidden Fruit *(1921)*
Forbidden Paths *(1917)*
A Gentleman of Leisure
  (1915)
A Gentleman of Paris *(1927)*
The Girl at Home *(1917)*
The Golden Fetter *(1917)*
Hawthorne of the U.S.A.
  (1919)
Honeymoon Lane *(1931)*
The House That Shadows
  Built *(1931)*
Hula *(1927)*
Jack Straw *(1920)*
The Letter *(1929)*
Lord Jim *(1925)*
The Lost Romance *(1921)*
Mama Loves Papa *(1933)*
Men Are Like That *(1929)*
Midsummer Madness *(1920)*
Mrs. Temple's Telegram
  (1920)
Morals *(1922)*
North of '36 *(1924)*

One Sunday Afternoon
  (1933)
Paramount on Parade
  Around the World *(1938)*
Paramount Silver Jubilee
  (1937)
Public Opinion *(1916)*
Queen High *(1930)*
The Rainbow Man *(1929)*
Redskin *(1929)*
The Round Up *(1920)*
Running Wild *(1927)*
The Secret Game *(1917)*
Secret Sin *(1915)*
The Shopworn Angel *(1928,
  incomplete)*
The Showdown *(1928)*
Sick-a-Bed *(1920)*
The Silent Enemy *(1930)*
The Soul of France *(1931)*
The Soul of Youth *(1920)*
Swing High, Swing Low
  (1937)
Tennessee's Partner *(1916)*
The Victoria Cross *(1916)*
The Whispering Chorus
  (1918)

Wings Over Ethiopia *(1935)*
Womanhandled *(1925)*
You Never Can Tell *(1920)*
You'd Be Surprised *(1926)*
Category II
Are You a Mason *(1934)*
Aren't We All *(1932)*
Carnet de Bal *(1937)*
Cave Man *(1926)*
The Cheat *(1915)*
The City That Stopped
  Hitler *(1943)*
Der Graf du Luxembourg
  (1915)
Grass *(1925)*
His Double Life *(1933)*
Holiday for Henrietta *(1915)*
Make Me a Star *(1932)*
Service for Ladies *(1932)*
The Spoilers *(1929)*
Tabu *(1931)*
Wolf Song *(1929)*
Category III
The Mad Parade *(1931)*
Little Orphan Annie *(1938)*
White Thunder *(1930)*

APPENDIX 1
MEMBERS OF FIAF

The Fédération Internationale des Archives du Film/The International Federation of Film Archives (FIAF) has its headquarters at rue Franz Merjay 190, 1180 Brussels, Belgium. Those archives whose names are preceded by an asterisk (*) are observer members; all others are full members of FIAF.

Albania

Arkivi Shteteror i Filmit I.R.P.S. Te
  Shqiperise
Rruga Aleksander Moisiu 76
Tirana

Algeria

*Cinémathèque Algérienne
Centre Algérien de la Cinématographie
rue Larbi Ben-M'Hidi 49
1600 Algiers

Angola

*Cinemateca Nacional de Angola
Caixa Postal 3512/Largo Luther King 4
Luanda

Argentina

Fundación Cinemateca Argentina
Corrientes 2092 piso 3°
1045 Buenos Aires

Australia

National Film and Sound Archive
GPO Box 2002/McCoy Circuit
Acton
Canberra, A.C.T. 2601

*The State Film Archives of Western
  Australia
Alexander Library Building
Perth Cultural Centre
Perth, W.A. 6000

Austria

Österreichisches Filmarchiv
Rauhensteingasse 5
1010 Vienna

Österreichisches Filmmuseum
Augustinerstrasse 1
A-1010 Vienna

Bangladesh

*Bangladesh Film Archive
Ministry of Information
Block No. 3, Gano Bhaban
Sher-E-Bangla Nagar
Dhaka-7

Belgium

Cinémathèque Royale/Koninklijk
  Filmarchief
rue Ravenstein 23
1000 Brussels

Bolivia

*Cinemateca Boliviana
Casilla 20271/Calle Pichincha Esq.
 Indaburo
La Paz

Brazil

Cinemateca Brasileira
Caixa Postal 12.900/Rua Volkswagen
04092 São Paulo

Cinemateca do Museu de Arte
 Moderna
Caixa Postal 44/Avenida Beira Mar
20000 Rio de Janeiro, R.J.

Bulgaria

Bulgarska Nacionalna Filmoteka
ul. Gourko 36
1000 Sofia

Canada

La Cinémathèque Québécoise
Boulevard de Maisonneuve est 335
Montréal, H2X 1K1

Moving Image and Sound Archives
 Division
National Archives of Canada
395 Wellington Street
Ottawa, K1A 0N3

China

Zhongguo Dianying Ziliaoguan
Xin Wai Dajie 25B
Beijing

Colombia

*Cinemateca Distrital
Carrera 7 No. 22-79
Bogotá, D.E.

Cuba

Cinemateca de Cuba
Calle 23, No. 1155
Vedado, Havana 4

Czechoslovakia

Československý Filmový Ústav —
 Filmový Archiv
Národni 40
11000 Prague 1

Denmark

Det Danske Filmmuseum
Store Sóndervoldstraede
1419 Copenhagen K

Ecuador

*Cinemateca Nacional del Ecuador
Casa de la Cultura Ecuatoriana
Casilla 3520/Av. 6 de Diciembre 794 y
 Tarqui
Quito

Egypt

*Al-Archive Al-Kawmy Lil-Film
Egyptian Film Center
City of Arts
Pyramids Avenue
Guiza

Finland

Suomen Elokuva-Arkisto
PL 177/Pursimiehenkatu 29-31
00151 Helsinki

France

Cinémathèque de Toulouse
rue Roquelaine 3
31000 Toulouse

La Cinémathèque Française
rue du Colisée 29
F-75008 Paris

*Cinémathèque Universitaire
U.E.R. d'Art et d'Archéologie
rue Michelet 3
F-75006 Paris

*Musée du Cinéma de Lyon
rue Jean Jaurès 69
691000 Villeurbanne

Service des Archives du Film du. Centre
National de la Cinématographie
78390 Bois d'Arcy

Germany

Bundesarchiv-Filmarchiv
Postfach 320/Potsdamer St. 1
D-5400 Koblenz

Deutsches Institut für Filmkunde
Schaumainkai 41
D-6000 Frankfurt/M 70

Deutsches Institut für
Filmkunde/Filmarchiv
Langenbeckstr. 9
D-6200 Wiesbaden

*Filmmuseum/Münchner
Stadtmuseum
St. Jakobs-Platz 1
D-8000 Munich 2

Staatliches Filmarchiv [der DDR]
Hausvogteiplatz 3/4
1080 Berlin

Stiftung Deutsche Kinemathek
Pommernallee 1
1000 Berlin 19

Greece

Tainiothiki Tis Ellados
Canari Street 1
10671 Athens

Hungary

Magyar Filmintezet/Filmarchívum
P.Box 114 PF 25/Budakeszi ut 51/b
H-1021 Budapest

Iceland

*Kvikmyndasafn Islands
P.O. Box 320/Laugavegur 24
101 Reykjavik

India

National Film Archive of India
Law College Road
Poona 411 004

Indonesia

*Sinematek Indonesia
Pusat Perfilman "H. Usmar Ismail"
Jl. Haji Rangkayo Rasuna Said
12950 Jakarta

Iran

*Film-Khane-ye Melli-e Iran
P.O. Box 5158
Ministry o Ershad-e Eslami
11365 Tehran

Israel

Archion Israeli Leseratim/Jerusalem
Cinematheque
P.O. Box 8561/Hebron Road
91083 Jerusalem

Italy

Cineteca Italiana
Villa Comunale
Via Palestro 16
1-20121 Milan

Cineteca Nazionale
Via Tuscolana 1524
00173 Rome

Museo Nazionale del Cinema
Palazzo Chiablese
Piazza San Giovanni 2
10 122 Turin

Korea [North]

Choson Minjujui Inmingonghwaguk
Kugga Yonghwa Munhongo
15 Sochangdong
Central District
Pyongyang

Korea [South]

Korean Film Archive
K.P.O. Box 605/34-5, 3-ka
Namsan-Dong-Ku
Seoul 100

Luxembourg

*Cinémathèque Municipale de
Luxembourg

Place Guillaume 28
1648 Luxembourg

Mexico

Cineteca Nacional
Av. México-Coyoacán 389
03330 Mexico City D.F.

Filmoteca de la Unam
Apartado Postal 45-002/San Ildefonso
 43
06020 Mexico City D.F.

Netherlands

Nederlands Filmmuseum
Vondelpark 3
1071 AA Amsterdam

New Zealand

The New Zealand Film Archive
P.O. Box 9544/82 Tory Street
Wellington

Nicaragua

*Cinemateca de Nicaragua
Apartado Postal 4642
Managua

Norway

Norsk Filminstitutt
Postboks 482 Sentrum/Grav Wedels
 plass 1-5
0105 Oslo 1

Philippines

*Film Archives of the Philippines
Manila Film Center, CCP Complex
P.O. Box 1394
Manila 2801

Poland

Filmoteka Polska
ul. Pulawska 61
00975 Warsaw

Portugal

Cinemateca Portuguesa

Rua Barata Salgueiro 29
1200 Lisbon

Russia [former U.S.S.R.]

Gosfilmofond
Belye Stolby
Moscow 142050

Spain

Filmoteca Española
Carretera Dehesa de la Villa
28040 Madrid

Sweden

Cinemateket—Svenska Filminstitutet
PB 27126/Filmhuset, Borgvägen 1-5
S-102 52 Stockholm

Switzerland

Cinémathèque Suisse
Case postale 2512/Allée Ernest
 Ansermet 3
1003 Lausanne

Turkey

Sinema-TV Enstitü Sü
Kislaönü—Besiktas
Istanbul

United Kingdom

Imperial War Museum
Department of Film
Lambeth Road
London SE1 6HZ

National Film Archive
21 Stephen Street
London W1P 1PL

United States of America

*Human Studies Film Archives
National Museum of Natural History
Room E307
Smithsonian Institution
Washington, DC 20560

International Museum of Photography
 at George Eastman House

900 East Avenue
Rochester, NY 14607

Motion Picture, Broadcasting and
  Recorded Sound Division
Library of Congress
Washington, DC 20540

The Museum of Modern Art
Department of Film
11 West 53rd Street
New York, NY 10019

National Center for Film and Video
  Preservation at the American Film
  Institute
John F. Kennedy Center for the Per-
  forming Arts
Washington, DC 20566

UCLA Film and Television Archive
University of California
Melnitz Hall
405 Hilgard Avenue
Los Angeles, CA 90024

*Wisconsin Center for Film and
  Theater Research Film Archive
816 State Street
Madison WI 53706

Uruguay

*Archivo Nacional de la Imagen
Sarandi 430
Montevideo

Cinemateca Uruguaya
Casilla 1170/Lorenzo Carnelli 1311
Montevideo

Vatican City

*Filmoteca Vaticana
00120 Città del Vaticano

Venezuela

*Cinemateca Nacional de Venezuela
Apartado Postal 17045/Museo de Cien-
  cias Naturales
Plaza Morelos
Caracas 1015-A

Vietnam

*Vien Tu Lieu Phim Viet Nam
Hoang Hoa Tham 62
Hanoi

Yugoslavia

Jugoslovenska Kinoteka
Knez Mihajlova 19/1
11000 Belgrade

APPENDIX 2
MAJOR U.S. NONCOMMERCIAL FILM ARCHIVES

Academy of Motion Picture Arts and
  Sciences
8949 Wilshire Boulevard
Beverly Hills CA 90211
(310) 247-3000

AFL-CIO Film and Photo Archives
George Meany Center for Labor Studies
1000 New Hampshire Avenue
Silver Springs MD 20903

American Archives of the Factual Film
Iowa State University
Ames IA 50011
(515) 294-6672

American Library of Radio and
  Television
Thousand Oaks Library
1401 East Janss Road
Thousand Oaks CA 91362
(805) 497-6282

American Museum of Natural History
Film Archives
Central Park West and 79th Street
New York NY 10024
(212) 769-5419

Anthology Film Archives
32-34 Second Avenue
New York NY 10003
(212) 505-5181

Arizona State University
2231 East Del Rio Drive
Tempe AZ 85282
(602) 965-6375

Bishop Museum
1525 Bernice Street
Honolulu HI 96817
(808) 848-4182

Boston University Film Archive
College of Communication
640 Commonwealth Avenue
Boston MA 02215
(617) 353-3498

Central New England Film Archives
305 Whitney Street
Leominster MA 01453

Circus World Museum, Library and
  Research Center
426 Water Street
Baraboo WI 53913
(608) 356-8341

Folger Shakespeare Library
201 East Capitol Street SE
Washington DC 20003
(202) 544-4600

Harvard University Film Archive
Carpenter Center for the Visual Arts

24 Quincy Street
Quincy MA 02138
(617) 495-4700

Hoover Institution on War, Revolution
and Peace
Stanford University
Stanford CA 94305-6010
(415) 723-3563

Indiana University
Audio-Visual Center
Bloomington IN 47405-5901
(812) 335-2103

Indiana University
Black Film Center
Department of Afro-American Studies
Bloomington IN 47405
(812) 855-2684

International Museum of Photography
at George Eastman House
900 East Avenue
Rochester NY 14607
(716) 271-3361

Kansas City Jazz Film Archives
Grant Hall
4420 Warwick
Kansas City MO 64111
(816) 363-1110

Kansas City Museum
Film Department
3218 Gladstone Boulevard
Kansas City MO 64123
(816) 483-8300

Library of Congress
Motion Picture, Broadcasting and
Recorded Sound Division
Washington DC 20540
(202) 707-5840

Louis Wolfson II Media Center
Miami-Dade Public Library
101 West Flagler Street
Miami FL 33130
(305) 375-4527

Martin and Osa Johnson Safari
Museum
16 South Grant
Chanute KS 66720
(316) 431-2730

Minnesota Historical Society
690 Cedar Street
St. Paul MN 55101
(612) 296-1275

Mississippi Department of Archives and
History
P.O. Box 571
Jackson MS 39205-0571
(601) 359-6874

Museum of Broadcast Communications
800 South Wells
Chicago IL 60607-4529
(312) 987-1500

Museum of Modern Art
Film Department
11 West 53rd Street
New York NY 10019
(212) 708-9602

Museum of Radio & Television
25 West 52nd Street
New York NY 10022
(212) 752-4690

Mystic Seaport Museum
P.O. Box 6000
Mystic CT 06355-0990
(203) 572-0711

National Aeronautics and Space Administration (NASA)
Film/Video Distribution Library
1020 Bay Area Boulevard, Suite 102
Houston TX 77058
(713) 486-9606

National Archives and Records
Administration
Motion Picture, Sound and Video
7th and Pennsylvania Avenue NW
Washington DC 20408
(202) 786-0041

National Cable TV Center and
    Museum
Pennsylvania State University
211 Mitchell Building
University Park PA 16802
(814) 865-1874

National Center for Jewish Film
Brandeis University
Waltham MA 02254
(617) 899-7044

National Jewish Archive of
    Broadcasting
The Jewish Museum
1109 Fifth Avenue
New York NY 10128
(212) 860-1886

National Museum of Communications
University of North Texas
Box 13108
Denton TX 76203
(817) 565-2537

Nebraska State Historical Society
1500 R Street
Lincoln NE 68501
(402) 471-2926

New Mexico State Records Center &
    Archives
Historical Film Collection
404 Montezuma
Santa Fe NM 87503
(505) 827-8860

New York Public Library at Lincoln
    Center
111 Amsterdam Avenue
New York NY 10023
(212) 870-1659 (Dance)
(212) 870-1641 (Theatre)

Northeast Historic Film
Route 175
Blue Hill Falls ME 04615
(207) 374-2109

Oklahoma Historic Film Repository
University of Science and Arts

Chickasha OK 73018
(405) 224-3140

Oregon Historical Society
Film Archives
1230 SW Park Avenue
Portland OR 97205
(503) 222-1741

Pacific Film Archive
University Art Museum
2625 Durant Avenue
Berkeley CA 94720
(415) 642-1412

Penn State University
Fred Waring's America
220 Special Services Building
University Park PA 16802
(814) 863-2911

Purdue University
Public Affairs Video Archives
West Lafayette IN 47907
(317) 494-9630

Smithsonian Institution
Human Studies Film Archives
Washington DC 20560
(202) 357-3349

Smithsonian Institution
National Air and Space Museum Film
    Archives
Washington DC 20560
(202) 357-4721

Southern California Library for Social
    Studies and Research
6120 South Vermont Avenue
Los Angeles CA 90044
(213) 759-6063

Southwest Film/Video Archives
Southern Methodist University
P.O. Box 4194
Dallas TX 75275
(214) 373-3665

UCLA Film and Television Archive
1015 North Cahuenga Boulevard

Hollywood CA 90038
(213) 462-4921

University of Alaska
Fairbanks AK 99775-1120
(907) 474-7296

University of Arizona
Film Collection
1325 East Speedway Boulevard
Tucson AZ 85721
(602) 621-3282

University of Kentucky
Audiovisual Archives
111 King Library North
Lexington KY 40506-0039
(606) 257-8634

University of North Carolina at Chapel
  Hill
Wilson Library
Chapel Hill NC 27599-3908
(919) 962-0114

University of South Carolina
Newsfilm Library
Columbia SC 29208
(803) 777-6841

University of Texas
Harry Ransom Humanities Research
  Center
P.O. Drawer 7219
Austin TX 78713-7219
(512) 471-9124

Vanderbilt University
Television News Archive
Nashville TN 37240-0007
(615) 322-2927

Vermont Historical Society
109 State Street
Montpelier VT 05602
(802) 828-2291

WGBH Educational Foundation
125 Western Avenue
Boston MA 02134
(617) 492-2777

West Virginia Department of Culture
  and History
The Cultural Center
Capitol Complex
Charleston WV 25305
(304) 348-0230

Will Rogers Memorial
P.O. Box 157
Claremore OK 74018
(918) 341-0719

Wisconsin Center for Film and Theater
  Research
Film Archive
816 State Street
Madison WI 53706
(608) 262-0585

WSB Television News Film Archive
University of Georgia
South PJ Auditorium
Athens GA 30602
(404) 542-1582

Yale Film Study Center
Box 174, Yale Station
New Haven CT 06520
(203) 432-0148

APPENDIX 3
MAJOR NON-U.S.
COMMERCIAL FILM
AND VIDEO LIBRARIES

Australian Broadcasting Corporation
Box 4444
Crows Nest
New South Wales 2065
Australia
(02) 950-3269

BBC Enterprises Limited
Library Sales
Windmill Road
Brentford, Middlesex TW8 9NF
United Kingdom
(081) 568-7986

Benelux Press b.v.
Postbox 269
2270 AG Voorburg
Netherlands
(070) 870470

Boulton Hawker Films Limited
Hadleigh
Ipswich, Suffolk IP7 5BG
United Kingdom
(0473) 822-235

British Movietone News
North Orbital Road
Uxbridge, Middlesex UB9 5HQ
United Kingdom
(0895) 833071

Camera g & p
Via Parini 9
20121 Milan, Italy
(2) 659-8184

CBC Enterprises
P.O. Box 6000
Station A
Montreal, Quebec H3C 3A8
Canada
(514) 597-7824

Central Independent Television PLC
Central House
Broad Street
Birmingham B1 2JP
United Kingdom
(021) 643-9898

Danmarks Radio
TV-Byen
2860 Søborg
Copenhagen, Denmark
(1) 671-233

East Anglia Film Archive
University of East Anglia
Norwich, Norfolk
United Kingdom
(0603) 56161

Editmedia TV
C/rosellón 205
08008 Barcelona, Spain
(3) 218-9784

Education & Television Films Limited
247a Upper Street
London N1 1RU
United Kingdom
(071) 226-2298

Fame (Film Archive Management and
   Entertainment)
Imperial Studios
Maxwell Road
Borehamwood, Herts WD6 1WE
United Kingdom
(081) 207-6446

Film World Research
4/14 Dickson Avenue
Artarmon, New South Wales 2064
Australia
(02) 438-1888

Filmfinders Limited
61 The Hall
Blackheath
London SE3
United Kingdom
(081) 852-4156

Granada Television Film Library
Manchester M60 9EA
United Kingdom
(061) 832-7211

Huntley Archives Limited
22 Islington Green
London N1 8DU
United Kingdom
(071) 226-9260

Independent Television News Limited
Library Sales
ITN House
48 Wells Street
London W1P 4DE
United Kingdom
(071) 637-2424

Index Stock Shots
12 Charlotte Mews
London W1P 1LN
United Kingdom
(071) 637-8741

Jack Chisholm Film Productions Ltd.
229 Niagara Street
Toronto, Ontario M6J 2L5
Canada
(416) 366-4933

Media Management ApS
Badstrestrassde 13
DK-1006 Copenhagen K, Denmark
(33) 91 02 11

Moving Image Research and Library
   Services Limited
First Floor
21-25 Goldhawk Road
London W12 8QQ
United Kingdom
(081) 740-4606

National Film Board of Canada
P.O. Box 6100, Station A
Montreal, Quebec H3C 3H5
Canada
(514) 333-4500

New Zealand National Film Unit
P.O. Box 46-002
Lower Hutt
New Zealand
(04) 672 059

Oxford Scientific Films Limited
Lower Road
Long Hanborough
Oxford OX7 2LD
United Kingdom
(0993) 881 881

Piet's Post Productions
Plantage Middenlaan 6
1018 DD Amsterdam
Netherlands
(020) 275 711

Radio Telefis Eireann
Donnybrook

Dublin 4, Eire
(01) 693 111

Survival Anglia Limited
Brook House
113 Park Lane
London W1Y 4DY
United Kingdom
(071) 321-0101

Swedish Television
Library Sales
S105 10 Stockholm, Sweden
(081) 784-7440

Thames Television
306 Euston Road
London NW1 3BB
United Kingdom
(071) 387-9494

TV House
Sturegatan 58
S114 36 Stockholm, Sweden
(8) 660-2700

Visnews
Cumberland Avenue
London NW10 7EH
United Kingdom
(01) 965-7733

World Backgrounds Imperial
    Studios
Maxwell Road
Borehamwood, Herts WD6 1WE
United Kingdom
(081) 207-4747

Worldwide Television News Corp.
31-36 Foley Street
London W1P 7LB
United Kingdom
(071) 323-3255

Yorkshire Television Film Library
The Television Centre
Leeds LS3 1JS
United Kingdom
(0532) 38283

APPENDIX 4
MAJOR U.S. COMMERCIAL
AND STOCK FOOTAGE
LIBRARIES

The following listing includes only the prominent film libraries. For a complete listing of all libraries, with descriptions as to holdings and policies, readers are referred to *Footage 89*, edited by Richard Prelinger and Celeste R. Hoffnar (published by Prelinger Associates, Inc., 430 West 14th Street, Room 403, New York NY 10014). Those libraries specializing in black-and-white archival footage are designated by an asterisk (*); all other libraries primarily hold color footage or a mixture of both.

Action Sports Adventure
330 West 42nd Street
New York NY 10036
(212) 594-6834

*John E. Allen, Inc.
116 North Avenue
Park Ridge NJ 07656
(201) 391-3299

*Archive Film Productions, Inc.
530 West 25th Street
New York NY 10001
(212) 620-3955

Britannica Films & Video
425 North Michigan Avenue
Chicago IL 60611
(800) 554-9862

*Budget Films, Inc.
4590 Santa Monica Boulevard

Los Angeles CA 90029
(213) 660-0187

CBS News Archives
524 West 57th Street
New York NY 10019
(212) 975-2875

CBS/MTM Studios Library
4024 Radford Avenue
Studio City CA 91604
(818) 760-5422

Cameo Film Library
10620 Burbank Boulevard
North Hollywood CA 91601
(818) 980-8700

Stephen J. Cannell Film Library
7083 Hollywood Boulevard
Hollywood CA 90028
(213) 856-7444

*Chertock Associates, Inc.
185 West End Avenue
New York NY 10023
(212) 874-0797

The Cinema Guild
1697 Broadway, Room 802
New York NY 10019
(212) 246-5522

Cinenet
2235 First Street, Suite 111
Simi Valley CA 93065
(805) 527-0093

Dick Clark Media Archives
3003 West Olive Avenue
Burbank CA 91510
(818) 841-3003

Coe Film Associates, Inc.
65 East 96th Street
New York NY 10128
(212) 831-5355

Columbia Pictures Television Film
    Library
4729 Alla Road
Marina del Rey CA 90291
(213) 827-5937

Bill Delaney Films
483 Mariposa Drive
Ventura CA 93001
(805) 653-2699

Larry Dorn and Associates
5550 Wilshire Boulevard, Suite 303
Los Angeles CA 90036
(213) 935-6266

Dreamlight Images, Inc.
932 North La Brea Avenue
Hollywood CA 90038
(213) 850-1996

*Em Gee Film Library
6924 Canby Avenue, Suite 103
Reseda CA 91335
(818) 981-5506

Energy Productions, Inc.
12700 Ventura Boulevard
Studio City CA 91604
(818) 508-1444

*Festival Films
2841 Irving Avenue South
Minneapolis MN 55408
(612) 870-4744

The Film Bank
3306 West Burbank Boulevard
Burbank CA 91505
(818) 841-9176

Film Search
111 Fifth Avenue
New York NY 10003
(212) 529-6700

Film/Video Stock Shots, Inc.
3151 Cahuenga Boulevard West
Los Angeles CA 90068
(213) 850-1900

Films Incorporated
5547 North Ravenswood Avenue
Chicago IL 60640
(800) 323-4222

*Fish Films, Inc.
4548 Van Noord Avenue
Studio City CA 91604
(818) 905-1071

Sherman Grinberg Film Libraries, Inc.
1040 North McCadden Place
Hollywood CA 90038
(213) 464-7491
    and
630 Ninth Avenue
New York NY 10036
(212) 765-5170

Halcyon Days Productions
12 West End Avenue, 5th Floor
New York NY 10023
(212) 397-8785

H.B. Halicki Productions
17902 South Vermont Avenue

Gardenia CA 90247
(213) 770-1744

*Imageways
412 West 48th Street
New York NY 10036
(212) 265-1287

Ivy Films, Inc.
165 West 46th Street, Suite 414
New York NY 10036
(212) 382-0111

Jalbert Productions, Inc.
775 Park Avenue
Huntington NY 11743
(516) 351-5878

Janus Films, Inc.
888 Seventh Avenue, 4th Floor
New York NY 10106
(212) 753-7100

Kesser Stock Library
21 S.W. 15 Road
Miami FL 33129
(305) 358-7900

*Killiam Shows, Inc.
6 East 39th Street
New York NY 10016
(212) 679-8230

*Kino International
333 West 39th Street, Suite 503
New York NY 10018
(212) 629-6880

Lorimar Film Library
4000 Warner Boulevard
Burbank CA 91522
(818) 954-5174

MacGillivray Freeman Films, Inc.
Box 205
South Laguna CA 92677
(714) 494-1055

Merkel Films, Inc.
Box 722
Carpinteria CA 93013
(805) 648-6448

*Movietone News, Inc.
460 West 54th Street
New York NY 10019
(212) 408-8450

NBC News Video Archive
30 Rockefeller Plaza
New York NY 10112
(212) 664-3797

NFL Films, Inc.
330 Fellowship Road
Mt. Laurel NJ 08054
(609) 778-1600

Paramount Pictures Film Library
5555 Melrose Avenue
Los Angeles CA 90038
(213) 468-5510

Kit Parker Films
1245 Tenth Street
Monterey CA 93940
(408) 649-5573

Petrified Films, Inc.
430 West 14th Street, Room 404
New York NY 10014
(212) 242-5461

Picture Start, Inc.
221 East Cullerton, 6th Floor
Chicago IL 60616
(312) 326-6233

Producers Library Service
1051 N. Cole Avenue
Hollywood CA 90038
(213) 465-0572

Pyramid Film & Video
Box 1048
Santa Monica CA 90406
(213) 828-7577

Ron Sawade Cinematography
3724 Berry Drive
Studio City CA 91604
(818) 769-1737

*Shields Archival
6671 Sunset Boulevard

Hollywood CA 90028
(213) 962-1899

The Source Stock Footage Library, Inc.
1709 South 29 Place
Tucson AZ 85710
(602) 298-4810

Rick Spalla/Hollywood Newsreel Syn-
    dicate, Inc.
1622 North Gower Street
Hollywood CA 90028
(213) 469-7307
    and
301 West 45th Street
New York NY 10036
(212) 765-4646

The Stock House
6922 Hollywood Boulevard, Suite 621
Hollywood CA 90028
(213) 461-0061

*Streamline Film Archives
109 East 29th Street
New York NY 10016
(212) 696-2616

Tropical Visions Video, Inc.
62 Halaulani Place
Hilo HI 69720
(808) 935-5557

*UCLA Film and Television Archive
Commercial Services Division

1015 North Cahuenga Boulevard
Hollywood CA 90038
(213) 466-8559

Universal Pictures Film Library
100 Universal City Plaza
Universal City CA 91608
(818) 777-1695

Video Tape Library Ltd.
1509 North Crescent Heights, Suite 2
Los Angeles CA 90046
(213) 656-4330

WTN/Worldwide Television News
    Corporation
1995 Broadway
New York NY 10023
(213) 362-4440

Warner Bros. Film Library
4000 Warner Boulevard
Burbank CA 91522
(818) 954-5018

White Production Archives, Inc.
    (WPA)
604 Davis Street
Evanston IL 60201
(708) 328-2221

Wildlife Film Library
25191 Rivendell
El Toro CA 92630
(714) 830-7845

APPENDIX 5
SUBJECT GUIDE TO U.S. FILMS
PRESERVED IN U.S. ARCHIVES

This list provides a basic guideline, by company, personality or series, to which films are preserved by which archives. It is not intended to imply that an archives has preserved all the films of that subject, or that another archives does not have some related titles. Of course, the fact that an archives has preserved certain films does not mean that those films are available for viewing. A listing of the holdings of the Museum of Modern Art has been published: *The Film Catalog: A List of Holdings in the Museum of Modern Art*, edited by Jon Gartenberg (Boston: G.K. Hall, 1985). Also, the American Film Institute has published a listing of its collection at the Library of Congress: *Catalog of Holdings: The American Film Institute Collection and the United Artists Collection at the Library of Congress* (Washington, DC: American Film Institute, 1978). Both of these listings are out-of-date.

American Biograph shorts: The Museum of Modern Art
Fred Astaire–Ginger Rogers features: The Library of Congress
Black Films: The Library of Congress
Frank Capra productions: The Library of Congress
Lon Chaney features: International Museum of Photography at George Eastman
    House
Maurice Chevalier features: UCLA Film and Television Archive
Columbia features and short subjects: The Library of Congress
De Forest Phonofilms: The Library of Congress
Cecil B. DeMille features: International Museum of Photography at George
    Eastman House
Edison productions: The Museums of Modern Art
Douglas Fairbanks features: The Museum of Modern Art
Fox features and short subjects: The Musem of Modern Art
Greta Garbo features: International Museum of Photography at George Eastman
    House
D.W. Griffith features and short subjects: The Musem of Modern Art

William S. Hart features and short subjects: International Museum of Photography
    at George Eastman House
Hearst Metrotone News: UCLA Film and Television Archive
Thomas H. Ince features and short subjects: International Museum of Photography
    at George Eastman House
George Kleine features and short subjects: The Library of Congress (see *The George
    Kleine Collection of Early Motion Pictures in the Library of Congress*, compiled
    by Rita Horwitz and Harriet Harrison. Washington DC: Library of Congress,
    1980)
Harold Lloyd features: UCLA Film and Television Archive
Ernst Lubitsch sound features: UCLA Film and Television Archive
M-G-M features and short subjects: International Museum of Photography at
    George Eastman House
Rouben Mamoulian features: UCLA Film and Television Archive
The March of Time series: National Archives and Records Service
F.W. Murnau U.S. features: The Museum of Modern Art
George Pal cartoons: UCLA Film and Television Archive
Paramount silent features: The Library of Congress
Paramount pre–1948 sound features: The Library of Congress and UCLA Film and
    Television Archive
Popular Science series: UCLA Film and Television Archive
RKO features: The Library of Congress
Wallace Reid features: The Library of Congress (preservation of *The Golden Fetter*
    [1917], *Hawthorne of the U.S.A.* [1917], *Excuse My Dust* [1920], *Sick-a-Bed*
    [1920], *The Love Special* [1921], and *The Affairs of Anatol* [1921])
Republic features and short subjects: UCLA Film and Television Archive
David O. Selznick features: The Museum of Modern Art
William Desmond Taylor: The Library of Congress (preservation of *The Soul of
    Youth* [1920], *Beyond* [1921] and *Morals* [1921])
20th Century–Fox features and short subjects: The Museum of Modern Art and
    UCLA Film and Television Archive
Universal features and short subjects: The Library of Congress
Universal News: National Archives and Records Service
Vitaphone short subjects: The Library of Congress and UCLA Film and Television
    Archive
Warner Bros. pre–1948 sound features: The Library of Congress
Lois Weber features and short subjects: The Library of Congress

APPENDIX 6
RECOMMENDATION
FOR THE
SAFEGUARDING AND
PRESERVATION OF
MOVING IMAGES

Adopted by the General Conference of the United Nations Educational, Scientific and Cultural Organization (UNESCO) at its 21st session in Belgrade, Yugoslavia, on October 27, 1980.

Considering that moving images are an expression of the cultural identity of peoples, and because of their educational, cultural, artistic, scientific and historical value, form an integral part of a nation's cultural heritage, . . .

Considering that moving images also provide a fundamental means of recording the unfolding of events and, as such, constitute important and often unique testimonies, of a new dimension, to the history, way of life and culture of peoples and to the evolution of the universe,

Noting that moving images have an increasingly important role to play as a means of communication and mutual understanding among all the peoples of the world . . .

Noting furthermore that many elements of the moving image heritage have disappeared due to deterioration, accident or unwarranted disposal, which constitutes an irreversible impoverishment of that heritage,

Recognizing the results yielded by the efforts of specialized institutions to save moving images from the dangers to which they are exposed, . . .

Considering at the same time that the appropriate measures to ensure the safeguarding and preservation of moving images should be taken with due regard for freedom of opinion, expression and information, recognized as an essential part of human rights and fundamental freedoms inherent in the dignity of the human being, for the need to strengthen peace and international understanding and for the legitimate position of copyright holders and of all holders of other rights in moving images, . . .

The General Conference of the United Nations Educational, Scientific and Cultural Organization, meeting in Belgrade from 23 September to 28 October 1980, at its twenty-first session,

Adopts, this twenty-seventh day of October 1980, the present Recommendation.

The appropriate measures should be taken to ensure that the moving image heritage is afforded adequate physical protection from the depredations wrought by time and by the environment. Since poor storage conditions accelerate the deterioration process to which the material supports are continuously subject and may even lead to their total destruction, moving images should be preserved in officially recognized film and television archives and processed according to the highest archival standards. Furthermore, research should be specifically directed towards the development of high quality and lasting support-media for the proper safeguarding and preservation of moving images, . . .

Access should be made available as far as possible to the works and information sources represented by moving images which are acquired, safeguarded and preserved by public and private non-profit-making institutions. Their utilization should not prejudice either the legitimate rights or the interests of those involved in the making and exploitation thereof, in accordance with the provisions of the Universal Copyright Convention, the Berne Convention for the Protection of Literary and Artistic Works and the Convention for the Protection of Performers, Producers of Phonograms and Broadcasting Organizations, and national legislation, . . .

To ensure that moving images forming part of the cultural heritage of countries are systematically preserved, Member States are invited to take measures whereby officially recognized archives are able to acquire for safeguarding and preservation any part or all of their country's national production. Such measures may include, for example, voluntary arrangements with the holders of rights for the deposit of moving images, acquisition of moving images by purchase or donation or the institution of mandatory deposit systems through appropriate legislation or administrative measures, . . .

Foreign producers, and those responsible for the public distribution of moving images made abroad, should be encouraged, in accordance with the spirit of this Recommendation and without prejudice to the free movement of moving images across national borders, to deposit voluntarily in the officially recognized archives of the countries in which they are publicly distributed a copy of moving images of the highest archival quality, subject to all the rights there in, . . .

Member States are invited to associate their efforts in order to promote the safeguarding and preservation of moving images which form part of the cultural heritage of nations, . . .

Technical cooperation should be provided in particular to developing countries, in order to ensure or facilitate the adequate safeguarding and preservation of their moving image heritage.

Member States are invited to co-operate for the purpose of enabling any State to gain access to moving images that relate to its history or culture and of which it does not hold either pre-print material or projection copies. . .

APPENDIX 7
RESTORING
JOSEF VON STERNBERG'S
THE SAGA OF ANATAHAN

The following report was prepared by Film Technology Company, Inc., on its 1975-1976 restoration of Josef von Sternberg's *The Saga of Anatahan*. It is one of the most detailed and exhaustive documents available on an individual restoration project, and is reprinted here by kind permission of Ralph Sargent, president of Film Technology Company, Inc.

Background

Josef von Sternberg's *The Saga of Anatahan*, completed in early 1953, was first shown in Japan in July of 1953 and in the U.S. during the spring and fall of 1954. Though it had been well received in Europe, the film received poor to mixed reviews in the U.S. where critics objected to the film's slow pacing and to the lack of erotic and sensational elements which the basic story seemed to require.

In 1958, Sternberg decided to modify the film to increase its commercial potential, and so he wired his cameraman in Japan to shoot some new and more explicit sequences featuring the leading actress, Negishi. Sternberg selected several of these shots, printed them along with pieces of sound track duped from the 1953 version, and spliced these short sequences into the existing release prints of *Anatahan*. In each instance, when putting in the new nude shots, Sternberg removed the equivalent footage from the prints. He also cut out several brief sections to drop repetitious shots of ocean waves, and to eliminate certain lines of dialogue and narration which had provoked unwanted laughter from audiences. The picture and sound quality of the new scenes did not match the adjacent scenes in the release prints, so the overall effect was disturbingly uneven.

184

During the 1950s and 1960s, the film was variously titled *Anatahan, Ana-ta-han, The Saga of Anatahan, The Devil's Pitchfork, The Only Woman on Earth,* and *Fever Over Anatahan.* Each time the title was changed, a new main title was spliced into the prints.

In December of 1975, Film Technology Co. was put in charge of recon-structing *Anatahan.* The Company received the following materials for this purpose.

1. *Composite fine grain* (safety) of the original 1953 release version, from George Eastman House.

2. *Positive print* of the 1958 modified version, from Twyman Films.

3. *Original picture negative* (part nitrate, part safety), of the 1953 ver-sion. This and the remaining materials were from Mrs. von Sternberg.

4. *Original mixed sound track negative* (nitrate) of the 1953 version.

5. *Original music track negative* (nitrate).

6. *Original Japanese dialogue/sound effects track negative* (nitrate).

7. *Original picture negative of 1958 nude shots* (safety, nitrate).

8. *Various trims,* out-takes, pieces of negative and fine grain left over from Josef von Sternberg's 1958 revision of the film.

One important element missing was the original English narration sound track; we had neither a negative nor a positive print at our disposal.

The above materials were in the following condition:

1. *Composite fine grain* — safety stock, complete and in good condition. Picture quality was satisfactory for duping purposes; however, there were some scene-to-scene mistimings and a few flashes on shot changes. The sound quality was only fair. The recording of Mr. von Sternberg's narration was noisy, muffled and badly mixed with the rest of the track elements. The poor com-posite sound track was not an exclusive fault of the fine grain, but was common to all negatives and prints of the 1953 version.

2. *Positive print of 1958 revised version.* Made on safety stock, this print was in fair condition. Some footage was missing and there were a considerable number of splices, most likely caused by print damage over the years. The nude shots were spliced in and the track level and picture timing of these did not match the rest of the print. Some scenes had been deleted causing bad jumps in the sound track and noisy splices. Generally, the print was badly timed and much of the beauty of Josef von Sternberg's photography was lost; in addition, flashes occurred on many shot changes as the result of improperly placed tim-ing notches. This will be discussed later in this report.

3. *Original picture negative.* The negative was comprised of about 80% safety and 20% nitrate film. All head and tail leaders were nitrate; this caused the head and tail scenes of most reels to have picture deterioration consisting of yellow-brownish or green colored stains and splotches. Many splices were coming apart. There were edge tears and torn sprocket holes in reels two, three, seven and eight with several very bad tears of one to two feet in length across

the center of the picture. These had been repaired with ordinary Scotch tape. Some abrasions and scratches were noted on both base and emulsion in reels two, four, five, six, eight and nine. Reels two, three, four and seven had frames replaced with clear leader slugs. Damaged perforations were found on reels six and eight. Most timing notches were misplaced by two-three frames.

4. *Original mixed sound track negative.* This negative was completely on nitrate stock and showed signs of beginning deterioration. The general quality of the sound track was poor.

5. *Original music track.* This negative was completely on nitrate stock and was in good condition. The sound quality of the track was poor to fair with a recorded-in hum. It did not sync exactly with any version of finished film.

6. *Original Japanese dialogue/sound effects track negative.* This negative was completely on nitrate stock and was in good condition. The sound quality of the track was poor to fair with a recorded-in hum. It did not sync exactly with any version of finished film.

7. *Original picture negative of 1958 nude shots.* This footage was on safety stock and comprised about 500 feet of miscellaneous nude scenes not used in either the 1958 or 1976 versions of the film.

8. *Trims, out-takes.* All on safety stock, these consisted of pieces removed from 1958 release prints. One set had been spliced together into a roll marked "Guide to Changes." Other rolls comprised fine grain positives and dupe negatives of various nude shots. A number of main title replacement negatives and fine grains for alternate titles were found. This material was useful for determining how Mr. von Sternberg had modified the release prints in 1958; otherwise, it was not needed for the reconstruction.

Differences Between Original Negative, Fine Grain and 1958 Positive Print

Several differences between the negative, fine grain, and print were noted. The *fine grain*, as discussed earlier, represented the film as originally finished and released in 1953. The 1958 *positive print* differed from the fine grain in the following respects:

Reel One: The original main title, *The Saga of Anatahan*, had been replaced with a new main title reading, *Anatahan*. The sound track had been duped from a release print and the whole was just spliced in. At 886 feet, there was a cut of 11 feet, apparently to eliminate an unwanted line of narration: "All by himself—or was he all by himself?".

Reel Two: At 73 feet, there was a cut of 85 feet; this has been replaced with a new nude sequence running about 90 feet showing the heroine taking a bath and being watched by Japanese soldiers. This new piece of film had a duped section of the original music track, but was missing narration and sound effects. The track level, and general looking picture density did not match the rest of the print. Narration missing: "(Some of us — sooner than the others, longed for something more than bread alone — and we watched her — and we watched each other.) The walls of the huts were thin. There were no secrets. She had been out collecting shells as usual — his way of paying her a compliment was to call her 'shell crazy.' The rains stopped — nothing lasts forever — though the waves of the ocean lasted long." (*Note:* Portion in parentheses was restored in 1976 version.)

At 347 feet, there was a cut of 16 feet, eliminating most of a shot of ocean waves and the following narration: "Tides lifted and the tides fell. We watched the waves approach and we watched them recede, and we tried to find a meaning where there was none."

Reel Three: At 522 feet, there was a new nude shot (seven feet long) of the heroine as she is thrown to the floor, which replaced the old, less explicit shot; the duped sound track was the same as the original; the picture quality and sound level of the new piece did not match the rest of the print.

Reel Four: At 16 feet, there was a ten foot cut of a shot of the ocean which eliminated the following narration: "We were free — free of all restraint — which only meant that we were slaves to our bodies."

Reel Five: At 80 feet, a new nude shot, seven feet long, was substituted for a portion of a shot of a group of men playing a musical instrument. The new shot consisted of the heroine standing nude on the beach in long shot. The sound track was duped and the quality of the section, both picture and track, did not match rest of print.

At 138 feet, a new nude shot, seven feet long, was added, showing the heroine running off beach; the sound track was completely silent.

At 383 feet, a cut of about five feet was made. This shot showed a man tuning a musical instrument.

Reel Six: At 68 feet, there was a cut of 14 feet which eliminated a shot of ocean waves and the following narration: "But, he missed the most important point — the enemy *was* on Anatahan — man's genius to destroy himself was in clear evidence."

Reel Seven: There was no difference between the 1953 fine grain and the 1958 print.

Reel Eight: At 654 feet, there were two new shots of about ten feet each which replaced the old single shot of trinkets in the hut. The first new shot showed the woman's breasts as she was manhandled and the second new shot showed her falling to the floor, nude, behind an overturned chair. The sound track was duped; and once again, overall quality did not match the rest of the print.

Reel Nine: At 71 feet, there was a cut of 22 feet which eliminated three shots of soldiers in the woods calling, "Keiko! Keiko! Keiko!"

At 367 ½ feet, a new nude shot eight feet long was substituted for an old shot of ocean waves. The new shot showed the heroine throwing off her clothes and walking into the ocean. The track was duped, etc.

When examined in 1975, the *original negative* matched the 1953 fine grain in every respect, except one: Two of the nude shots of the heroine bathing in a tub, shot by Sternberg's Japanese cameraman and used in reel *two* of the 1958 version, were spliced into reel *five* of the picture negative. This is at the very same place that the 1958 print had a different set of nude shots of the heroine on the beach. The fine grain consisted of a single long take which showed men playing a musical instrument and singing. Apparently, Josef von Sternberg, in recent years, decided to make this one change in the original negative. This appears to have been done years after the fine grain was made.

In one other respect, the original negative no longer matched the fine grain — physical condition. Virtually none of the tears, splotches, repairs, etc. in the negative appear in the 1953 fine grain. Most of the damage must have been done in the late 1950's and early 60's.

What To Do?

Picture

Several options were available to Film Technology Company, Inc. The picture negative could just be matched to the fine grain, thus restoring the film to its 1953 version. This could be accomplished by taking out the nude sequence in reel five and replacing the bad sections with dupe negative from fine grain, or:

The picture negative could be left alone, just fixing the damaged sections (i.e.: leave in nude bathing sequence in reel five) creating a new variant edition, or:

The negative could be matched to 1958 prints which had been assembled by Josef von Sternberg and the necessary repairs and replacement sections made from fine grain.

Sound

We could print from original nitrate mixed track negative, or:

Re-record from mixed positive track on the 1953 fine grain or 1958 positive print, or:

Make prints of original music, dialogue and effects tracks, transfer these to magnetic tracks, edit the mag tracks to match, then mix to make a new improved sound track.

According to Mrs. von Sternberg, her husband felt the 1958 revision of *Anatahan* was the final form in which he wished to leave the film. Therefore, she decided that we should proceed by changing the original negative to match the 1958 print. This meant cutting certain shots out, adding nude shots, repairing bad splices and tears in the negative, and replacing badly damaged sections with dupe negative made from the fine grain. Regarding the sound, it was decided to use the original track elements and re-mix to get a better result, because Sternberg's narration on the original 1953 sound track was very muffled and hard to understand. One major problem arose, however, when it was discovered that the original track for Sternberg's narration could not be found. It was then decided to make as good a recording as possible, by means of special filtering and equalization, of Sternberg's voice from the mixed track on the fine grain, then combine this voice recording with a re-mix of the original music, dialogue/effects tracks.

Reconstruction

Picture

The following operations had to be performed to prepare the picture negative for printing:

First, missing footage had to be filled in in the 1958 positive print to make it useable as the workprint for the new 1976 version. To do this, we compared the problem sections of the 1958 print with the 1953 fine grain, and spliced in slugs of leader to bring the 1958 print out to length.

We had to determine which sections of the original negative were too badly deteriorated, torn or damaged to use. The negative was carefully gone over and cards were filled out for each reel listing all defects, however small; then, we marked portions of the fine grain which needed to be duped to replace damaged shots in the picture negative. These pieces (about 30 in all) were printed, and spliced into the original picture negative. The remaining small tears, bad splices, etc. in the negative were repaired by means of re-cementing, repair tape, etc.

At this stage, all nitrate picture negative in good condition was left in the negative, in order to get the best projection prints and fine grain possible for the new 1976 version. Before shipping the final negative to AFI, the remaining nitrate pieces were replaced with safety negative duped from the fine grain.

The timing notches had to be standardized. The majority of the notches were consistently off by two and one half frames from the proper position. We could either fix all of these notches and make them standard, or we could leave these alone and move a smaller number of notches to make them consistent with these. The latter decision was made, and a special electronic delay unit was constructed to use when printing the film to avoid flashes on shot changes.

Finally, timing cards were prepared for the negative, cinex strips were made, and proper timing was determined for each scene in the film.

The picture negative was now ready to use for the first trial answer print.

Sound

The 18 rolls of separate nitrate track negatives were printed up and down on nine reels of safety positive film. Then these music and Japanese dialogue/effects tracks were transferred to separate rolls of magnetic stock while being carefully filtered, equalized and noise-suppressed. The recording of Josef von Sternberg's narration from the 1953 fine grain was given a similar treatment.

The music and dialogue/effects magnetic tracks were then cut to sync with the 1958 workprint. The narration magnetic track was also cut to fit, and pauses between words and sentences were slugged out so as to facilitate mixing this material with the other tracks. Skillful cutting and syncing of the narration track was imperative because bits of music and effects remained on the narration track and could have caused phasing problems in the final mix if not kept in perfect sync with the other elements.

After much testing and many rehearsals, the separate track elements — music, dialogue/effects and narration track — were mixed to make a combined final sound track on 35mm magnetic film. It was from this film that the final optical negative track was made.

Printing

After a complete cinexing and analysis of the cinex strips, the first trial print was made. At its first screening, many small, but significant exposure changes were made, and the timing cards marked accordingly. Because this print would eventually be sent to AFI, the decision was made to reprint certain reels and sections of reels so as to produce a smoother, more acceptable overall print.

Three release prints were made, all of excellent quality. Further refinements continued to be made while making print numbers one and two. Print number three came closest to perfection.

A 35mm composite fine grain, matching the number three release print in terms of timing, was also printed as protection and to use for making a 16mm reduction picture negative.

A 16mm reduction negative was made from the fine grain, and a 16mm optical sound track negative was transferred from the 35mm magnetic mixed track.

Further Negative Reconstruction

After the above materials were made and before sending the original picture negative to AFI/LOC, all remaining nitrate footage was eliminated and replaced with new safety dupe negative made from the Eastman House (1953) fine grain.

Trailer

A dupe picture negative and track negative for Josef von Sternberg's trailer for *Anatahan* were found in the trims and out-takes from the 1958 version. Both picture and track negatives were on safety stock so no restoration was necessary beyond replacing the main title (*The Only Woman on Earth* changed to *The Sage of Anatahan*).

Three 35mm prints and a composite fine grain were made from the negatives; the fine grain was then used to make a 16mm reduction picture negative, and a 16mm optical track negative was re-recorded from one of the positive prints.

Disposition of Elements

After finishing the reconstruction, all materials relating to *The Saga of Anatahan* were disposed of as follows:

1. Returned to George Eastman House:
   a. 35mm Safety composite fine grain (1953 version), nine reels.
2. Sent to Twyman Films, Inc.:
   a. Three 35mm safety release prints (1976 version), nine reels each.
   b. 16mm Reduction picture negative (1976 version), on five rolls.
   c. 16mm Optical track negative (1976 version), on five rolls.
   d. Three 35mm safety release prints of Trailer.
   e. 16mm Reduction picture negative of Trailer.
   f. 16mm Optical track negative for Trailer.
3. Sent to the Library of Congress/AFI:
   a. First trial answer print—35mm safety positive (1976 version), nine reels.
   b. 35mm Safety composite fine grain (1976 version), nine reels.
   c. 35mm Safety original picture negative (1976 version), nine reels.
   d. 35mm Safety optical track negative (1976 version), nine reels.
   e. 35mm Mixed magnetic track (1976 version), nine reels.
   f. 35mm Safety composite fine grain of Trailer.
   g. 35mm Safety picture negative of Trailer.
   h. 35mm Optical track negative of Trailer.
   i. 35mm Safety positive, fine grain, and negative of extra footage (1958 nude shots), about 500 feet total.
4. Returned to Mrs. von Sternberg:
   a. 35mm Safety workprint (1958 print modified for 1976 version).
   b. 16mm Magnetic track elements—music, Japanese dialogue/effects, narration, additional effects, and mixing sheets for reels one to nine.
   c. 35mm Safety up and down track prints—music and dialogue/effects tracks.
   d. Misc. 35mm safety trims, out-takes, etc. from Josef von Sternberg 1958 modification of film, and from 1976 reconstruction. Twenty-one cans.
   e. Quarter-inch protection tapes—narration, nine rolls.

   f. Quarter-inch protection tapes — final mixed track (1976 version),
      nine rolls.
5. Returned to UCLA Film Archives:
   a. 35mm Nitrate picture negative trims — shots removed before send-
      ing picture negative to AFI. One can, approximately 900 feet.
   b. 35mm Nitrate track negative — music, nine reels.
   c. 35mm Nitrate track negative — Japanese dialogue/effects, nine
      reels.
   d. 35mm Nitrate track negative — mixed sound track (1953 version),
      nine reels.

APPENDIX 8
THE SCANDINAVIAN WAY

The work of the film archives of Sweden, Norway, Denmark, and Finland is a model which could, and should, be followed by film archives throughout the world. When the Film Foundation was launched in 1990, to raise funding for American film preservation, one of its first activities was an appearance by the project's founders at the Cannes Film Festival, in an effort to stimulate similar programs in other countries. In reality, the Scandinavian countries have gone way beyond anything accomplished in the United States. All of the archives have adequate government funding for preservation. Each is operated in an efficient, yet sincere and enthusiastically personal fashion. Their individual storage facilities any archives in the world would be proud to own.

Cooperation between the four archives is highly productive and lacking in the politics which permeate so much of the archives movement in the United States and throughout much of the world. Individual archives in each of these countries can work together in a fashion which the multiple archives of the United States or, for example, Italy cannot. Because the Norsk Filminstitutt/Norwegian Film Institute has no laboratory facility available in its own country for archival work, it is able to send its nitrate for copying to the Swedish Film Institute laboratories at Rotebro. In the early eighties, the Norwegians found what proved to be the only complete print extant of Carl Th. Dreyer's 1928 classic, *The Passion of Joan of Arc*. It was located in the attic of a psychiatric hospital, a doctor at which had acquired the print around 1930 from Dreyer, a personal friend. Because of a backlog of films awaiting cataloging, the print's existence in the archives was not revealed until 1984, but immediately—as a matter of course—the Norwegians handed the film over to Det Danske Filmmuseum/The Danish Film Museum, the rightful place for its preservation in view of the nationality of the director.

Another important find of the Norwegian Film Institute was the only surviving print, albeit lacking the prologue and epilogue, of Mauritz Stiller's 1916 feature, *Vingarne/The Wings*, which is, questionably, the first film with a "gay" theme. The nitrate print was found at a flea market, and, because it was a Swedish production, it was handed over for preservation to the Swedish Film Institute.*

The Swedish Film Institute and to a certain extent its counterparts in Norway and Finland combine the cultural side of the motion picture with the commerical production end. The Swedish institute is located only a few minutes' walk from the center of Stockholm, in an impressive, if sterile-looking building called Filmhuset/The Film House. A block away is the home of Swedish television and immediately behind Filmhuset is a top secret military establishment. When the building was in the planning stages, architect Peter Celsing was told that no windows could be placed on the side of the building overlooking the military establishment; he responded with a blank wall on which is a large, peering eye.

The six-story Filmhuset was built in 1970 on land leased from the government. Approximately half of the building is occupied by the Swedish Film Institute, with the remainder leased to the Swedish National Board of Building and Planning.

The Institute has its origins in the Swedish Film Club, founded in October 1933, and Einar Lauritzen's Filmhistoriska Samlingarna/Film History Collection. The Institute itself was established in 1963, with funding provided through a 10 percent levy on the gross box-office receipts from all Swedish cinemas operating on a regular basis. The Institute's income was increased in 1972 through specific state subsidies—although, of course, as theatre attendance has dropped so has the Institute's box-office levy—and, in 1982, the Film and Video Agreement was signed, whereby the video industry agreed to pay the Institute 40 Swedish kronor on each videocassette of a feature film sold to the public, and 24 kronor for each short subject.

The Institute is administered by a board of directors, appointed by the government, and an executive director appointed by the board. The present director is a jovial and hands-on administrator, former film producer Anna-Lena Wibom, who had headed the Institute's archival program for many years and was also active in FIAF. She follows in the footsteps of such prestigious predecessors as Harry Schein and Jörn Donner, and is in the unique position of overseeing both the cultural and production activities of the Institute. It is as if the workload of the director of the Film Department of the Museum of Modern Art was combined with that of the C.E.O. of Warner Bros.

Of an average 30 films produced each year in Sweden, 25 are coproduced with the Swedish Film Institute. Approximately 60 percent of the Institute's budget goes to film production, and, on an average, one third of the budget for a feature film will be provided by the Institute. Additionally, it funds a number of short subjects, at least half of which are specifically films for children.

*Information on the Swedish Film Institute is taken in part from Slide, Anthony, "Sweden's Unique Film Institute," in American Cinematographer, March 1987, pp. 80–83.

Aside from funding and cofunding films, the Swedish Film Institute is very much involved in their production, with a complete studio facility within Filmhuset. Located on the building's second and third levels, the studio facilities include two studios with a total square area of 870 meters. The two studios can be combined into one, if necessary, and the largest of the two is also equipped with a tank. There are also makeup and dressing rooms, a prop room, metal and paint shops, and a full editing facility.

The Institute has an active publications program, which includes the technical magazine *TM* (the initials stand for *Teknik* and *Manniska*, or Technology and Man) and the popular bi-monthly journal *Chaplin*, which was founded as an independent film magazine by Bengt Forslund in 1959, and taken over by the Institute in 1965. The Publications Program, headed by Bertil Wredlund, is also responsible for the multivolume *Svensk Filmografi*, which documents in considerable detail all Swedish feature films produced between 1920 and 1969.

The top floor of the Filmhuset is given over to the Institute's cultural activities. Here are located the library, the clippings archives, and the still photographs and posters archives. All are open to the public at no charge and are efficiently and neatly organized in extreme. There are approximately 30,000 volumes in the library, which subscribes to more than 250 periodicals. It also receives scripts — usually the script girl's copy and a cutting continuity — for all films in which the Institute is involved. Despite is name, the clippings archives has no clippings. Once a clipping has been taken, it is immediately transferred to a microfiche and the original destroyed. As of 1983, the archives had microfiches available on 46,000 films, 13,000 film personalities and 700 general subjects.

Regular screenings of both new and classic films, comparable to those of the Museum of Modern Art or Pacific Film Archive are presented nightly in a 360-seat theatre named in honor of Swedish director Victor Sjöström. Additional screenings are also held in a theatre in downtown Stockholm. The audience is composed of members of the Film Club, and the program is under the direction of Gunner Almer.

Aside from the main theatre, there is also a 133-seat and a 15-seat theatre. All three theatres are served from a central projection room, with 16mm, 17.5mm and 35mm projectors, slide projectors, a PA system, and VTR and AV equipment. The theatres are equipped for mono, stereo, and Dolby sound, and when not in use for public screenings are utilized by staff to check archival prints, for screenings of dailies, and by the classes of the University of Stockholm.

Rolf Lindfors is curator of the archives, and he is one of those individuals with an obsessive zeal for accurate documentation, not only in terms of the Institute's holdings, but also any published filmographic volume. Ask Rolf what the Institute's holding is on a specific film, and he can immediately find the appropriate microfiche record and tell you exactly what he has.

Unlike the American archives and compatible with its fellow Scan-divanivan archives, the Swedish Film Institute is concerned only with the pres-ervation and restoration of Swedish films. If it has a nitrate print or negative for a non–Swedish title, it will contact the archives in the country of origin and offer to make the nitrate available if the film has not already been preserved there. It does, however, maintain a library of non–Swedish films in order to meet the needs of the Film Club. It also works in tandem with the other Scan-dinavian film archives in acquiring screening prints of non–Swedish films.

The day-to-day preservation activities of the Swedish Film Institute are coordinated by Inga Adolfsson. In 1985, she was responsible for the important restoration of Sweden's first color feature, *Klockorna i Gamla Stan/The Bells of the Old Town* shot in 1946 in Cinecolor. She worked carefully not only in ensuring that there was no problem with registration but also in creating a color style as close as possible to the original two-color Cinecolor, rather than modern Eastman Color.

All too often, other archives are willing to send out silent films which have only "flash titles" — that is, one frame of title — thus preventing the viewer from reading the captions or subtitles. Not only does this not happen in films from the Swedish Film Institute, but also the Institute will often insert new titles in Swedish, English, and French.

As already noted, the Institute maintains its own laboratory just outside of Stockholm, and this is utilized for both preservation work and general pro-cessing of contemporary productions.

The dedication to film preservation by the Swedish Film Institute and its predecessor is obvious. It must surely have influenced the International Federa-tion of Film Archives to hold its 1959 Congress in Stockholm — the meeting was attended by 40 delegates from 29 archives, with the Pole Jerzy Toeplitz presid-ing. (As Ernest Lindren of the National Film Archive commented in 1970, "Professor Toeplitz from Warsaw, with his fluent command of many lan-guages, his authority, his fairness, and his ability to interpret West to East and East to West, has held FIAF together with a remarkable unity for over 20 years."*)

Nothing better exemplifies the Swedish Film Institute's concern with both the commercial and archival aspects of the motion picture than its develop-ment of a film conditioning apparatus, which is marketed as the FICA cabinet by AB Film-Teknik (P.O. Box 1328, S-17126 Solna, Sweden). The FICA cabinet was developed in response to the need to safeguard color films by storing them at an extremely low temperature but at a constant relative humidity.

The FICA cabinet does away with the need for humidity control by side-stepping the issue. The film is placed in the cabinet for a period of between

---

*Lindren, Ernest, "The International Federation of Film Archives," Journal of the Society of Film and Television Arts, no. 39, spring 1970, p. 24.

four and seven days, during which time moisture is drawn from it. It is then placed in a special bag, made of three laminated layers—polyester, aluminum foil, and polyethylene. The bag is placed in a combined vacuum chamber-heat sealer. When the chamber is closed, the air is evacuated and the bag is automatically heat-sealed. The bag is placed in a film can, which is sealed with tape, and the film is now ready for cold storage. The film can be reused by leaving the bag at room temperature for 24 hours. What makes the FICA cabinet appealing to production companies, as much as archives, is that once the cabinet is installed, the cost of cold storage of the film is relatively cheap—and simple. The film can even be stored in a household refrigerator or freezer!

The FICA-method of cold film storage was first conceived in 1979, and was developed, after consultation with both Eastman Kodak and Agfa-Gevaert, by Hans-Evert Bloman and Roland Gooes of the Institute staff.

So determined has been the Swedish Film Institute in its work that its anticipates completion of the copying of all Swedish nitrate films by sometime in 1992. Director Wibom would like to expand the Institute work, and begin the location and restoration of "lost" films from the developing countries. "If something isn't done on this score, the future will regard it as a catastrophe comparable to the burning of the Alexandria Library," she told *Variety* in 1988.*

Like its Swedish counterpart, the Norwegian Film Institute is concerned with both the cultural and the business aspects of the motion picture industry. In association with the National Film Production Committee, it administers government grants for film production, usually comprising at least 55 percent of a feature film's budget. Since 1986, it has maintained the Register of Videogrammes, a listing, in part for censorship purposes, of all video tapes released for sale in Norway. Until 1985, when the National Centre for Screen Studies was founded, the Institute also operated as a film school. In 1990, it accepted responsibility for the representation of Norwegian films abroad, organizing both foreign sales and festival participation.

The Institute's activities are directed by Jan Erik Holst, who took over as managing director from Jon Stenklev in the fall of 1987.

The Norwegian Film Institute was established by parliament in 1955, and three years later became a member of FIAF. In 1984, it moved to its new headquarters in the basement of a beautifully restored 19th century military hospital in the old section of Oslo. The building houses the Institute's administrative offices, a small yet efficient library (and the only one of its kind in Norway) and a 120-seat theatre which presents nightly screenings for an often small but always enthusiastic audience.

The archives program is headed by Arne Pedersen, who has been with the

*Keller, J.R. Keith, "Economical 'Preservation-in-a-Bag' One of Swede Institute's Winners," Variety, June 1, 1988, p. 34.

Institute for more than 30 years. He expresses satisfaction with the government's funding of the transfer of all extant Norwegian nitrate films to safety, but regrets that the country does not have its own preservation laboratory. Realizing in 1990 that one million meters of nitrate film were still to be copied, Pedersen adopted three criteria for preservation: the importance of the film; its technical condition; and whether a copy is needed by an outside user, such as Norwegian television.* The Institute maintains acetate vaults on the outskirts of Olso, and nitrate vaults in the mountains.

With an annual budget of a little over $2 million, a total staff of 16 and a preservation staff of three, the Norwegian Film Institute offers both a friendly and informal atmosphere. Everyone on the staff does what needs to be done for the common good of the Institute and film preservation.

The Danish Film and Cinema Act of June 8, 1977, designated the Danish Film Museum as having responsiblity for the preservation of film, film stills, and other materials relating to film, and also the authority to collect and loan film literature and to disseminate knowledge on the history of cinema through screenings and other means. However, the Museum's origins go back long before 1977.

In the late 1930s, a group of critics and writers in Copenhagen conceived of the idea for a national film museum, and one of the first tasks that they were able to undertake was the sorting of film stills from Denmark's oldest and largest film company, Nordisk Films Kompagni. The first government support for the organization came in November 1941, when Dansk Kulturfilm, which produced short films for educational and cultural purposes, was authorized to fund the group's activities. In 1947, the museum was officially named Det Danske Filmmuseum/the Danish Film Museum, and that same year it became a member of the International Federation of Film Archives.

The Museum operated as a private institution, subsidized by the state, until 1958, when it became a part of Statens Film Central, the successor to Dansk Kulturfilm. The Film Act of May 27, 1964, removed the Museum from the administration of Statens Film Central and granted it status as an independent institution under the authority of the Ministry of Cultural Affairs. In 1966, the Museum moved to new premises at Store Søndervoldstraede, which it shared with the Danish Film Institute and the Film School.

More than 13,000 films are held by the Danish Film Museum, including approximately one quarter of the 1,400 or so produced Danish silent films, and some two thirds of all Danish sound films. Although the Museum had assumed that it had collected all surviving Danish film titles, it continues to receive "lost" films from as far away as Brazil and Spain. It has a complete collection of the films of Carl Th. Dreyer and approximately 30 of the 75 films made by the great Danish actress Asta Neilsen. Since 1964, the Museum has auto-

---

*Conversation with Arne Pedersen, April 29, 1990.

matically received one archival copy and one projection print of every released Danish film.

The films are stored in 24 temperature and humidity-controlled vaults in Bagsvaerd, near Copenhagen, a facility which the Museum took over in January 1962. It does not operate its own laboratory for film preservation, but relies on Denmark's only 16mm and 35mm film laboratory, Johan Ankerstjerne A/S, which is owned by Nordish Films Kompagni.

Aside from the film collection, the Museum operates an extensive library—the largest of its type in the country—containing books, periodicals, scripts, clippings, film stills, and posters. A permanent exhibition of film equipment is on display on the second floor at Store Søndervoldstraede, and two traveling exhibits—on Carl Th. Dreyer and Asta Nielsen—are continually in demand.

The Danish Film Museum first began regular film screenings in January 1949, and acquired its first theatre facility in September of the same year. Currently, films are screened three times a day, from Mondays through Thursdays, except during the summer months, and additional film screenings are presented at Århus in Jutland. Since 1954, the Museum has published the quarterly film journal *Kosmorama*. The entire operation is guided by the affable Ib Monty, a respected name throughout the world in the archival film field.*

A visit to the vaults of Suomen Elokuva-Arkisto/the Finnish Film Archive, located at Otaniemi on the campus of Helsinki's Technical University, is rather like visiting a vast nuclear war shelter, hewn out of solid earth. In fact, the vaults can be used in time of a nuclear holocaust. They are approached through double doors, wide enough to allow a truck access.

Two of the six vaults in the complex house the Archive's holdings of the best copies of paper materials (such as posters and still photographs) and a collection of museum artifacts (such as projectors and cameras). Three of the vaults, maintained at 7° centigrade and 50 percent relative humidity, hold deposited copies of both Finnish and foreign films. Original negatives, master archival copies and color prints are stored in a separate vault kept at −7° centigrade and 25 percent relative humidity. So-called "levelling chambers" are used for the transition of the films from cold storage to normal temperature conditions. The entire complex is a magnificent example of modern technology being utilized in close collaboration with the best of contemporary archival film standards.

The Archive's nitrate collection is housed at Tuusula, 25 miles outside of Helsinki. Far smaller than the safety vaults, the nitrate vaults are maintained at 7° centigrade and 50 percent relative humidity. Owned by the Archive, the vaults are serviced, interestingly enough, by an explosives manufacturing company. Unlike many American nitrate vaults, which are close to residential

Thanks to Ib Monty for providing information on the Danish Film Museum.

property, the Finnish Film Archive nitrate vaults are more than half a mile from the nearest buildings.

The main offices of the Finnish Film Archive are situated on one rented floor of a former factory complex close to the center of Helsinki. The Archive also rents two bomb shelters, one of which houses material from Suomi-Filmi (the country's oldest production company), the assets of which are jointly owned by the Archive and the Finnish Broadcasting Company, which purchased the television rights to the company's films in 1986. Materials stored here will eventually be moved to Otaniemi, when extension of the vaults there is completed, possibly in 1995.

The Finnish Film Archive was officially founded on April 24, 1957, but attempts at creating a national film archives date back to the 1930s. State subsidies began in 1962, and the Archive became a state-run organization on March 1, 1979. It is administered by a self-governing board, comprising representatives from various national film and television groups, as well as the Ministry of Education (of whose Art Department the Archive is a part). The director of the Archive (Kaarle Stewen) has responsibility for its screening program, the loan of films, the in-house library, publications, cataloging, and research. The Archive's major research project is publication of *Filmografia Fennica*, a detailed study of all feature-length Finnish films from 1907 to present. On a regular basis, the Archive screens two or three feature films a night at its own theatre, the Orion Cinema, located in the heart of the capital. The theatre dates back to the early teens and is reminiscent of small, suburban American or European motion picture theatres. The assistant director (Timo Muinonen) is responsible for the acquisition and preservation of the Archive's film and paper holdings.

In 1984, the Finnish Government decreed that as of September 1 of that year, one print of all films (foreign and domestic) presented on a commercial basis in Finland must be deposited with the Archive. One country whose distributors are notably lax in observing the law is the United States of America. In addition, one copy of all videocassettes of which more than 50 have been sold in Finland must be deposited with the Archive.

State subsidies for film preservation began in 1972, and by 1975, the Archive was copying 200,000 meters of film a year. Since then, the number has decreased to between 30,000 and 70,000 meters a year. The physical preservation work is handled by a private laboratory, Finnlab, the only laboratory currently operational in the country.

As of December 1990, the Finnish Film Archive held 8,300 prints of foreign feature films, 2,700 prints of Finnish feature films, approximately 16,000 prints of foreign short films, and 12,000 prints of Finnish short films. There are many duplicate copies. About 2,700,000 meters of film are either

Thanks to Timo Muinonen for providing factual information on the Finnish Film Archive.

original acetate negatives or master safety copies made from nitrate originals by the Archive. The Archive also has a collection of 8,500 videocassettes, 1,600,000 still photographs, and 130,000 posters.*

American archives can learn much from their Scandinavian counterparts. Obviously, there is a need for a closer, possibly federally-mandated, relationship between U.S. archives and film producers, as exists in the Scandinavian countries. Archival standards, particularly in terms of long-term storage, are higher there than in the United States. Above all, one is struck by a lack of the political maneuvering and in-fighting which has become so much a part of the American archival film field in recent years. The emphasis in Scandinavia is on preservation, with individuals and archives working together towards the common goal.

BIBLIOGRAPHY 1
GENERAL WORKS

Akermark, Margareta, editor. *Remembering Iris Barry*. New York: Museum of Modern Art, 1980.

Aldridge, L., and J.W. "Television's Yesterday Preserved." *American Film*, vol. 1, no. 10 (Sept. 1976), 70, 75.

"The American Film Institute Blasts Off." *Film Society Review*, Dec. 1967, 7–14.

Anderson, Phil. "Archivists and Exhibitors: Balancing (Conflicting?) Needs on Shoestring Budgets." *Media Arts*, vol. 2, no. 5/6 (winter/spring 1990), 22–23.

Ball, Edward. "The Good, the Bad, the Forgettable: The Influence of Film Archives." *The Independent*, March 1987, 18–21.

Barry, Iris. "The Film Library and How It Grew." *Film Quarterly*, vol. 22, no. 4 (summer 1969), 2ff.

_____. "In Search of Films." *Sight and Sound*, vol. 16, no. 62 (summer 1947), 65–67.

Borde, Raymond. "Archivists and the Industry Aren't Always in Step, But They're Learning to Tango." *Variety*, June 1, 1988, 36.

Borger, Lenny. "Cinémathèque Française, World's Warehouse of Film, Hits Stride in Preservation on 50th Anni." *Variety*, Jan. 8, 1986, 8.

_____. "Laborious Effort Is Required by Cinémathèque Curators to Classify, Let Alone Restore, Langlois' Legacy." *Variety*, Oct. 1, 1986, 31, 44.

Bowser, Eileen. "'Lost' Films Are Found in the Most Unexpected Places." *The New York Times*, section D, June 25, 1978, 17, 22.

Bowser, Eileen, and John Kuiper. *A Handbook for Film Archives*. Brussels: FIAF, 1980.

Bradley, John. "LC Plans Its Film Program." *Library Journal*, Nov. 15, 1946, 1595.

Brownlow, Kevin. "The Dark Is Light Enough." *Films in Review*, vol. 26, no. 1 (Jan. 1975), 13–16.

"Can Films Be Preserved." *Motography*, vol. 13, no. 14 (April 3, 1915), 1.

Canby, Vincent. "The Festival Makes a Potent Case for Preservation." *The New York Times*, Oct. 21, 1984, C23.

_____. "The Fight to Preserve Old Films, Good and Bad." *The New York Times*, Oct. 30, 1977, 17, 33.

Card, James. "The Historical Motion-Picture Collections at George Eastman House." *Journal of the SMPTE*, vol. 68, no. 3 (March 1959), 143–146.

Carey, Gary. *Lost Films*. New York: Museum of Modern Art, 1970.

Chamberlain, Stephen C. "Point of View: Preserving the Present for the Future." *SMPTE Journal*, vol. 91, no. 3 (March 1982), 227–228.

203

Champlin, Charles. "AFI's Major Mission as Preserver." *Los Angeles Times* Calendar, May 13, 1986, 1, 6.
Ciment, Michel. "Preservation: The Legacy of Langlois." *American Film*, vol. 22, no. 12 (Dec. 1986), 17–19.
Cleveland, D. "East Anglian Film Archive." *Framework*, autumn 1980, 44–45.
Cohn, Lawrence. "Col's Film Preservation Efforts to be Toasted at N.Y. Museum." *Variety*, Oct. 29, 1986, 6, 45.
_____. "Fox Archival Restoration Projects Rejuvenates 80 Vintage Titles." *Variety*, April 21, 1982, 7, 28.
Collins, Tom. "The Reel Thing: Resurrecting 'Lost' Films." *The Wall Street Journal*, March 12, 1985, 32.
"Color Problem." *Sight and Sound.* vol. 50, no. 1 (winter 1980-81), 12–13.
Crain, Mary Beth. "The Fine Art of Film Restoration." *L.A. Weekly*, Jan. 18, 1985, 39.
Culhane, John. "Nitrate Won't Wait." *American Film*, vol. 2, no. 5 (March 1977), 54–59.
"'Decade of Preservation' Begins with Ceremonial Benefit in L.A." *Variety*, July 6, 1983, 8, 29.
"Discover Industry's Pioneer Films in Library of Congress." *Daily Variety*, June 7, 1943, 1, 3.
Edelman, Rob. "Color Fading: Raging Bull." *Films in Review*, vol. 31, no. 10 (Dec. 1980), 607–608.
Ehrenstein, David. "Scorsese's Quest to Preserve Film Quality." *Los Angeles Herald-Examiner*, April 10, 1981, D27.
_____. "On Film, What's New Is What's Old." *Los Angeles Herald-Examiner* Weekend, Feb. 10, 1989, 13.
Everson, William K., "Film Treasure Trove: The Film Preservation Program at 20th Century-Fox." *Films in Review*, vol. 25, no. 10 (Dec. 1974), 595–610.
_____. "Should Everything Be Saved." *Films in Review*, vol. 29, no. 9 (Nov. 1978), 541–544, 563.
_____. "Discoveries of the Seventies." *Focus on Films*, Oct. 1980, 45–47, 52.
F.B. "Preserving the Cinema: The Art of Keeping Films Alive." *The Hollywood Reporter*, 47th anniversary edition, Nov. 1977, 80.
"Fade to Pink." *Premiere*, Dec. 1980, 7.
"FIAF—at 50." *Variety*, June 1, 1988, 33–63.
"Film Archives Fire Report: Blame Govt. and Goofs." *Daily Variety*, Jan. 25, 1980, 11.
"Film Restoration: Keeping Old Films Alive." *American Cinemeditor*, fall/winter 1979-80, 10–11.
Fisher, Bob. "Restoring Historic Films as a Life Work." *American Cinematographer*, vol. 61, no. 7 (July 1980), 678–679, 692–693.
Fleming, Charles. "Rescuing Dreams from the Dust." *Los Angeles Herald-Examiner* Weekend, Feb. 19, 1988, 6–7.
Fox, Michael. "PFA Offers Window on World of Cinema." *Release Print*, May 1990, 8–9.
Gartenberg, Jon. "Archiving of the Moving Image in the Twenty-First Century." *Historical Journal of Film, Radio & Television*, vol. 4, no. 2 (1984), 220–221.
_____. "The Brighton Project: The Archives and Research." *Iris*, vol. 2, no. 1 (1984), 5–16.
_____. *The Film Catalog: A List of Holdings in the Museum of Modern Art.* Boston: G.K. Hall, 1985.
_____. "Griffith at MOMA." *Films in Review*, vol. 32, no. 2 (Feb. 1981), 91–104.

Gerard Lilian. "The Study and Preservation of Films at the Museum of Modern Art." *Film Comment*, vol. 5, no. 3 (fall 1969), 12–15.

Gillet, John. "Gold Tinted." *Sight and Sound*, vol. 44, no. 2 (spring 1975), 85.

————. "Munich's Cleaned Pictures." *Sight and Sound*, vol. 47, no. 1 (winter 1977-78), 37–41.

Gilroy, Dan. "Film Archive Has Won Its Spurs by Fighting the Ravages of Time That Turn Moving Images to Dust." *Variety*, June 26, 1985, 31, 42.

Gitt, Robert. "Restoring Vitaphone Films." In *The Dawn of Sound*, editor Mary Lea Bandy. New York: Museum of Modern Art, 1989; 11–13.

Greenfield, Amy. "The Case of the Vanishing Videotape." *The Independent*, July-Aug. 1981, 17–18.

Gross, Linda. "Old Films Never Die: They *Fade*." *Los Angeles Times* Calendar, April 5, 1981, 2–4.

Haller, Robert A. "The Return of Anthology Film Archives." *Media Arts*, vol. 2, no. 5/6 (winter/spring 1990), 8.

Harmetz, Aljean. "Film History Being Lost by Oversight." *The New York Times*, March 24, 1987, C13.

Herrick, Doug. "Toward a National Film Gallery: Motion Pictures at the Library of Congress." *Film Library Quarterly*, vol. 13, no. 2/3 (1980), 5–25.

"History and Motion Pictures." *Views and Films Index*, vol. 1, no. 32 (Dec. 1, 1906), 1.

Hitchens, Gordon. "Anthology Film Archives Heroic Task to Save Old Pic Negatives." *Variety*, August 5, 1987, 6.

————. "Can Valuable Historical Films Be Entrusted to U.S. Archives?" *Variety*, January 3, 1979.

Hodsoll, Frank. "Film Preservation: A Large Piece of Americana Is Fading Away." *Daily Variety*, January 14, 1983, 28, 40, 60.

Into the Eighties. New York: Anthology Film Archives, undated.

Jacobson, Harlan. "Old Films Don't Die, But They Are Slowly Fading." *Daily Variety*, July 10, 1980, 1, 6.

Jeavons, Clyde. "Nitrate." *Sight and Sound*, vol. 47, no. 1 (winter 1977-78), 40–41.

————. "Sunken Treasure." *Sight and Sound*, vol. 52, no. 1 (winter 1982-83), 4.

Kahlenberg, Friedrich P. "Toward a Vital Film Culture: Film Archives in West Germany." *Quarterly Review of Film Studies*, vol. 5, no. 2 (spring 1980), 253–261.

Kauffmann, Stanley. "Troubles Noted." *The New Republic*, August 16, 1980, 34–35.

King, Andrea. "Raiders of Lost Negatives: Top Directors to Save Old Pics." *The Hollywood Reporter*, May 2, 1990, 1, 16.

Knight, Arthur. "I Remember MOMA." *The Hollywood Reporter*, April 21, 1978, 14, 19.

Koszarski, Richard. "Lost Films from the National Film Collection." *Film Quarterly*, vol. 23, no. 2 (winter 1969-70), 31–37.

————, George Lobell and Richard Corliss. "Lost and Found." *Film Comment*, vol. 7, no. 1 (spring 1971), 70–74.

Kuehl, Jerry. "The Historian and Film." *Sight and Sound*, vol. 45, no. 2 (spring 1976), 118–119.

Kula, Sam. "There's Film in Them Thar Hills!" *American Film*, vol. 4, no. 9 (July-Aug. 1979), 14–18.

Kupferberg, Audrey. "Archives." *Films in Review*, vol. 28, no. 1 (Jan. 1977), 53–55; no. 7 (Aug.-Sept. 1977), 427–428; no. 9 (Nov. 1977), 561–562.

Lamont, Austin. "The Search for Lost Films." *Film Comment*, vol. 7, no. 4 (winter 1971-72), 58–65.

Loynd, Ray. "Film and TV Preservation Goes National." *Daily Variety*, May 23, 1985, 1, 16.

McBride, Joseph. "Eight Form Preservation Band." *Daily Variety*, May 2, 1990, 1, 18.
_____. "Studio Mounts Re-Release Campaign Following Program to Restore TV, Pic Classics." *Daily Variety*, April 27, 1990, 1, 34, 43.
_____. "Studios Not Doing Enough to Stem Preservation Crisis, Says Rosen." *Daily Variety*, April 17, 1990, 12, 17.
Mercer, John. "Kemp Niver and the History of Cinema." *Journal of the University Film Association*, vol. 23, no. 3 (1971), 71–72.
"MOMA's Urgent Task: Save Those Films." *Variety*, June 26, 1985, 31, 106.
"Motion Picture Films of the National Archives of the U.S." *Science*, Sept. 6, 1935, 214.
Montgomery, Patrick. "Killiam Film Restorations." *Blackhawk Film Digest*, May 1979, 74.
Moskowitz, Gene. "Cinémathèque Fire." *Sight and Sound*, vol. 49, no. 4 (autumn 1980), 214.
"National Center Launches Initial Film & TV Preservation Efforts." *Variety*, May 29, 1985, 2.
"The National Film Archive." *Journal of the Society of Film and Television Arts*, no. 39 (spring 1970), entire issue.
Neuhaus, Cable. "Old Film Favorites May Never Die But, Just as Tragic, Warns an Expert, They Are Fading Away." *People*, March 16, 1981, unpaged.
"NFA Preserves the Nation's Film Heritage." *Screen International*, March 19, 1983, 26.
Niver, Kemp. *Early Motion Pictures: The Paper Print Collection in the Library of Congress*. Washington, DC: Library of Congress, 1985.
_____. "From Film to Paper to Film." *The Quarterly Journal of the Library of Congress*, vol. 21, no. 4 (Oct. 1964), 248–264.
_____. *Motion Pictures from the Library of Congress Paper Print Collection, 1894–1912*. Berkeley: University of California Press, 1967.
O'Connell, Bill. "Fade Out." *Film Comment*, vol. 15, no. 5 (Sept./Oct. 1979), 11–18.
O'Doherty, Brian. "Film Preservation: It's About Time." *Arts Review*, vol. 1, no. 2 (winter 1984), 16–18.
O'Konor, Louise. "Anthology Film Archives." *Filmrutan*, vol. 15, no. 1 (1972), 38–39.
O'Leary, Liam. "A Very Private Archive: Cinema in Ireland." *Historical Journal of Film, Radio & Television*, vol. 1, no. 2 (Oct. 1981), 183–187.
Perkins, Les. "Restoring Animation Art." *Disney News*, winter 1986, 35, 37.
Perry, Ted. "Will Experimental Film Disappear?" *American Film*, vol. 3, no. 10 (Sept. 1978), 6.
Pettigrew, Jim, Jr. "A Fresh Look at Old Movies." *Sky*, June 1986, 123–129.
Poe, William. "Preservation of Research Sources: Film and Videotape." *Humanities Report*, Oct. 1982, 13–17.
The Preservation of Motion Picture Film: Handling, Storage, Identification. Los Angeles: Hollywood Museum, 1964.
"Preservation to Protect Film Heritage, Kodak Says." *Back Stage*, Nov. 21, 1980, 10, 16, 26.
Problems of Selection in Film Archives: Proceedings of the FIAF Symposium at Karlovy Vary. Brussels: FIAF, 1981.
Reynolds, Herbert. "What Can You Do for Us, Barney? Four Decades of Film Collecting: An Interview with James Card." *Image*, vol. 20, no. 2 (June 1977), 13–31.
Roud, Richard. *A Passion for Films: Henri Langlois and the Cinémathèque Française*. New York: Viking Press, 1983.
Rowan, Bonnie. *Scholars' Guide to Washington, DC: Film and Video Collections*. Washington, DC: Smithsonian Institution Press, 1981.

Sanburn, Curt. "The Race to Save America's Film Heritage." *Life*, July 1985, 68–73, 77, 80.

"Scholar and Screen." *The Quarterly Journal of the Library of Congress*, vol. 21, no. 4 (Oct. 1964), 265–269.

Scorsese, Martin. "Letter." *Film Comment*, vol. 16, no. 1 (Jan.-Feb. 1980), 79.

Sharples, Win, Jr. "The Past—to the Rescue." *American Film*, vol. 2, no. 2 (Nov. 1976), 2.

Shepard, David. "The Search for Lost Films." *Film Comment*, vol. 7, no. 4 (winter 1971-72), 58–64.

Short, R.K.M. "Twentieth Century-Fox Movietone News Collection at the University of South Carolina." *Historical Journal of Film, Radio & Television*, vol. 1, no. 1 (March 1981), 70–72.

Silver, Charles. "History of the Museum of Modern Art." *Historical Journal of Film, Radio & Television*, vol. 1, no. 2 (Oct. 1981), 182–183.

Smith, Anthony. "Mixing Chemistry with Culture: Preserving Film and Television." *Screen Digest*, May 1981, 87–91.

_____. "The Problem of the Missing Film." *Sight and Sound*, vol. 57, no. 2 (spring 1988), 84–86.

Smith, Steven. "Restorer Lauds N.Y. Film Work." *Los Angeles Times* Calendar, Oct. 29, 1985, 1, 5.

Snedaker, Kit. "The Boulevard of Broken Dreams." *Los Angeles Herald-Examiner* California Living, Nov. 21, 1971, 26–29, 34–35.

Sokolov, Bernie. "Vanishing Images." *Films in Review*, vol. 37, no. 2 (Nov. 1986), 538–541.

Spehr, Paul C. "The Color Film Crisis." *American Film*, vol. 5, no. 2 (Nov. 1979), 56–61.

Stanbrook, Alan. "As It Was in the Beginning." *Sight and Sound*, vol. 59, no. 1 (winter 1989-90), 28–32.

Stein, Elliott. "Well Preserved." *Village Voice*, July 12, 1988, 55.

Sterne, Herb. "Iris Barry: The Attila of Films." *Rob Wagner's Script*, vol. 21, no. 702 (April 14, 1945), 14–15.

Stites, Tom. "Preserving the Joys of Jazz on Film Is a Project of Note in Kansas City." *Chicago Tribune*, section 5, Nov. 26, 1985, 1, 3.

Sussex, Elizabeth. "Preserving." *Sight and Sound*, vol. 53, no. 4 (autumn 1984), 237–238.

Swerdlow, J. "Is All the News Fit to Save?" *American Film*, vol. 4, no. 7 (May 1979), 8–9.

Torgon, S. "Hardy Har Har!" *American Film*, vol. 12, no. 1 (Oct. 1986), 10–11.

Turner, George. "Restoration... Slowly But Surely." *American Cinematographer*, April 1986, 128.

"U.S. Film Archive Fires: Neglect & Goof." *Variety*, Jan. 23, 1980, 7, 100.

Usai, Paolo Cherchi. "The Unfortunate Spectator." *Sight and Sound*, vol. 56, no. 3 (autumn 1987), 170–174.

Utterback, W.H., Jr. "An Opinion on the Nitrate Film Fire, Suitland, Maryland, 7 December 1978." *Journal of the University Film Association*, vol. 32, no. 3 (summer 1980), 3–16.

van Vliet, M. "The UNESCO Recommendation for the Safeguarding and Preservation of Moving Images." *EBU Review*, vol. 32, no. 3 (May 1981), 16–18.

Vesselo, Arthur. "Searchlight on Veterans." *Sight and Sound*, vol. 8, no. 31 (autumn 1939), 109–111.

Ward, Alex. "Gone with the Nitrate." *NEA Cultural Post*, May/June 1977, 8–9.

Weinberg, Herman G. "Lost Ones." *Film Comment,* vol. 5, no. 3 (fall 1969), 6–10.
Werner, Gosta. "Frame by Frame: Scandinavian Film Reconstruction." *Quarterly Journal of the Library of Congress,* summer/fall 1980, 332–341.
"Whitney Starts World Film Federation to Cooperate on Films' Archives." *Motion Picture Herald,* Nov. 5, 1938, 31.
Wiener, R.M.M. "Color Film Often Doomed at Birth—in the Lab." *Box Office,* May 4, 1980, 1, 5, 30.
————. "Scorsese Asks Industry Help to Save Films." *Box Office,* May 12, 1980, 1, 4.
————. "Vanishing Art: Fading Color Threatens Film Archives." *Box Office,* April 28, 1980, 1, 8, 14.
Wigle, Shari. "Where Film Industry Stores Its Canned Goods." *Los Angeles Times* Calendar, Sept. 8, 1968, 18.
Williams, L. "Focus on Education: Berkeley's Lively Archive." *American Film,* vol. 3, no. 9 (July-Aug. 1978), 72, 75.

BIBLIOGRAPHY 2
TECHNICAL WORKS

Adelstein, Peter Z., C. Loren Graham and Lloyd E. West. "Preservation of Motion-Picture Color Film Having Permanent Value." *Journal of the Society of Motion Picture and Television Engineers,* vol. 79, no. 11 (Nov. 1970), 1011–1018.

Bertram, H. Neal, Michael K. Stafford and David R. Mills. "The Print Through Phenomenon." *Journal of the Audio Engineering Society,* vol. 28, no. 10 (Oct. 1980), 690–705.

Bertram, H. Neal, and Edward F. Cuddihy. "Kinetics of the Humid Aging of Magnetic Recording Tape." *IEEE Transcriptions on Magnetics,* vol. 18, no. 5 (Sept. 1982), 993–999.

Blair, George A. "The Care and Preservation of Motion Picture Negatives." *Transactions of the Society of Motion Picture Engineers,* May 1922, 22.

The Book of Film Care. Rochester, NY: Eastman Kodak Company, Motion Picture and Audiovisual Markets Division, 1983.

Bradley, John G. "Film Vaults: Construction and Use." *Journal of the Society of Motion Picture Engineers,* vol. 53, no. 2 (Aug. 1949), 193–206.

_____. "Specifications on Motion Picture Film for Permanent Records." *Journal of the Society of Motion Picture Engineers,* vol. 48, no. 2 (Feb. 1947), 167–170.

Brems, Karel A.H. "The Archival Quality of Film Bases." *SMPTE Journal,* vol. 97, no. 12 (Dec. 1988), 991–993.

Brown, Harold G. "Problems of Storing Film for Archive Purposes." *British Kinematography,* May 1952, 150–162.

Calhoun, J.M. "The Preservation of Motion-Picture Film." *American Archivist.* July 1967, 517–525.

Carroll, J.F., and John M. Calhoun. "Effect of Nitrogen Oxide Gases on Processed Acetate Film." *Journal of the SMPTE,* vol. 64, no. 9 (Sept. 1955), 501–507.

La Conservation des Films. Brussels: FIAF, 1965.

Cuddihy, Edward F. "Aging on Magnetic Recording Tape." *IEEE Transactions on Magnetics,* vol. 16, no. 4 (July 1980), 558–568.

Cummings, James W., Alvin C. Hutton and Howard Silfin. "Spontaneous Ignition of Decomposing Cellulose Nitrate Film." *Journal of the Socity of Motion Picture and Television Engineers,* vol. 54, no. 3 (March 1950), 268–274.

Flory, John. "Doomsday for Film: The Crisis in Motion-Picture Archives." *Journal of the Society of Motion Picture Engineers,* vol. 72, no. 5 (May 1963), 410–412.

Gooes, Roland, and Hans-Evert Bloman. "An Inexpensive Method for Preservation and Long-Term Storage of Color Film." *SMPTE Journal,* vol. 92, no. 12 (Dec. 1983), 1314–1316.

Green, Leonard A. "Retirement Can Be Profitable." *SMPTE Journal*, vol. 92, no. 9 (Sept. 1983), 951–953.

Gregory, Carl Louis. "Printers for Old and Shrunken Film: Report of the Committee on Preservation of Film." *Journal of the Society of Motion Picture Engineers*, vol. 35, no. 12 (Dec. 1940), 599.

_____. "Resurrection of Early Motion Pictures." *Journal of the Society of Motion Picture Engineers*, vol. 42, no. 3 (March 1944), 159–169.

Hill, J.R., and C.G. Weber. "Stability of Motion Picture Films as Determined by Accelerated Aging." *Journal of the Society of Motion Picture Engineers*, vol. 27, no. 6 (Dec. 1936), 677–690.

Hunt, C. Bradley. "Corrective Reproduction of Faded Color Motion Picture Prints." *SMPTE Journal*, vol. 90, no. 7 (July 1981), 591–596.

Ih, Charles S. "A Holographic Process for Color Motion Picture Preservation." *SMPTE Journal*, vol. 87, no. 12 (Dec. 1978), 832–834.

Kleindienst, Wolf, and Ingelore Schwandt. "A Special Copying Apparatus for 35mm Film with Damaged Perforation." *SMPTE Journal*, vol. 90, no. 11 (Nov. 1981), 1090–1093.

Kopperl, D.F., and C.C. Bard. "Freeze/Thaw Cycling of Motion-Picture Films." *SMPTE Journal*, vol. 94, no. 8 (Aug. 1985), 826–827.

Lindgren, Ernest H. "Preservation of Cinematograph Film in the National Film Archive." *British Kinematography*, October 1968, 290–292.

Mugford, Peter. "Search for Permanent Pictures: Metal Film." *Journal of the SMPTE*, vol. 83, no. 6 (June 1974), 508.

Patterson, Richard. "The Preservation of Color Films." *American Cinematographer*, vol. 62, no. 7 (July 1981), 694–697, 714–720; no. 8 (Aug. 1981), 792–799, 816–822.

Perkins, Fred W. "Preservation of Historical Films." *Transactions of the Society of Motion Picture Engineers*, vol. 10, no. 27 (Jan. 1927), 80.

Preservation and Restoration of Moving Images and Sound: A Report to the FIAF Preservation Commission. Brussels: FIAF, 1986.

"Report of the Committee on the Preservation of Film." *Journal of the Society of Motion Picture Engineers*, vol. 20, no. 6 (June 1933), 523–530.

Sargent, Ralph. *Preserving the Moving Image*. Washington, DC: Corporation for Public Broadcasting/National Endowment for the Arts, 1974.

Schou, Henning, and Dominic Case. "An Experimental Quality Control Program for Printing Archival Films." *SMPTE Journal*, vol. 96, no. 12 (Dec. 1987), 1180–1185.

Shifrin, Art. "Researching and Restoring Pioneer Talking Pictures: The 70th Anniversary of the Theatrical Release of Kinetophone." *SMPTE Journal*, vol. 92, no. 7 (July 1983), 739–751.

Volkmann, Herbert. *Film Preservation*. London: British Film Institute, 1966.

West, L.E. "Preservation of Motion-Picture Color Films Having Permanent Value." *Journal of SMPTE*, vol. 88, no. 11 (Nov. 1979), 1011–1018.

Wheeler, Jim. "Videotape Storage: How to Make Your Videotapes Last for Decades...or Centuries." *American Cinematographer*, vol. 64, no. 1 (Jan. 1983), 23–25.

Woodward, J.G. "Stress Demagnetization in Videotapes." *IEEE Transactions on Magnetics*, vol. 18, no. 6 (Nov. 1982), 1812–1817.

BIBLIOGRAPHY 3
COLORIZATION AND
THE NATIONAL FILM
PRESERVATION BOARD

Allen, Woody. "The Great Colorization Debate." *Screen Actor,* fall 1987, 13–14.

Armstrong, Scott. "Now They're Using Computers to Color Black-and-White Movies." *Christian Science Monitor,* Oct. 16, 1984, 25, 27.

Baker, Russell. "The Well-Trashed Act." *The New York Times,* section 2, Nov. 26, 1986, 27.

Bennetts, Leslie. "'Colorizing' Film Classics: A Boon or a Bane?" *The New York Times,* August 5, 1986, 1, 21.

Bierbaum, Tom. "*Topper* 1st Off the Block Using Colorization Process." *Daily Variety,* April 19, 1985, 6.

Canby, Vincent. "'Colorization' Is Defacing Black and White Film Classics." *The New York Times,* section 2, Nov. 2, 1986, 1, 21.

――――. "Through a Tinted Glass, Darkly." *The New York Times,* section 2, Nov. 30, 1986, 19, 24.

"Capra to Congress: Pass Film Preservation Act." *Daily Variety,* June 16, 1988, 2, 15.

Corliss, Richard. "Raiders of the Lost Art." *Time,* Oct. 20, 1986, 98.

Desowitz, Bill. "Colorized *34th* a Ratings Hit." *The Hollywood Reporter,* Dec. 5, 1985, 1, 19.

Dileski, Paul. "DGA to Take Battle Against Colorization to U.S. Senate." *The Hollywood Reporter,* April 13, 1987, 1, 15.

Dowd, Maureen. "Movie Stars Testify Against Film Coloring." *The New York Times,* May 13, 1987, 22.

Elmer-DeWitt, Philip. "Play It Again, This Time in Color." *Time,* Oct. 8, 1984, 83.

Fantel, Hans. "Foes of Colorization See Red over Black and White." *The New York Times,* section 2, June 19, 1988, 30.

Farber, Stephen. "Will Colorizing Revitalize Old TV Series?" *The New York Times,* section 2, June 7, 1987, 35.

Gelman, Morrie. "Turner Orders Color for 24 B & W Features." *Daily Variety,* May 20, 1986, 1, 19.

Grove, Martin A. "The Money of Color." *The Hollywood Reporter,* April 2, 1987, 6.

Harris, Paul. "C'Right Office Shows True Colors." *Daily Variety,* March 16, 1989, 1, 30.

――――. "House OK's Nat'l Pic Commission." *Daily Variety,* June 30, 1988, 1, 34.

_____. "Nat'l Film Panel Up to Reagan." *Daily Variety,* Aug. 10, 1988, 1, 19.
_____. "Reagan Signs Film Preservation Bill." *Daily Variety,* Sept. 26, 1988, 1, 8.
_____, and Joseph McBride. "U.S. Cites 25 Pix in First Cut." *Daily Variety,* Sept. 20, 1989, 1, 23.
"Hope Is Slim for Legislation to Ban Film Coloring." *The New York Times,* June 19, 1988, 44.
Huntington, Tom. "Black and White in Color." *Saturday Review,* Nov./Dec. 1985, 10–11.
Krauthammer, Charles. "*Casablanca* in Color? I'm Shocked, Shocked!" *Time,* January 12, 1987, p. 82.
Lev, Michael. "Little Gold in Coloring Old Films." *The New York Times,* section 2, Nov. 11, 1989, 1, 21.
Locher, Mark. "Colorization Goes to Washington." *Screen Actor,* fall 1987, 11.
Markle, Wilson. "The Development and Application of Colorization." *SMPTE Journal,* vol. 93, no. 7 (July 1984), 632–635.
Matthews, Jack. "Film Directors See Red Over Ted Turner's Movie Tinting." *Los Angeles Times,* part 6, Sept. 12, 1986, 1, 10.
_____. "How Kane Triumphed over Turner in B & W." *Los Angeles Times* Calendar, Feb. 26, 1989, 6, 26–27.
Maurer, Joseph. "Color Spectography: Film of a Different Color." *Emmy,* May/June 1984, 60, 62.
McBride, Joseph. "Pic Preservers Mum on Next Titles." *Daily Variety,* Feb. 20, 1990, 1, 24.
McCarthy, Todd. "Color Institute B & W When It Comes to Vintage Films." *Daily Variety,* Oct. 2, 1986, 1, 28.
McWilliams, Peter A. "Adding Color to Black-and-White Movies Is a Splendid Idea." *TV Guide,* June 27, 1987, 34–35.
Molotsky, Irvin. "Colored Movies Ruled Eligible for Copyright." *The New York Times,* June 20, 1987, 12.
"National Film Preservation Board: DGA Responds to MPAA's Jack Valenti." *Daily Variety,* Aug. 1, 1988, 14, 17.
Robb, David. "Academy Shuns Colorizing Flap." *Daily Variety,* Dec. 22, 1986, 3, 27.
_____. "Huston's Cup Overfloweth with Harsh Words for B & W Colorizing and Ted Turner." *Daily Variety,* Nov. 14, 1986, 1, 35.
_____. "Nat'l Pic Commission Proposed." *Daily Variety,* June 10, 1988, 1.
Rogers, Ginger. "Color Me Indignant." *Screen Actor,* fall 1987, 15.
Rothman, Cliff. "Color Videos in Store for B & W Library Fare." *The Hollywood Reporter,* June 25, 1984, 1, 12.
Sarris, Andrew. "The Color of Money." *Village Voice,* Feb. 24, 1987, 50.
Schiller, Suzanne Ilen. "Black and White and Brilliant: Protecting Black-and-White Films from Color Recoding." *Hastings Journal of Communications and Entertainment Law,* spring 1987, 523–543.
Sørensen, Peter. "Black and White in Color." *Technology Illustrated,* Oct. 1983, 28–31.
Stewart, James. "Our Films Ain't Broke—Don't Fix 'Em." *Screen Actor,* fall 1987, 14.
Valenti, Jack. "Nat'l Film Preservation Board Is a Dangerous Chink in Showbiz' Armor." *Daily Variety,* July 20, 1988, 10.
Vitale, Joseph. "Black and White And Green." *Channels of Communications,* Jan. 1987, 17.
Wharton, Dennis. "Altered Pic Label Rules Lenient." *Daily Variety,* Aug. 21, 1990, 1, 30.
_____, and Joseph McBride. "Second Wave of Classic Pix Cited." *Daily Variety,* Oct. 19, 1990, 1, 22–23.

BIBLIOGRAPHY 4
SPECIFIC PROJECTS

Most film restoration or preservation projects are never discussed in print. Therefore, this section is limited to those restorations which are not necessarily the most important in terms of film history, but which have been the subject of considerable public attention. As most archivists would agree, the smaller, less "glamorous" restoration efforts are often just as time consuming and can sometimes be more complex. Dates of restoration reflect the years the projects were completed.

The Bat Whispers (1931)

(1988 restoration by Robert Gitt for the UCLA Film and Television Archive)
MacQueen, Scott. "A Gathering of Bats." *American Cinematographer*, vol. 69, no. 9 (Sept. 1988), 34–40.

Becky Sharp (1935)

(1984 restoration by Robert Gitt for the UCLA Film and Television Archive)
Desowitz, Bill. "Three-Strip 'Sharp' Sharpened for Full-Color N.Y. Fest Debut." *The Hollywood Reporter*, Aug. 31, 1984, 1, 25.
Flint, Peter B. "Mamoulian's Color Classic Restored." *The New York Times*, Sept. 16, 1984, C17.
Gitt, Robert, and Richard Dayton. "Restoring *Becky Sharp*." *American Cinematographer*, vol. 65, no. 11 (Nov. 1984), 99–104.
Kart, Larry. "Celluloid Salvation: 'Sharp' Screening Shows How Technology Can Save Art." *The Chicago Tribune*, section 13, July 14, 1985, 12–13.
King, Susan. "Pioneer Film Director with a Colorful Past." *Los Angeles Herald-Examiner*, Nov. 15, 1984, E6.
Slide, Anthony. "The Return of *Becky Sharp*." *Films in Review*, vol. 36, no. 3 (March 1985), 148–153.
Thomas, Kevin. "*Becky Sharp:* A Glorious Technicolor Restoration." *Los Angeles Times* Calendar, Nov. 11, 1984, 19.

The Big Trail (1930)

(1985 restoration by Peter Williamson for the Museum of Modern Art)
Haver, Ron. "Trail Blazing." *American Film*, vol. 11, no. 7 (May 1986), 17–19.

The Black Pirate (1926)
(1972 restoration by Harold Brown for the National Film Archive)
Andrews, Nigel. "Resurrecting the Pirate." *BFI News*, Jan. 1973, 3.

The Blot (1921)
(1975 restoration by Robert Gitt for the American Film Institute)
Slide, Anthony. "Restoring 'The Blot'." *American Film*, vol. 1, no. 1 (Oct. 1975), 71–72.

The Bullfighter and the Lady (1951)
(1986 restoration by Robert Gitt for the UCLA Film and Television Archive)
"Boetticher's 'Bullfighter' Restored, Screens Tonight." *Daily Variety*, July 18, 1986, 6.
Wilmington, Michael. "An *Ole!* for 'Bullfighter' Director." *Los Angeles Times*, part 6, July 18, 1986, 12.

A Corner in Wheat (1909)
(1975 restoration by Eileen Bowser for the Museum of Modern Art)
Bowser, Eileen. "The Reconstitution of 'A Corner in Wheat'." *Cinema Journal*, vol. 15, no. 2 (spring 1976), 42–52.

Doctor X (1932)
(1986 restoration by Robert Gitt for UCLA Film and Television Archive)
MacQueen, Scott. "*Doctor X*— A Technicolor Landmark." *American Cinematographer*, vol. 67, no. 6 (June 1986), 34–42.

The Glenn Miller Story (1954)
(1984 restoration by Universal Pictures)
Harmetz, Aljean. "Universal to Reissue 'Glenn Miller Story'." *The New York Times*, Nov. 17, 1984.
McCarty, Todd. "Restored 'Glen Miller' Pic Wildly Received at Cannes." *Daily Variety*, May 20, 1985, 12.
Siskel, Gene. "Stereo Version of *Glenn Miller Story* a Sound Piece of Show Business Nostalgia." *Chicago Tribune*, section 13, May 12, 1985, 2.
"Story Behind Restored Pic Told by Stewart." *Variety*, May 20, 1985.

Gone with the Wind (1939)
(1988 restoration by YCM Laboratory for Turner Entertainment)
Alexander, Max. "Once More, the Old South in All Its Glory." *The New York Times*, January 29, 1989.
May, Richard P. "Scarlett Returns in a Refreshed *GWTW*." *American Cinematographer*, vol. 70, no. 4 (April 1989), 36–39.
Vaughn, Christopher. "Turner's Restored 'GWTW' Poised to Take Nation by Storm." *The Hollywood Reporter*, Jan. 16, 1989, 12.

Hell's Angels (1930)
(1988 restoration by Robert Gitt for UCLA Film and Television Archive)
"Hughes' 'Hell's Angels' Color Restored by UCLA." *Daily Variety*, Jan. 20, 1989, 73.

Intolerance (1916)
(1898 restoration by Peter Williamson for the Museum of Modern Art)
Alexander, Max. "Griffith's 'Intolerance' Is Given the Blush of Youth." *The New York Times*, Oct. 1, 1989.
Canby, Vincent. "Seeing 'Intolerance' Is Hard Work." *The New York Times*, Oct. 29, 1989, H15, H17.

Cohn, Lawrence. "N.Y. Embraces 'Intolerance' in Reconstructed Pic Bow." *Daily Variety*, Oct. 4, 1989, 2, 19.
Crutchfield, Will. "Clues and Adornment: The Score of 'Intolerance'." *The New York Times*, Oct. 2, 1989.
Everson, William K. "*Intolerance*." *Films in Review*, vol. 61, no. 1/2 (Jan./Feb. 1980), 16–20.
Hansen, Miriam, "Griffith's Real *Intolerance*." *Film Comment*, vol. 25, no. 5 (Sept.-Oct. 1989), 28–29.

Lawrence of Arabia (1962)
(1988 restoration by Robert Harris for Columbia Pictures)
Ansen, David, with Constance Guthrie. "Saved from the Sands of Time." *Newsweek*, Feb. 6, 1989, 75.
Benson, Sheila. "'Lawrence' Restored: Nothing Can Touch It." *Los Angeles Times* Calendar, Feb. 15, 1989, 1, 4.
Broeske, Pat H. "Restored 'Lawrence' Conquers New York Premiere Audience." *Los Angeles Times* Calendar, Feb. 6, 1989, 1, 10.
Collins, Glenn. "'Lawrence of Arabia' the Way It Should Be." *The New York Times*, Dec. 15, 1988.
Corliss, Richard. "A Masterpiece Restored to the Screen." *Time*, Feb. 6, 1989, 62–63.
Denby, David. "Riddle of the Sands." *New York Magazine*, Feb. 13, 1989, 78.
"L.A. 'Lawrence' Benefit Ups Pic-Preservation Coffers." *Variety*, Feb. 15, 1989, p. 9.
Maslin, Janet. "'Lawrence' Seen Whole." *The New York Times*, Jan. 29, 1989.
Parsi, Paula. "'Lawrence' Premiere Spotlights Film Center Preservation Efforts." *The Hollywood Reporter*, Feb. 8, 1989, p. 10, 18.
"Revamped 'Lawrence of Arabia' Due Out in Fall from Columbia." *Variety*, May 18, 1988, 41.
Rothman, Cliff. "The Resurrection of 'Lawrence of Arabia'." *Los Angeles Times* Calendar, Jan. 29, 1989, 22–23, 26–30.
Siegel, Fern. "Reconstructing Film History." *Box Office*, Oct. 1989, 18, 20.
"Top-to-Bottom Redo for Lean's 'Lawrence' Epic." *Daily Variety*, May 9, 1988, 1, 21.

Lost Horizon (1937)
(1986 restoration by Robert Gitt for the American Film Institute)
Farber, Stephen. "Cuts in Film 'Lost Horizon' Restored." *The New York Times*, Sept. 3, 1986, C19.
Frank, Sam. "Lost Footage of 'Lost Horizon'." *Los Angeles Times*, part 4, Feb. 25, 1977, 13.
————. "'Lost Horizon': Reconstructing a Capra Classic One Frame at a Time." *Chicago Tribune*, section 13, August 19, 1984, 10.
————. "*Lost Horizon* Finds Shangri-La (Finally)." *L.A. Reader*, July 26, 1985, 7.
————. "*Lost Horizon* — A Timeless Journey." *American Cinematographer*, April 1986, 30–39.
————. "*Lost Horizon* Losses Restored." *American Cinematographer*, July 1987, 46–51.
Kehr, Dave. "Restoration Revives Lost 'Lost Horizon'." *Chicago Tribune*, August 21, 1986.
McCarthy, Todd. "AFI Screens Results — So Far — of Search for Lost 'Horizon' Scenes." *Daily Variety*, Oct. 22, 1979, 4, 9.
Sarris, Andrew. "Footage Fetish: Recovering 'Lost Horizon'." *Village Voice*, Sept. 23, 1986, 55, 66.

Thomas, Kevin. "The Lost and Found of 'Horizon'." *Los Angeles Times* Calendar, June 28, 1986, 1,8.

Macbeth (1948)
    (1980 restoration by Robert Gitt for UCLA Film and Television Archive)
Kauffmann, Stanley. "Restored and Revisited." *The New Republic*, July 26, 1980, 24–25.
"UCLA Archivist Reconstructs Orson Welles' Original 'Macbeth'." *Variety*, May 7, 1980, 144.

Nanook of the North (1922)
    (1976 restoration by David Shepard for International Film Seminars)
Dobi, Steve. "Restoring Robert Flaherty's *Nanook of the North*." *Film Library Quarterly*, vol. 10, no. 1/2 (1977), 7–18.

Napoléon (1927)
    (1980 restoration by Kevin Brownlow for the National Film Archive)
Alexander, Max. "'Napoleon' Campaigns in the Battle for Preservation." *The New York Times*, June 16, 1989, C20.
Brownlow, Kevin. "Abel Gance's Epic *Napoleon* Returns from Exile." *American Film*, vol. 6, no. 4 (Jan.-Feb. 1981), 28–32, 70–72.
_____. "'Napoleon' – A Triumphant Return." *The New York Times*, section 2, Oct. 11, 1981, 19.
_____. *Napoleon: Abel Gance's Classic Film*. New York: Alfred A. Knopf, 1983.
Everson, William K. "The Many Lives of 'Napoleon'." *Film Comment*, Jan./Feb. 1981, 21–23.
Insdorf, Annette. "'Napoleon' – Rescuing an Epic Film." *The New York Times*, section 2, Jan. 18, 1981, 1.
Kroll, Jack. "Movies: A Lost Epic Regained." *Newsweek*, Feb. 2, 1981.
Millar, Gavin. "The Rescue of Napoleon." *The Listener*, vol. 110, no. 2833 (Nov. 3, 1983), 39.

Queen Kelly (1928)
    (1984 restoration by Dennis Doros and Donald Krim for Kino International)
Koszarski, Richard. "A Film That Almost Got Away." *American Film*, vol. 10, no. 5 (March 1985), 15–18.

Sadie Thompson (1928)
    (1987 restoration by Dennis Doros for Kino International)
Kupferberg, Audrey, and Rob Edelman. "*Sadie Thompson:* The Restoration and Recreation of a Lost Classic." *Sightlines*, vol. 20, no. 4/vol. 21, no. 1 (summer/fall 1987), 20–22.

The Sea Hawk (1940)
    (Videotape restoration)
Anderson, Judy. "Errol Flynn's Lost Love Scene." *Video*, March 1986, 96–99, 138.

Spartacus (1960)
    (1991 restoration by Robert Harris and Robert Lawrence for Universal/MCA)
Grove, Martin A. "Hollywood Report." *The Hollywood Reporter*, Jan. 31, 1991, 10; Feb. 1, 1991, 14.
Sheehan, Henry. "The Fall & Rise of Spartacus." *Film Comment*, vol. 27, no. 2 (March-April 1991), 57–63.

A Star Is Born (1954)

(1983 restoration by Ronald Haver for the Academy of Motion Picture Arts and Sciences)

Harmetz, Aljean. "Missing Star Is Found." *The New York Times,* April 15, 1983, C10.

Harvey, Stephen. "Thanks to a Sleuth, 'A Star Is Born' Takes on New Lease of Life." *The New York Times,* section 2, July 3, 1983, 11–12.

Haver, Ron. "A Star Is Born Again." *American Film,* July/August 1983, 28–33, 59.

Haver, Ronald. *A Star Is Born: The Making of the 1954 Movie and Its 1983 Restoration.* New York: Alfred A. Knopf, 1988.

Holt, Chris. "*A Star Is Born:* Reconstructing the Original Version." *American Cinematographer,* vol. 65, no. 2 (Feb. 1984), 38–48.

Maslin, Janet. "Restoration: Save It for the Lovable Movies." *The New York Times,* section 2, Aug. 28, 1983, 15, 18.

Pollock, Dale. "'A Star Is Born' as a Movie Is Reborn." *Los Angeles Times* Calendar, April 15, 1983, 1, 15.

"Restored 'Star' Event Highlights Broad Film Preservation Battle." *Variety,* June 22, 1983, 6.

Way Down East (1920)

(1984 restoration by Peter Williamson for the Museum of Modern Art)

Gunning, Tom. "Rebirth of a Movie." *American Film,* Oct. 1984, 18–19, 93.

INDEX